Twentieth Century Opera in England and the United States

Cameron Northouse

G. K. HALL & CO., 70 LINCOLN STREET, BOSTON, MASS.

Library of Congress Cataloging in Publication Data

Northouse, Cameron.
    Twentieth century opera in England and the United
States.

    Bibliography: p.
    Includes index.
    1. Opera--England--Bibliography. 2. Opera--
United States--Bibliography. I. Title.
ML128.O4N7   016.7821   76-1012
ISBN 0-8161-7896-8

Contents

Preface

During the twentieth century, contemporary operas
by English and American composers and librettists have
been virtually ignored by the major opera institutions
and by the vast majority of the opera-going public. To
be sure, some of these works have ascended to the level
of the great opera houses, but, even in these few instances, the number of performances has been limited
and, generally, only in one season. The possible rea-
sons for this situation are reasonably complex and in-
volve a number of factors. However, the result is
evident: the opera culture, those individuals (composers, librettists, performers, producers, audiences,
historians, financial contributors, musicologists, and
others) who are interested in opera, has become divided.
The more numerous segment of the opera culture, the
"dominant opera culture," adheres to very strict definitions of the term "opera."* If a particular work vio-
lates the definitional construct of "opera," then the
work is rejected, occasionally with angry outbursts of
shock and amazement but more conventionally by non-
attendance and low ticket sales. Fundamentally opposed
to the strict constructionist view of opera is a far

---

*Most of these definitions include some or all of the
following statements: English is a language unfit to be
sung; the libretto of an opera is the least important
aspect of the work; opera must have continuous music;
opera, like symphonic music, should be "felt" rather than
intellectually understood; twentieth century opera should
conform to the rules of composition of nineteenth century
opera.

less numerous group of individuals, "the opera sub-
culture," which tends to see opera as a flexible art
form which depends on dynamic innovation and change. The
split between these two groups has led to an unrelenting
incoherence in the twentieth century opera culture.
While composers and librettists have continually pro-
duced operas of merit, they have not been given the sub-
stantial financial and social support of the dominant
opera culture, at least not the high degree of support
that has been expended on the institutionalization of
pre-twentieth century opera. While well over 2500
operas have been written by English and American composers and librettists during the twentieth century,
almost all of them are unknown except to a very small
audience.

The following lists are attempts to trace some of
the basic details of the twentieth century opera sub-
culture. The first section, "First Performances of
Twentieth Century English and American Operas," lists in
chronological order by date of first performance the
details of 1612 operas. In no instance can any of the
following lists be considered as complete, a fact which
is adequately indicated by the second section, "Additional Operas Lacking Complete Performance Information."

Section two is a list of 941 operas about which
little is known in most instances other than the title
and composer of the work.

Appendix A, "Operas Based on Literary Works,"
attempts to give some indication of the type of literary
works that have been used by composers and librettists
during the twentieth century. Not only is the use of
twentieth century literary works of some interest, but,
also, beginning in the 1920's and continuing to the
present, a number of writers primarily known for their
literary works began to take an active interest in
writing opera libretti. Some of these writers are W. H.
Auden, Gertrude Stein, E. M. Forster, Tennessee Williams,
William Carlos Williams, Edna St. Vincent Millay, Arnold
Bennett, Ted Hughes, Anne Sexton, John Updike, and

others. Not since the late eighteenth century have so
many literary figures participated in the composition of
operas. The last opera libretto before the 1920's by a
writer of recognized literary importance was The Village
Coquettes by Charles Dickens in 1836. The names of
librettists and their works can be located in the index.

Appendix B, "Published Operas," is a checklist of
basic bibliographical information on scores, vocal
scores, and libretti. In addition to operas by English
and American composers and librettists, each list also
includes, where appropriate, information on Canadian,
Australian, Irish, Welsh, Scottish, South African, New
Zealander, and Indian composers, librettists, operas,
and first performances. Operas by composers from non-
English-speaking countries, but which were written to
libretti by English-speaking librettists, are also included, such as W. H. Auden's three libretti for Hans
Werner Henze. Some will disagree with this procedure
and, also, the inclusion of operas by composers who
immigrated to English-speaking countries, operettas, and
some contemporary works that do not accomodate them-
selves to various a priori definitions of "opera," but
the intent here is to provide as clear a picture as is
possible of twentieth century opera and the opera sub-
culture's development in England and the United States.

The following items are indexed at the end of the
volume: composers, opera titles, librettists, literary
titles, and literary authors. The names of the composers are designated by "(c)" following the name; opera
titles have no following designation; librettists are
designated by "(l)" following the name; literary titles
are designated by an asterisk (*) following the title;
literary authors are designated by an asterisk (*)
following the name. The arrangement is alphabetical.

For their advice and assistance in obtaining the
information in this book and its preparation, I give my
thanks to Donna M. Northouse, Morse Peckham, J. Michael
Foster, and Eric Walter White.

Preface

Anyone possessing information on operas not contained
in the following, listings without complete information,
or entries which are in error are encouraged to write to
Cameron Northouse.

I. FIRST PERFORMANCES OF TWENTIETH CENTURY
ENGLISH AND AMERICAN OPERAS

This section is a chronological listing by the date of first performance of twentieth century operas. The format for each entry is:

Composer's name
OPERA TITLE. City of first performance.
Educational Institution of first performance if applicable. Date. Librettist's name

1900

1   Herbert, Victor
THE VICEROY. San Francisco. 12 Feb. Harry B. Smith

2   MacCunn, Hamish
THE MASQUE OF WAR AND PEACE. London. 13 Feb.

3   Warren, Richard Henry
PHYLLIS. New York. 7 May

4   Walthew, Richard Henry
THE ENCHANTED ISLAND. London. 8 May

Twentieth Century Opera

1901

5   Daniels, Mabel Wheeler
      THE COURT OF HEARTS. Cambridge, Massachusetts.
      2 Jan.

6   Stanford, Charles Villiers
      MUCH ADO ABOUT NOTHING. London. 30 May.
      Julian R. Sturgis

7   Chadwick, George Whitfield
      JUDITH. Worcester, Massachusetts. 26 Sept.
      William Chauncey Langdon

8   Coleridge-Taylor, Samuel
      TOUSSAINT L'OUVERTURE. London. 26 Oct.

9   Fanciulli, Francesco
      PRISCILLA, THE MAID OF PLYMOUTH. Norfolk,
      Virginia. 1 Nov.

10   DeKoven, Reginald
      MAID MARIAN. Philadelphia. 4 Nov. Harry B.
      Smith

1902

11   Lincke, Paul
      LYSISTRATA. London. 31 Mar.

12   German, Sir Edward
      MERRIE ENGLAND. London. 2 Apr. Basil Hood

13   Smyth, Dame Ethel
      DER WALD. Berlin. 9 Apr. Composer; in German

14   Luders, Gustav
      KING DODO. New York. 12 May. Frank Pixley

1903   First Performances

15   ____.
        THE PRINCE OF PILSEN. Boston. 21 May

16   Bunning, Herbert
        PRINCESS OSRA. London. 14 July

17   Edwards, Julian
        WHEN JOHNNY COMES MARCHING HOME AGAIN. Detroit.
        6 Oct.

                        1903

18   Paine, John Knowles
        AZARA. Boston. 7 Mar.

19   Moore, Homer
        THE NEW WORLD. St. Louis. 18 May. excerpts

20   Mildenberg, Albert
        WOOD-WITCH. New York. 25 May. Composer

21   Herbert, Victor
        BABES IN TOYLAND. Chicago. 17 June

22   Freeman, Harry Lawrence
        AFRICAN KRAAL. Chicago. 30 June

23   Howland, William Legrand
        SARRONA. Bruges. 3 Aug. Composer (Sarrona
        was the first opera by an American composer pro-
        duced in Europe)

24   MacAlpin, Colin
        THE CROSS AND THE CRESCENT. London. 22 Sept.

25   Caryll, Ivan
        THE DUCHESS OF DANTZIC. London. 17 Oct.
        H. Hamilton

26   Herbert, Victor
        BABETTE. Washington, D. C.   9 Nov.   Harry B.
        Smith

27   Butler, O'Brien
        MUIRGHEIS. Dublin.   7 Dec.   (Muirgheis was the
        first opera to have a Gaelic libretto)

1904

28   Delius, Frederick
        KOANGA. Elberfeld. 30 Mar. C. F. Keary;
        performed in a German translation

29   Maclean, Alexander Morvaren
        THE KING'S PRICE. London. 29 Apr.

30   Daniels, Mabel
        ALICE IN WONDERLAND CONTINUED. Brookline,
        Massachusetts. 20 May

31   Luders, Gustav
        THE SHO-GUN. New York. 10 Oct. George Ade

32   Herbert, Victor
        IT HAPPENED IN NORDLAND. Harrisburg. 21 Nov.

1905

33   Mackenzie, Sir Alexander Campbell
        THE KNIGHTS OF THE ROAD. London. 27 Feb.
        Lytton

34   Webber, Amherst
        FIORELLA. London. 7 June. Performed in Italian

35   Herbert, Victor
      MISS DOLLY DOLLARS. Rochester. 31 Aug.

36   ______.
      WONDERLAND. Buffalo. 14 Sept.

37   ______.
      MLLE. MODISTE. Trenton, New Jersey. 7 Oct.
      Henry Blossom

38   Coerne, Louis Adolphe
      ZENOBIA. Bremen, Germany. 1 Dec. Performed in
      German

1906

39   Converse, Frederick S.
      THE PIPE OF DESIRE. Boston. 31 Jan. George
      Edward Barton. (The Pipe of Desire was the first
      American opera to be staged by the Metropolitan
      Opera Company, 18 Mar. 1909)

40   Walthew, Richard Henry
      THE GARDENERS. London. 12 Feb.

41   DeLara, Isidore
      SANGA. Nice. 21 Feb. Performed in French

42   Gatty, Nicholas
      GREYSTEEL, OR THE BEARSARKS COME TO SURNADALE.
      London. 1 Mar. Reginald Gatty

43   Sousa, John Phillip
      THE FREE LANCE. Springfield, Massachusetts.
      26 Mar.

44   D'Erlanger, Frederic
      TESS. Naples. 10 Apr. Illica; performed in
      Italian

45   Maclean, Sir Alexander Morvaren
        DIE LIEGESGEIGE. Mainz, Germany. 15 Apr.
        Performed in German.

46   Eggers, Anton C.
        NINA. New York. 1 May

47   Freeman, Harry Lawrence
        VALDO. Cleveland. ? May

48   Pirani, Eugenio
        BLACK BLOOD. New York. 3 June

49   Herbert, Victor
        THE RED MILL. Buffalo, New York. 3 Sept.

50   Smyth, Dame Ethel
        STRANDRECHT. Leipzig. 11 Nov. H. Brewster;
        original libretto in French; performed in German

51   Lehman, Liza
        THE VICAR OF WAKEFIELD. London. 12 Nov.

52   Herbert, Victor
        DREAM CITY. New York. 25 Dec.

1907

53   Nevin, Arthur
        POIA. Pittsburgh. 16 Jan.

54   Herbert, Victor
        THE TATTOOED MAN. Baltimore. 11 Feb.

55   Delius, Frederick
        A VILLAGE ROMEO AND JULIET (ROMEO UND JULIA AUF
        DEM DORFE). Berlin. 21 Feb. C. F. Keary;
        performed in a German translation by Jelka Delius

56   German, Sir Edward
      TOM JONES. London. 17 Apr. Alexander M.
      Thompson and Charles H. Taylor

57   Gleason, Frederick Grant
      OTHO VISCONTI. Chicago. 4 June. Composer

58   DeLara, Isidore.
      SOLÉA. Cologne. 12 Dec. J. Richepin; performed
      in a German translation by Neitzel

                              1908

59   Holbrooke, Josef
      THE STRANGER. London. ? Mar. W. E. Grogan

60   Leps, Wassili
      ANDON. Philadelphia. 28 May

61   Herbert, Victor
      ALGERIA. Atlantic City. 24 Aug.

62   ______.
      LITTLE NEMO. Philadelphia. 28 Sept.

63   ______.
      THE PRIMA DONNA. Chicago. 5 Oct.

64   Edwards, Julian
      THE PATRIOT. New York. 23 Nov.

65   Harling, William Frank
      ALDA. Boston. 7 Dec.

1909

66   Naylor, Edward Woodall
        THE ANGELUS. London. **27 Jan.** Thornely

67   Hadley, **Henry**
        SAFIÉ. Mayence, Germany. 6 Apr. Edward
        Oxenford; performed in German

68   Leps, Wassili
        HOSHI-SAN. Philadelphia. 21 May. John Luther
        Long

69   Hadley, **Henry**
        THE CULPRIT FAY. Grand Rapids, Michigan.
        28 May

70   Maclean, Alexander Morvaren
        MAÎTRE SEILER. London. 20 Aug.

71   Herbert, Victor
        THE ROSE OF ALGERIA. Wilkes-Barre, Pennsylvania.
        11 Sept.

72   ______.
        OLD DUTCH. Wilkes-Barre, Pennsylvania. 6 Nov.

73   Holbrooke, Josef
        PIERROT AND PIERRETTE. London. 11 Nov. W. E.
        Grogan

74   Gatty, Nicholas Comyn
        DUKE OR DEVIL. Manchester. 16 Dec. I. Gatty

1910

75   Coleridge-Taylor, Samuel
        ENDYMION'S DREAM. Brighton. 3 Feb.

76   O'Dwyer, Robert
        EITHNE. Dublin. 16 May. O'Ceallaigh; performed
        in Gaelic

77   Clutsam, George H.
        A SUMMER NIGHT. London. 23 July. Composer

78   DeLeone, Francesco B.
        A MILLIONAIRE'S CAPRICE. Naples. 26 July

79   Florida, Pietro
        PAOLETTA. Cincinnati. 29 Aug. Paul Jones

80   Hoschna, Carl L.
        MADAME SHERRY. New York. 30 Aug.

81   Herbert, Victor
        NAUGHTY MARIETTA. Syracuse, New York. 24 Oct.
        Rida Johnson Young

82   Berge, Irene Marius
        CORSICA. Kingston, New York. 26 Oct.

83   Breil, Joseph Carl
        LOVE LAUGHS AT LOCKSMITHS. Portland, Maine.
        27 Oct. Composer

84   Stewart, H. L.
        THE ORACLE. San Francisco. 12 Nov.

85   Herbert, Victor
        WHEN SWEET SIXTEEN. Springfield, Massachusetts.
        5 Dec.

86   Tonning, Gerald
        LEIF ERICSSON. Seattle. 10 Dec. C. M. Thuland

First Performance   1911

87   D'Erlanger, Frederic
        NOËL. Paris. 28 Dec. J. Ferrier and P. Ferrier;
        performed in French

                           1911

88   Patton, Willard
        POCAHONTAS. Minneapolis. 4 Jan.

89   Herbert, Victor
        NATOMA. Philadelphia. 25 Feb. Joseph D.
        Redding

90   Converse, Frederick S.
        THE SACRIFICE. Boston. 3 Mar. Composer and
        John Macy

91   Caryll, Ivan
        THE PINK LADY. New York. 13 Mar.

92   Klein, Manuel
        BOW SING. New York. 20 Mar.

93   Herbert, Victor
        MLLE. ROSITA. Boston. 27 Mar. Joseph Herbert.
        (Mlle. Rosita was later titled The Duchess)

94   Delli Ponti, R. and Else Gregori
        HASCHISCH. Turin. 21 Apr.

95   Herbert, Victor
        THE ENCHANTRESS. Washington, D. C. 9 Oct.
        Fred DeGresac and Harry B. Smith

1912

96   Houseley, Henry
     NARCISSUS AND ECHO. Denver. 30 Jan. S. Frances
     Houseley

97   _____.
     PYGMALION. Denver. 30 Jan. S. Frances
     Houseley

98   Delara, Isidore
     LES TROIS MASQUES. Marseilles. 24 Feb. Méré;
     performed in French

99   Kirkpatrick, Howard
     OLAF. Lincoln, Nebraska. 5 Mar.

100 Damrosch, Walter
     THE DOVE OF PEACE. New York. 14 Mar. Wallace
     Irvin

101 Parker, Horatio
     MONA. New York. 14 Mar. Brian Hooker.

102 Moore, Mary Carr
     NARCISSA. Seattle. 22 Apr. Composer's mother

103 DeLara, Isidore
     NAÏL. Paris. 22 Apr. Bois; performed in
     French

104 Holbrooke, Josef
     THE CHILDREN OF DON. London. 15 June. T. E.
     Ellis

105 Herbert, Victor
     THE LADY OF THE SLIPPER. Philadelphia. 8 Oct.

106   Friml, Rudolf
        THE FIREFLY. Syracuse, New York. 14 Oct. Otto
        Harbach

                            1913

107   Hanson, William F.
        THE SUN DANCE. Vernal, Utah. 20 Feb.

108   Damrosch, Walter
        CYRANO. New York. 27 Feb. William J. Henderson

109   Maclean, Alexander Moraven
        WALDIDYLL. Berlin. 23 Mar. Performed in
        German

110   Herbert, Victor
        SWEETHEARTS. Baltimore. 24 Mar. Fred DeGresac
        and Harry B. Smith

111   Hochman, Arthur
        FIAMETTA. New York. 6 Apr. A trial rehearsal

112   Allen, Paul Hastings
        MILDA. Venice. 12 Apr. Performed in Italian

113   Cardillo, Salvatore Napoleone
        ROMILDA. New York. 14 Oct.

114   Herbert, Victor
        THE MADCAP DUCHESS. Rochester, New York. 13 Oct.
        David Stevens and Justin Huntly McCarthy

115   Allen, Paul Hastings
        IL FILTRO. Genoa. 26 Oct. Performed in
        Italian

116   Tonning, Gerard
        ALL IN A GARDEN FAIR. Seattle. 1 Nov. Mrs.
        H. W. Powell

117   Friml, Rudolf
        HIGH JINKS. Syracuse, New York. 3 Nov.

118   Miles, P. Napier
        WESTWARD HO! London. 4 Dec. E. F. Benson

                            1914

119   Herbert, Victor
        MADELEINE. New York. 24 Jan. Grant Stewart

120   Drake, Earl R.
        THE BLIND GIRL OF CASTEL-CUILLE. Chicago.
        19 Feb.

121   Romberg, Sigmund
        THE MIDNIGHT GIRL. New York. 23 Feb.

122   Mackenzie, Sir Alexander Campbell
        THE CRICKET ON THE HEARTH. London. 6 June.
        Julian R. Sturgis

123   Holbrooke, Josef
        DYLAN, SON OF THE WAVE. London. 4 July. T. E.
        Ellis

124   Boughton, Rutland
        THE IMMORTAL HOUR. Glastonbury. 26 Aug.
        Composer

125   ______.
        THE CHAPEL IN LYONESSE. Glastonbury. ? Aug.

126   Herbert, Victor
        THE DÉBUTANTE. Atlantic City. 21 Sept.

127   _____.
        THE ONLY GIRL. Atlantic City. 1 Oct..

128   Etten, Jane Van
        GUIDO FERRANTI. Chicago. 29 Dec.

                        1915

129   Parker, Horatio
        FAIRYLAND. Los Angeles. 1 July. Brian Hooker

130   Romberg, Sigmund
        THE BLUE PARADISE. New York. 5 Aug.

131   Bainton, Edgar Leslie
        THE CRIER BY NIGHT. Glastonbury. 11 Aug.
        Composer

132   _____.
        OITHONA. Glastonbury. 11 Aug. Composer

133   Herbert, Victor
        PRINCESS PAT. Atlantic City. 23 Aug.

134   Enna, Emil
        THE DAWN OF THE WEST. Portland, Oregon. 7 Nov.

135   Friml, Rudolf
        KATINKA. Morristown, New Jersey. 2 Dec. Otto
        Harbach

136   'Boughton, Rutland
        BETHLEHEM. Glastonbury. 28 Dec. (Coventry
        Nativity Play)

1916

137   Stanford, Charles Villiers
        THE CRITIC, OR AN OPERA REHEARSED. London.
        14 Jan. Lewis C. James

138   Bucharoff, Simon
        THE LOVER'S KNOT. Chicago. 15 Jan. Cora
        Bennett-Stephenson

139   Smyth, Dame Ethel
        THE BOATSWAIN'S MATE. London. 28 Jan. Com-
        poser

140   Allen, Paul Hastings
        L'ULTIMO DEI MOICANI. Florence. 24 Feb.
        Zangarini; performed in Italian

141   Beach, John
        PIPPA'S HOLIDAY. Paris. 29 Mar. Performed in
        French

142   Boughton, Rutland
        THE ROUND TABLE. Glastonbury. 14 Aug. Composer
        and Reginald Buckley

143   Raybould, Clarence
        THE SUMIDA RIVER. Glastonbury. 15 Aug. Marie
        Stopes

144   Holst, Gustav
        SAVITRI. London. London School of Opera.
        5 Dec. Composer

1917

145   Herbert, Victor
        EILEEN. Cleveland. 1 Jan. Henry Blossom. (The
        original title for Eileen was Hearts of Erin)

146   Gerrish-Jones, Abbie
        THE SNOW QUEEN. San Francisco. 9 Feb. Gerard
        Wismer Hoffman

147   Moore, Homer
        LOUIS XIV. St. Louis. 16 Feb.

148   DeKoven, Reginald
        THE CANTERBURY PILGRIMS. New York. 8 Mar.
        Percy MacKaye

149   LaPrade, Ernest
        XANTHA. London. 23 Mar.

150   Tonning, Gerard
        BLUE WING. Seattle. 18 May

151   Romberg, Sigmund
        MAYTIME. New York. 7 Aug.

152   Herbert, Victor
        HER REGIMENT. Springfield, Massachusetts.
        22 Oct. William LeBaron

153   Guerrieri, Stefano
        EVANDRO. New York. 23 Nov. Performed in
        Italian

154   Hadley, Henry
        AZORA, DAUGHTER OF MONTEZUMA. Chicago. 26 Dec.
        David Stephens

                            1918

155   Nevin, Arthur Finley
        A DAUGHTER OF THE FOREST. Chicago. 5 Jan.
        Randolph Hartley

1919   First Performances

156   Cadman, Charles Wakefield
        SHANEWIS, OR THE ROBIN WOMAN. New York.
        23 Mar. Nelle Richmond Eberhart

157   Heckscher, Celeste de Longpre
        THE ROSE OF DESTINY. Philadelphia. 2 May.
        Composer

158   Belcher, Mary Williams
        THE LEGEND OF RONSARD AND MADELON. Cleveland.
        Cleveland University. ? June

159   Witmark, Isidore
        SHANGHAI. London. 28 Aug.

160   Hadley, Henry
        BIANCA. New York. 15 Oct. Grant Stewart

161   Herbert, Victor
        THE VELVET LADY. Philadelphia. 23 Dec.

1919

162   Breil, Joseph Carl
        THE LEGEND. New York. 12 Mar. Jacques Byrne

163   Hugo, John Adam
        THE TEMPLE DANCER. New York. 12 Mar. J. Bell-
        Ranke

164   Boughton, Rutland
        THE MOON MAIDEN. Glastonbury. 23 Apr. Marie
        Stopes

165   Parry, Joseph
        BLODWEN (WHITE FLOWER). Colwyn Bay. 29 Apr.
        Performed in Welsh

First Performances   1920

166   Herbert, Victor
        ANGEL FACE. Chicago. 8 June

167   Delius, Frederick
        FENNIMORE UND GERDA. Frankfurt. 21 Oct.
        Composer; performed in German

168   Gatty, Nicholas Comyn
        PRINCE FERELON, OR, THE PRINCESS'S SUITORS.
        London. Florence Ettlinger Opera School.
        27 Nov. Composer

169   Herbert, Victor
        MY GOLDEN GIRL. Stamford, Connecticut. 19 Dec.

                        1920

170   Dekoven, Reginald
        RIP VAN WINKLE. Chicago. 2 Jan. Percy Mackaye

171   Barkworth, John Edmund
        ROMEO AND JULIET. Middlesborough, England.
        7 Jan. Composer

172   Maclean, Alexander Morvaren
        QUENTIN DURWARD. Newcastle-on-Tyne. 13 Jan.
        Ross

173   Hadley, Henry
        CLEOPATRA'S NIGHT. New York. 31 Jan. Alice
        Leal Pollock

174   Zimbalist, Efrem
        HONEYDEW. Stamford, Connecticut. 19 Mar.

175   Herbert, Victor
        OUI, MADAME. Philadelphia. 22 Mar.

176   Gatty, Nicholas Comyn
        THE TEMPEST. London. 17 Apr. Reginald Gatty

1921   First Performances

177   Clokey, Joseph W.
        THE PIED PIPER OF HAMELIN. Miami, Ohio. Miami
        University. 14 May. Anna J. Bieswenger

178   Herbert, Victor
        THE GIRL IN THE SPOTLIGHT. Stamford,
        Connecticut. 7 July

179   Boughton, Rutland
        THE BIRTH OF ARTHUR. Glastonbury. 16 Aug.
        Composer and Reginald Buckley

180   Cadman, Charles Wakefield
        THE SUNSET TRAIL. San Diego. 23 Aug. Moyle

181.   Somerville, Sir Arthur
        DAVID GARRICK. London. 9 Dec. Composer

1921

182   DeLara, Isidore
        LE TROIS MOUSQUETAIRES. Cannes. 3 Mar. Cain
        and Payla; performed in French

183   Phillips, Montague
        THE REBEL MAID. London. 12 Mar.

184   Berners, Lord (Gerald Tyrwhitt)
        LA CARROSE DU SAINT-SACREMENT. Paris. 24 Apr.
        Performed in French

185   Carey, Clive
        ALL FOOL'S DAY. Glastonbury. 29 Aug. T. M.
        Baretti

186   Campbell, Colin Macleod
        THAÏS AND TALMAAE. Manchester. 13 Sept. Bourne

First Performances

187   McCoy, William J.
        EGYPT. Berkeley, California. 17 Sept.

188   Romberg, Sigmund
        BLOSSOM TIME. New York. 29 Sept.

                        1922

189   Rootham, Cyril
        THE TWO SISTERS. Cambridge, England. 14 Feb.
        M. Fausset.

190   Romberg, Sigmund
        THE ROSE OF STAMBOUL. New York. 7 Mar.

191   Moore, Mary Carr
        THE FLAMING ARROW. San Francisco. 27 Mar.
        Sarah Pratt Carr

192   Hager, George
        PAN. Seattle Cornish School. 21 Apr.

193   Noyes-Greene, Edith
        OSSEO. Boston. 9 May. Lillie Fuller Mirriam

194   Vaughan Williams, Ralph
        THE SHEPHERDS OF THE DELECTABLE MOUNTAINS.
        London. Royal College of Music. 11 July. Com-
        poser. (The Shepherds of the Delectable Moun-
        tains was later incorporated into The Pilgrim's
        Progress)

195   'Boughton, Rutland
        ALKESTIS. Glastonbury. 26 Aug.

196   Herbert, Victor
        ORANGE BLOSSOMS. Philadelphia. 4 Sept.

1923

197   Browne, John Lewis
        LA CORSICANA. Chicago. 4 Jan. Stuart Maclean;
        performed in an Italian translation

198   Stearns, Theodore
        SNOWBIRD. Chicago. 13 Jan. Composer

199   Chadwick, George Whitfield
        LOVE'S SACRIFICE. Chicago. 1 Feb.

200   Farner, Eugene Adrian
        THE WHITE BUFFALO MAID. Boise, Idaho. 26 Apr.

201   Holst, Gustav
        THE PERFECT FOOL. London. 14 May. Composer

202   Ware, Harriet
        UNDINE. Baltimore. Peabody Conservatory.
        19 May

203   Smyth, Dame Ethel
        FÊTE GALANTE. Birmingham, England. 4 June.
        Shanks; performed in French

204   Venth, Carl
        PAN IN AMERICA. Asheville, North Carolina.
        13 June

205   Palmer, Geoffrey Molyneux
        SRUTH NA MAOILE. Dublin. 25 July. O'Ceallaigh;
        .performed in Gaelic

206   Reiser, Alois
        GOBI. New York. 29 July

207   Freeman, Harry Lawrence
       VENDETTA. New York. 12 Nov.

208   Bath, Hubert
       BUBBLES. Belfast. 26 Nov. Composer

209   Armstrong-Gibbs, Cecil
       THE BLUE PETER. London. 11 Dec. A. P. Herbert

1924

210   Pound, Ezra
       LE TESTAMENT DU FRANCOIS VILLON. Paris. ? Jan.
       Composer; performed in French and English. (The
       revised version of Le Testament was broadcast on
       BBC, 26 Oct. 1931)

211   Freer, Eleanor Everest
       THE LEGEND OF THE PIPER. South Bend, Indiana.
       28 Feb.

212   Carter, Ernest Trow
       THE WHITE BIRD. Chicago. 6 Mar. Brian Hooker

213   Mackenzie, Sir Alexander Campbell
       SAINT JOHN'S EVE. Liverpool. 16 Apr. E.
       Farjeon

214   Herbert, Victor
       THE DREAM GIRL. New Haven. 22 Apr.

215   Stewart, Humphrey J.
       THE HOUND OF HEAVEN. San Francisco. 24 Apr.

216   Blakeslee, Samuel Earle
       THE LEGEND OF WIWASTE. Ontario, California.
       Chaffey Junior College. 25 Apr.

1924

First Performances

217   DeLeone, Francesco B.
        ALGALA. Akron, Ohio. 23 May. Cecil Fanning

218   Armstrong-Gibbs, C.
        MIDSUMMER MADNESS. Hammersmith, England. 3 July.
        Clifford Bax

219   Vaughan Williams, Ralph
        HUGH THE DROVER. London. 14 July. Harold H.
        Child

220   Boughton, Rutland
        THE SERAPHIC VISION. Glastonbury. 8 Aug.

221   Friml, Rudolf and Herbert Stothart
        ROSE-MARIE. Atlantic City. 18 Aug.

222   Boughton, Rutland
        THE QUEEN OF CORNWALL. Glastonbury. 21 Aug.
        Composer

223   ______.
        AGINCOURT. Glastonbury. 26 Aug. Composer

224   Bantock, Granville
        THE SEAL WOMAN. Birmingham, England. 27 Sept.
        Margery Kennedy-Fraser

225   Miles, Philip Napier
        FIRE FLIES. Clifton, England. 13 Oct. Julian
        R. Sturgis

226   ______.
        MARKHEIM. Clifton, England. 13 Oct. Composer

227   Bucharoff, Simon
        SAKAHRA. Frankfurt. 29 Oct. Isabel Buckingham;
        performed in German

First Performances   1925

228   Romberg, Sigmund
        THE STUDENT PRINCE. New York. 2 Dec.

229   Kirkpatrick, Howard
        LA MENUETTE. Lincoln, Nebraska. 8 Dec. H. B.
        Alexander

                            1925

230   Saminsky, Lazare
        GAGLIARDA OF A MERRY PLAGUE. New York. 22 Feb.
        Composer

231   Redding, Joseph D.
        FAY-YEN-FAH. Monte Carlo. 26 Feb. Charles
        Templeton Crocker

232   Cadman, Charles Wakefield
        THE GARDEN OF MYSTERY. New York. 20 Mar. Nelle
        Richmond Eberhardt.

233   Savini, Alexander
        XENIA. New York. 21 Mar.

234   Holst, Gustav
        AT THE BOAR'S HEAD. Manchester. 3 Apr.
        Composer

235   Stanford, Charles Villiers
        THE TRAVELLING COMPANION. Liverpool. 30 Apr.
        Henry Newbolt

236   Arnstein, Ira B.
        THE SONG OF DAVID. New York. 17 May

237   Scott, Cyril Meir
        THE ALCHEMIST. Essen. 28 May. Composer;
        performed in a German translation

1926   First Performances

238   Patterson, Franklin
        THE ECHO. Portland, Oregon. 9 June. Composer

239   Smyth, Dame Ethel
        ENTENTE CORDIALE. London. Royal College of Music.
        22 July. Composer

240   Friml, Rudolf
        THE VAGABOND KING. New York. 15 Sept.

241   Breil, Joseph Carl
        DER ASRA. Los Angeles. 24 Nov. Composer

242   Franchetti, Aldo
        NAMIKO-SAN. Chicago. 11 Dec.

243   Clokely, Joseph W.
        THE NIGHTINGALE. Miami, Ohio. Miami University.
        12 Dec. Willis Knapp-Jones

244   Harling, W. Franke
        A LIGHT FROM ST. AGNES. Chicago. 26 Dec.

                            1926

245   Freer, Eleanor Everest
        MASSIMILLIANO, OR THE COURT JESTER. Lincoln,
        Nebraska. 19 Jan. Elia W. Peattie

246   Shaw, Martin
        MR. PEPYS. London. 11 Feb. Clifford Bax

247   Reynolds, Alfred
        THE POLICEMAN'S SERENADE. Hammersmith, England.
        10 Apr. A. P. Herbert

248   Lyford, Ralph
        CASTLE AGRAZANT. Cincinnati. 29 Apr. Composer

First Performances   1927

249   Knowlton, E. Bruce
        THE MONK OF TOLEDO. Portland, Oregon. 10 May.
        Composer

250   Engels, Peter Joseph
        KING SOLOMON. New York. 26 May. Partial
        performance; performed in German

251   Venth, Carl
        THE REBEL. Fort Worth, Texas. 29 May. Composer

252   Grove, Issac Van
        THE MUSIC ROBBER. Cincinnati. 4 July. Richard
        L. Stokes

253   Harling. W. Franke
        DEEP RIVER. Lancaster, Pennsylvania. 18 Sept.

254   Bryson, Ernest
        THE LEPER'S FLUTE. Glasgow. 15 Oct. J. Colvin

255   Bimoni, Alberto
        WINONA. Portland, Oregon. 11 Nov. Perry
        Williams

256   Romberg, Sigmund
        THE DESERT SONG. New York. 30 Nov. Otto
        Harbach, Oscar Hammerstein II and Frank Mandel

257   Cadman, Charles Wakefield
        A WITCH OF SALEM. Chicago. 8 Dec. Nelle
        Richmond Eberhart

1927

258   Romberg, Sigmund
        MY MARYLAND. Atlantic City. 10 Jan.

259   Taylor, Deems
        THE KING'S HENCHMAN. New York. 17 Feb. Edna
        St. Vincent Millay

260   Giglio, Clement.
        THE WHITE SISTER. Paterson, New Jersey. 29 Mar.
        Performed in Italian

261   Lester, William
        EVERYMAN. Chicago. 24 Apr. Composer

262   Braine, Robert
        THE WANDERING JEW. New York. 14 May.
        E. Temple Thurston

263   Collingwood, Lawrence Arthur
        MACBETH. London. 12 Nov. Composer

264   Romberg, Sigmund
        THE NEW MOON. Philadelphia. 22 Dec.

                           1928

265   Friml, Rudolf
        THE THREE MUSKETEERS. New York. 13 Mar.
        William A. McGuire

266   Ozier, Julius
        THE BRIDGE OF BAGDAD. Kansas City, Missouri.
        ? Mar. Excerpts

267   Virzi, Salvatore
        VANNA. New York. 9 Apr. Performed in Italian;
        performance collapsed after one act

268   Hanson, William F.
        TÄM-MÄN-NÄCÚP. Provo, Utah. 8 May

269   Appleton, Adeline Carola
        THE WITCHES' WELL. Tacoma, Washington. ? May.
        Composer; excerpts

270   Freeman, Harry Lawrence
        VOODOO. New York. 10 Sept.

271   Knowlton, E. Bruce
        WAKUTA. Portland, Oregon. 14 Oct. Composer

272   Shaw, Martin
        WATERLOO LEAVE. Norwich, England. 12 Nov.
        Clifford Bax

                            1929

273   Holbrooke, Josef
        BRONWEN, DAUGHTER OF LLYER. Huddersfield.
        1 Feb. T. E. Ellis

274   Vaughan Williams, Ralph
        SIR JOHN IN LOVE. London. Royal College of
        Music. 21 Mar. Composer

275   Engel, A. Lehman
        PIERROT OF THE MINUTE. Cincinnati. Cincinnati
        College. 8 Apr.

276   Knowlton, E. Bruce
        THE WOODSMAN. Portland, Oregon. 4 Apr.
        Composer

277   Blitzstein, Marc
        TRIPLE SEC. Philadelphia. 6 May. Ronald Jeans

278   Goosens, Eugene
        JUDITH. London. 25 June. Arnold Bennett

1930   First Performances

279   Coward, Noel
       BITTER SWEET. London. 21 Aug. Composer

280   Loomis, Clarence
       YOLANDA OF CYPRUS. Hamilton, Ontario. 9 Oct.
       Cole Young Rice

281   Romberg, Sigmund
       NINA ROSE. Detroit. 22 Oct.

282   Shaw, Martin
       AT THE SIGN OF THE STAR. London. 6 Dec.
       Barclay Baron

283   Lawrence, Charles W.
       ATSUMORI. Seattle, Washington. University of
       Washington. 11 Dec.

284   Knowlton, E. Bruce
       CHARLOTTE. Portland, Oregon. 11 Dec. Composer

285   Coates, Albert
       SAMUEL PEPYS. Munich. 21 Dec. W. P. Drury and
       R. Pryce; performed in a German translation

286   Freer, Eleanor Everest
       A CHRISTMAS TALE. Houston, Texas. 27 Dec.

                          1930

287   LaViolette, Wesley
       SHYLOCK. Chicago. 9 Feb. Excerpts

288   Flick-Stegner, Charles L.
       DORIAN GRAY. Aussiz, Bohemia. 1 Mar. Performed
       in German

289   Lester, Thomas William
       MANABOZO. Chicago. 26 Mar. Private performance
       of excerpts

First Performances   1931

290   Skilton, Charles Sanford
         THE SUN BRIDE. New York. 17 Apr. Lillian
         White Spencer

291   Antheil, George
         TRANSATLANTIC. Frankfurt. 25 May. Composer;
         performed in German

292   Forrest, Hamilton
         CAMILLE. Chicago. 10 Dec. Composer

293   Gatty, Nicholas Comyn
         KING ALFRED AND THE CAKES. London. 10 Dec.
         Reginald Gatty

                         1931

294   Dunhill, Thomas Frederick
         TANTIVY TOWERS. London. 6 Jan. A. P. Herbert

295   Freer, Eleanor Everest
         FRITIHOF. Chicago. 1 Feb.

296   Loeffler, Charles Martin
         EVOCATION. Cleveland. 5 Feb.

297   Taylor, Deems
         PETER IBBETSON. New York. 7 Feb. Composer and
         Constance Collier

298   Clokey, Joseph W.
         OUR AMERICAN COUSIN. Claremont, California.
         2 Mar. Willis Knapp-Jones

299   James, D.
         PAOLO AND FRANCESCA. Rochester, New York.
         Eastman School of Music. 2 Apr.

300   Marsh, William J.
      THE FLOWER OF FAIR PEKING. Dallas, Texas.
      23 Apr.

301   Rogers, Bernard
      THE MARRIAGE OF AUDE. Rochester, New York.
      22 May. Charles Rodda

302   Shaw, Martin
      THE THORN OF AVALON. London. 6 June. Barclay
      Baron

303   Freer, Eleanor Everest
      A LEGEND OF SPAIN. Milwaukee. 19 June.

304   Moore, Mary Carr
      LOS RUBIOS. Los Angeles. 10 Sept. Neeta
      Marquis

305   Leigh, Walter
      THE PRIDE OF THE REGIMENT, OR CASHIERED FOR HIS
      COUNTRY. Midhurst, England. 19 Sept.
      V. C. Clinton-Bradley and Scobie Mackenzie

306   Oberndorfer, Marx E.
      ROSEANNE. Chicago. 25 Oct. Nan Bagby Stevens

307   Knowlton, E. Bruce
      ANTONIO. Portland, Oregon. 27 Oct. Composer

308   Gruenberg, Louis
      JACK AND THE BEANSTALK. New York. Juilliard.
      19 Nov. John Erskine

309   Benjamin, Arthur
      THE DEVIL TAKE HER. London. Royal College of
      Music. 1 Dec. Allan Collard

310   Schmidt, Karl
        THE LADY OF THE LAKE. Chicago. 6 Dec. Wallace
        Taylor Hughes

311   Carter, Ernest
        THE BLONDE DONNA, OR THE FIESTA OF SANTA BARBARA.
        Brooklyn. 8 Dec. Composer

1932

312   Manning, Edward
        RIP VAN WINKLE. New York. 12 Feb.

313   Hageman, Richard
        TRAGÖDIE IN AREZZO. Freiburg-im-Breisgau.
        18 Feb. Arthur Goodrich; performed in German
        (Performed in New York at the Metropolitan Opera
        on 4 Feb. 1937 under the title Caponsacchi)

314   Reynolds, Alfred
        DERBY DAY. Hammersmith, England. 24 Feb.
        A. P. Herbert

315   Tovey, Sir Donald
        THE BRIDE OF DIONYSUS. Edinburgh. 25 Apr.
        R. C. Trevelyan

316   Moore, Mary Carr
        DAVID RIZZIO. Los Angeles. 26 May. Emmanuel
        Mapelson Browne

317   Graham, Shirley
        TOM-TOM. Cleveland. 30 June. Composer

318   Loomis, Clarence
        A NIGHT IN AVIGNON. Indianapolis. ? July.
        Cole Young Rice

Twentieth Century Opera

First Performances

319   Weber, Bertha
      THE MYSTERIOUS CHARACTERS OF MR. FU. Oakland,
      California. 7 Oct.

320   Luening, Otto
      EVANGELINE. New York. Columbia University.
      29 Dec. Composer

1933

321   Gruenberg, Louis
      THE EMPEROR JONES. New York. 7 Jan. Kathleen
      DeJaffa

322   Leigh, Walter
      THE JOLLY ROGER, OR, THE ADMIRAL'S DAUGHTER.
      Manchester, England. 13 Feb. V. C. Clinton-
      Bradley and Scobie Mackenzie

323   Hadley, Henry
      A NIGHT IN OLD PARIS. New York. 22 Feb.

324   Rosenthal, Manuel
      BOOTLEGGERS. Paris. 2 May.

325   Hanson, Howard
      MERRY MOUNT. Ann Arbor, Michigan. University
      of Michigan. 20 May. Richard L. Stokes

326   Haile, Eugene
      HAROLD'S DREAM. Woodstock, New York. 30 June.

327   Cadman, Charles Wakefield
      THE WILLOW TREE. New York. 3 Oct. Nelle
      Richmond Eberhart

328   Lehner, Derrick N.
      THE HARVEST. San Francisco. 14 Oct.

329   Dunhill, Thomas Frederick
       HAPPY FAMILIES. Guildford. 1 Nov.

330   Wad, Emmanuel
       SWING LOW. Baltimore. 13 Dec.

1934

331   Holst, Gustav
       THE WANDERING SCHOLAR. Liverpool. 31 Jan.
       Clifford Bax

332   Thomson, Virgil
       FOUR SAINTS IN THREE ACTS. Hartford, Connecticut.
       28 Feb. Gertrude Stein

333   Antheil, George
       HELEN RETIRES. New York. Juilliard. 28 Feb.
       John Erskine

334   Freer, Eleanor Everest
       LITTLE WOMEN. Chicago. 2 Apr.

335   Collingwood, Lawrence Arthur
       MACBETH. London. 12 Apr. Composer

336   Kroll, Louis
       MME. BUTTERFLY RECOVERS. New York. 20 May

337   Pemberton, Charles E.
       THE PAINTER OF DREAMS. Los Angeles. University
       of Southern California. ? May

338   Allen, Gilbert
       STEAL AWAY. New York. 26 July.

339   Boughton, Rutland
       THE LILY MAID. Gloucester. 10 Sept. Composer

340   Giannini, Vittorio
        LUCEDIA. Munich. 20 Oct. Karl Flaster; per-
        formed in a German translation of the original
        Italian libretto

341   Lloyd, George
        IERNIN. London. 6 Nov. W. Lloyd

342   D'Antalffy, D.
        ONTEORA'S BRIDE. New York. 15 Nov.

343   Weinberg, Jacob
        HECHALUTZ. New York. 25 Nov.

344   Lehner, Derrich Norman
        THE NECKLACE OF THE SUN. Oakland, California.
        ? Dec.

                        1935

345   Barlow, Samuel L. M.
        MON AMI PIERROT. Paris. 11 Jan. Sacha Guitry.
        (Mon Ami Pierrot was the first opera by an Amer-
        ican composer premiered at the Opera-Comique)

346   Seymour, John Laurence
        IN PASHA'S GARDEN. New York. 24 Jan.
        H. C. Tracy

347   Bennett, Robert Russell
        MARIA MALIBRAN. New York. Juilliard. 8 Apr.
        Robert A. Simon

348   Tietjens, Paul
        THE TENTS OF THE ARABS. New York. Columbia
        University. 7 Aug.

349   Boughton, Rutland
        THE EVER YOUNG. Bath. 9 Sept. Composer

350   Kroll, Louis
        LE BELLE, OR ANDRE GOES COMMERCIAL. New York.
        30 Sept.

351   Gershwin, George
        PORGY AND BESS. Boston. 30 Sept. DuBose
        Heyward and Ira Gershwin

352   Leginska, Ethel
        GALE. Chicago. 23 Nov. C. A. Dawson-Scott

353   Claflin, Avery
        HESTER PRYNNE. Hartford, Connecticut. 15 Dec.
        Dorothea Claflin

1936

354   Cole, Rossetter Gleason
        THE MAYPOLE LOVERS. Chicago. 9 Jan. Partial
        performance

355   Bimboni, Alberto
        THERE WAS A LITTLE GATE. New York. 11 Mar.

356   Lindsey, Edwin S.
        ELIZABETH AND LEICESTER. Chattanooga, Tennessee.
        University of Chattanooga. 21 Apr.

357   Vaughan Williams, Ralph
        THE POISONED KISS, OR THE EMPRESS AND THE
        NECROMANCER. Cambridge, England. 12 May.
        Evelyn Sharp

358   Shaw, Martin
        MASTER VALIANT. London. ? June. Barclay Baron

1937   First Performances

359   Thomas, Gertrude Auld
       HAZILA. Los Angeles. 27 Oct.

360   Lovingood, Penman
       MENELEK. New York. 16 Nov.

361   Coates, Albert
       PICKWICK. London. 20 Nov. Composer

362   Quilter, Roger
       JULIA. London. 3 Dec.

1937

363   Weill, Kurt
       THE ETERNAL ROAD. New York. 7 Jan.

364   Stoessel, Albert
       GARRICK. New York. Juilliard. 24 Feb.
       Robert A. Simon

365   Moore, Douglas
       THE HEADLESS HORSEMAN. Bronx, New York. 5 Mar.
       Stephen Vincent Benét

366   Moonie, W. B.
       THE WEIRD OF COLBAR. Glasgow. 22 Mar.
       G. M. Reith

367   Menotti, Gian-Carlo
       AMELIA AL BALLO. Philadelphia. 1 Apr. Composer

368   Hanson, William F.
       THE BLEEDING HEART OF TIMPANOGAS. Provo, Utah.
       7 Apr.

369   Copland, Aaron
       THE SECOND HURRICANE. New York. 21 Apr. Edwin
       Denby

370   Damrosch, Walter
        THE MAN WITHOUT A COUNTRY. New York. 12 May.
        Arthur Guiterman

371   Blitzstein, Marc
        THE CRADLE WILL ROCK. New York. 16 June.
        Composer

372   Goosens, Eugene
        DON JUAN DE MAÑARA. London. 24 June. Arnold
        Bennett

373   Gruenberg, Louis
        GREEN MANSIONS. New York. 17 Oct. Brian
        Hooker

374   Blitzstein, Marc
        I'VE GOT THE TUNE. New York. 24 Oct.

375   Vaughan Williams, Ralph
        RIDERS TO THE SEA. London. 30 Nov. (The
        libretto is the original J. M. Synge play with
        minor changes)

                            1938

376   Rubinstein, Beryl
        THE SLEEPING BEAUTY. New York. Juilliard.
        19 Jan. John Erskine

377   Strube, Gustav
        ROMONA. Baltimore. 28 Feb. Frederick Kummer

378   Alderman, Pauline
        BOMBASTES FURIOSO. Los Angeles. University of
        Southern California. 30 Apr.

1939   First Performances

379   Freer, Eleanor Everest
        THE BROWNINGS GO TO ITALY. Chicago. 11 May.

380   Kubik, Gail
        A MIRROR IN THE SKY. Eugene, Oregon. University
        of Oregon. 23 May. Jessamyn West

381   Giannini, Vittorio
        THE SCARLET LETTER. Hamburg. 2 June. Composer;
        performed in German

382   Wickham, Florence
        ROSALIND. Carmel, New York. 5 Aug.

383   Ruger, Morris Hutchen
        GETTYSBURG. Los Angeles. 23 Sept.

384   Weill, Kurt
        KNICKERBOCKER HOLIDAY. Hartford, Connecticut.
        24 Sept. Maxwell Anderson

385   Rubino, Pasquale
        IL FILO D'ARIANNA. New York. 24 Sept. Per-
        formed in Italian

386   Lloyd, George
        THE SERF. London. 20 Oct. W. Lloyd

387   Giannini, Vittorio
        BEAUTY AND THE BEAST. New York. 24 Nov.
        Robert A. Simon

1939

388   Von Donhoff, Baron Gabriel Wajditsch Verbovac
        HORUS. Philadelphia. 5 Jan. Composer

First Performances   1940

389   Giannini, Vittorio
        BLENNERHASSET. New York. 2 Feb. Philip Roll
        and Norman Corwin

390   Smith, Julia
        CYNTHIA PARKER. Denton, Texas. North Texas
        State Teachers College. 16 Feb.

391   Menotti, Gian-Carlo
        THE OLD MAID AND THE THIEF. New York. 22 Apr.
        Composer

392   Moses, Abram
        MELODY IN 'I'. Baltimore. 2 May

393   Moore, Douglas
        THE DEVIL AND DANIEL WEBSTER. New York. 18 May.
        Stephen Vincent Benét

394   Zádor, Eugen
        CHRISTOPHER COLUMBUS. New York. 8 Oct. Arch-
        duke Joseph Franz; original libretto in Hungarian;
        performance in an English translation

1940

395   Cheslock, Louis
        THE JEWEL MERCHANTS. Baltimore. Peabody Con-
        servatory. 26 Feb.

396   Lee, Dai Keong
        THE POET'S DILEMMA. New York. 12 Apr.

397   Baron, Maurice
        FRANCOIS VILLON. New York. 14 Apr.

398   Stramiello, Ernest
        MAGGIO FIORINTINO. New York. Brooklyn Academy
        of Music. 29 Apr.

1941   First Performances

399   Weill, Kurt
      LADY IN THE DARK. Boston. 30 Dec. Moss Hart

1941

400   Blitzstein, Marc
      NO FOR AN ANSWER. New York. 5 Jan. Composer

401   Loomis, Clarence
      THE FALL OF THE HOUSE OF USHER. Indianapolis.
      11 Jan.

402   Nordoff, Franklin
      THE MASTERPIECE. Philadelphia. 24 Jan.
      Franklin Brewer

403   Elmore, Robert
      IT BEGAN AT BREAKFAST. Philadelphia. 18 Feb.

404   Coates, Albert
      GAINSBOROUGH'S DUCHESS. Los Angeles. U. C. L. A.
      20 Apr.

405   Britten, Benjamin
      PAUL BUNYAN. New York. Columbia University.
      5 May. W. H. Auden

406   Krenek, Ernst
      TARQUIN. Poughkeepsie, New York. 13 May.

407   White, Clarence Cameron
      OUANGA. New York. New School for Social
      Research. 18 June. John Frederick Matheus

1942

408   Taylor, Deems
      RAMUNTCHO. Philadelphia. 7 Feb. Composer

409   Menotti, Gian-Carlo
        THE ISLAND GOD. New York. 20 Feb. Composer
        and Fleming McLeish

410   William, Henley
        TRANSIT THROUGH FIRE. Toronto. 8 Mar.

411   Thompson, Randall
        SOLOMON AND BALKIS. New York. 29 Mar. Composer

412   Lessner, George
        THE NIGHTINGALE AND THE ROSE. New York. 25 Apr.

413   Loomis, Clarence
        REVIVAL. Los Angeles. ? Apr.

414   Bacon, Ernest
        A TREE ON THE PLAINS. Spartanburg, South
        Carolina. Converse College. 2 May. Paul Horgan

415   Maganini, Quinto
        TENNESSEE PARTNER. New York. 28 May.

416   Damrosch, Walter
        THE OPERA CLOAK. New York. 3 Nov. Gretchen
        Damrosch Finletter

417   Wood, Joseph
        THE MOTHER. New York. Juilliard. 9 Dec. Hurd
        Hatfield

                        1943

418   Hageman, Richard
        THE CRUCIBLE. Los Angeles. 4 Feb.

419   Tauber, Richard
        OLD CHELSEA. London. 17 Feb.

420   Weill, Kurt
       ONE TOUCH OF VENUS. Boston. 17 Sept.
       S. J. Perelman and Ogden Nash

421   William, Henley
       BREBEUF AND HIS BRETHEN. Toronto. 26 Sept.

422   Savine, Alexander
       THE GIRL FROM SANJAK. Chicago. 3 Oct.

423   Bennett, Robert Russell
       CARMEN JONES. New York. 9 Dec. Oscar
       Hammerstein II

1944

424   Gray, Cecil
       THE WOMEN OF TROY. London. 5 Apr. Composer

425   Wagenaar, Bernard
       PIECES OF EIGHT. New York. Columbia University.
       10 May. Edward Eager

426   Bainton, Edgar Leslie
       THE PEARL TREE. Sydney. 20 May. R. C. Trevelyan

427   Brand, Max
       THE GATE. New York. 23 May

428   Siegmeister, Elie
       SING OUT, SWEET LAND. Hartford, Connecticut.
       9 Nov.

1945

429   Lourié, Arthur
       THE FEAST DURING THE PLAGUE. Boston. 5 Jan.

430   Romberg, Sigmund
        UP IN CENTRAL PARK. New York. 27 Jan.

431   Beach, Mrs. H. H. A.
        CABILDO. Athens, Georgia. University of Georgia.
        27 Feb.

432   Lockwood, Normand
        THE SCARECROW. New York. Columbia University.
        9 May. Dorothy Lockwood and Percy MacKaye

433   Virzi, Salvatore
        IL CANCELLETO D'ORO. New York. 18 May

434   Britten, Benjamin
        PETER GRIMES. London. 7 June. Montague Slater

435   Bennett, Robert Russell
        THE ENCHANTED KISS. New York. 30 Dec. Robert A.
        Simon

                        1946

436   William, Henley
        DEIDRE OF THE SORROWS. Toronto. 20 Apr.

437   Menotti, Gian-Carlo
        THE MEDIUM. New York. 8 May. Composer

438   Gundry, Inglis
        THE PARTISANS. St. Pancras. 28 May. Composer

439   Britten, Benjamin
        THE RAPE OF LUCRETIA. Glyndebourne. 12 July.
        Ronald Duncan

440   Weill, Kurt
        STREET SCENE. Philadelphia. 16 Dec. Elmer Rice
        and Langston Hughes

1947

441   Rogers, Bernard
        THE WARRIOR. New York. 11 Jan. Norman Corwin

442   Menotti, Gian-Carlo
        THE TELEPHONE. New York. 18 Feb. Composer

443   Smith, Julia
        THE GOOSEHERD AND THE GOBLIN. New York. 22 Feb.
        Josephine Fetter-Royle

444   Sessions, Roger
        THE TRIAL OF LUCULLUS. Berkeley, California.
        University of California-Berkeley. 18 Apr.

445   Smith, Julia
        THE STRANGER OF MANZANO. Dallas, Texas.
        Southern Methodist University. 6 May

446   Thomson, Virgil
        THE MOTHER OF US ALL. New York. Columbia Uni-
        versity. 7 May. Gertrude Stein

447   Britten, Benjamin
        ALBERT HERRING. Glyndebourne. 20 June. Eric
        Crozier

1948

448   Anders, Emile
        KING HARALD. New York. Hunter College. 7 Jan.

449·   Allen, Paul Hastings
        'O MUNASTERIO. New York. 11 Jan. Performed in
        Italian

450   Bergensen, Baldwin
        FAR HARBOR. New York. Hunter College. 22 Jan.

451   Hopkins, Anthony
        LADY ROHESIA. London. 17 Mar. Composer

452   Doellner, Robert
        ESCAPE FROM LIBERTY. Hartford, Connecticut.
        1 Apr.

453   Collins, Anthony
        CATHERINE PARR. New York. 9 May. Maurice
        Barring

454   Freed, Isadore
        THE PRINCESS AND THE VAGABOND. Hartford, Con-
        necticut. Hartt College. 13 May. Pearl
        Cleveland Wilson

455   Allen, Paul Hastings
        MAMZELLE FIGARO. Lindenhurst, New York. 20 May.
        Composer; performed in Italian

456   Weill, Kurt
        DOWN IN THE VALLEY. Bloomington, Indiana.
        Indiana University. 14 July. Arnold Sundgaard

457   Virzi, Salvatore
        SULAMITA. New York. 19 Dec.

                        1949

458   Byrd, William Clifton
        LYNEIA. Cincinnati. University of Cincinnati.
        20 Jan.

459   Moore, Douglas
        WHITE WINGS. Hartford, Connecticut. Hartt Col-
        lege. 9 Feb. Composer

460   Kalmanoff, Martin
        FIT FOR A KING. New York. 13 Feb. Atra Bear

461   Moore, Douglas
        THE EMPEROR'S NEW CLOTHES. New York. 19 Feb.
        Raymond Abrashkin

462   Benjamin, Arthur
        PRIMA DONNA. London. 23 Feb. Cedric Cliffe

463   Baylor, Murray
        BY GEMINI. Galesburg, Illinois. Knox College.
        2 Mar.

464   Still, William Grant
        THE TROUBLED ISLAND. New York. 31 Mar.
        Langston Hughes

465   Gundry, Inglis
        AVON. Scala. 11 Apr. Composer

466   Floyd, Carlisle
        SLOW DUSK. Syracuse, New York. Syracuse Uni-
        versity. 2 May. Composer

467   Bacon, Ernst
        A DRUMLIN LEGEND. New York. Columbia Univer-
        sity. 9 May. Helen Carus

468   Phillips, Burrill
        DON'T WE ALL. Rochester, New York. Eastman
        School of Music. 9 May. Alberta Phillips

469   Bimboni, Alberto
        IN THE NAME OF CULTURE. Rochester, New York.
        Eastman School of Music. 9 May. Norma
        Stelzenbach

First Performances   1950

470   Britten, Benjamin
        THE LITTLE SWEEP. Aldeburgh. 14 June. Eric
        Crozier (The Little Sweep is the third act of
        Let's Make an Opera)

471   Meyerowitz, Jan
        SIMOON. Tanglewood (Lenox, Massachusetts) 2 Aug.
        John P. Stevens

472   Jacobi, Frederick
        THE PRODIGAL SON. Stanford, California. Stan-
        ford University. ? Aug. Herman Voaden

473   Novello, Ivor
        KING'S RHAPSODY. London. 15 Sept.

474   Bliss, Arthur
        THE OLYMPIANS. London. 29 Sept. J. B. Priestley

475   Weill, Kurt
        LOST IN THE STARS. New York. 30 Oct. Maxwell
        Anderson

476   Blitzstein, Marc
        REGINA. New York. 31 Oct. Composer

477   Bucci, Mark
        THE BOOR. New York. Finch College. 29 Dec.

478   Kupferman, Meyer
        IN A GARDEN. New York. Finch College. 29 Dec.
        (Gertrude Stein play)

                            1950

479   Robb, John Donald
        LITTLE JO. Albuquerque, New Mexico. 18 Jan.
        Robert Bright

1950   First Performances

480   Meyerowitz, Jan
        THE BARRIER. New York. Columbia University.
        18 Jan. Langston Hughes

481   Overton, Hall
        THE ENCHANTED PEAR TREE. New York. Juilliard.
        7 Feb. John Thompson, Jr.

482   Menotti, Gian-Carlo
        THE CONSUL. Philadelphia. 1 Mar. Composer

483   Collingwood, Lawrence Arthur
        THE DEATH OF TINTAGILES. London. 16 Apr.

484   Dello Joio, Norman
        THE TRIUMPH OF ST. JOAN. Bronxville, New York.
        Sarah Lawrence. 9 May. Composer (See The
        Trial at Rouen produced in New York 16 Apr. 1959)

485   Foss, Lukas
        THE JUMPING FROG OF CALAVERAS COUNTY. Blooming-
        ton, Indiana. Indiana University. 18 May.
        Jean Karsavina

486   Rogers, Bernard
        THE VEIL. Bloomington, Indiana. Indiana Uni-
        versity. 18 May

487   Scarmolin, A. Louis
        AN INTERRUPTED SERENADE. Lindenhurst, Long
        Island. 19 May

488   Rivington, Hill
        MR. BELLAMY COMES HOME. London. 13 Oct.
        Martin R. Holmes

489   Haubiel, Charles
        SUNDAY COSTS FIVE PESOS. Charlotte, North Caro-
        lina. Piedmont Junior High School. 6 Nov.
        Josephine Niggli

First Performances   1951

490   Kreutz, Arthur
        ACRES OF SKY. Fayetteville, Arkansas. Univer-
        sity of Arkansas. 16 Nov. Zoe Lunde Schiller

491   Easdale, Brian
        THE CORN KING. London. 21 Nov. Naomi Mitchison

492   Moore, Douglas
        PUSS 'N BOOTS. New York. ? Nov. Raymond
        Abrashkin

493   Franchetti, Arnold
        THE LION. New London, Connecticut. 16 Dec.

1951

494   Kalmanoff, Martin
        NOAH AND THE STOWAWAY. New York. 18 Feb. Atra
        Bear

495   Moore, Douglas
        GIANTS IN THE EARTH. New York. N. Y. U. 28 Mar.
        Arnold Sundgaard

496   Williams, R. R.
        THE INTRODUCTION. Greencastle, Indiana. De Pauw
        University. 13 Apr.

497   Floyd, Carlisle
        THE FUGITIVES. Tallahassee, Florida. Florida
        State University. 17 Apr. Composer

498   Johnson, Lockrem
        A LETTER TO EMILY. Seattle. 22 Apr. Composer

499   Wolfe, Jacques
        MISSISSIPPI LEGEND. New York. 24 Apr.

1951   First Performances

500   Vaughan Williams, Ralph
PILGRIM'S PROGRESS. London. 26 Apr. Composer

501   Krenek, Ernst
DARK WATERS. Los Angeles. University of Southern California. 2 May. Composer

502   Mennini, Louis
THE WELL. Rochester, New York. Eastman School of Music. 8 May. Composer

503   Lloyd, George
JOHN SOCMAN. Bristol. 15 May. William Lloyd

504   Martinelli, Rodolfo
ALONE I STAND. New York. Brooklyn Academy of Music. 18 May

505   Fore, Burdette
ARIA DA CAPO. Stockton, California. College of the Pacific. 19 May

506   Berl, Paul
JUDGEMENT DAY. New York. Hunter College. 28 May

507   List, Kurt
THE WISE AND THE FOOLISH. New York. 2 June.

508   Easdale, Brian
THE SLEEPING CHILDREN. Cheltenham, England. 9 July. Tyrone Gutherie

509   Hopkins, Anthony
THE MAN FROM TUSCANY. Canterbury. 20 July. Christopher Hassall

510   Tranchell, Peter
THE MAYOR OF CASTERBRIDGE. Cambridge, England. 28 July. Composer

511   Haufrecht, Herbert
        BONEY QUILLEN. Chicester, New York. 18 Aug.
        Composer

512   More, Margaret
        THE MERMAID. Birmingham, Alabama. 4 Sept.
        Claudine Currey

513   Stravinsky, Igor
        THE RAKE'S PROGRESS. Venice. 11 Sept.
        W. H. Auden and Chester Kallman

514   Brown, J. Harold
        KING SOLOMON. Cleveland. 28 Sept.

515   Tamkin, David
        THE DYBBUK. New York. 4 Oct. Alex Tamkin

516   Helm, Everett B.
        ADAM AND EVE. Wiesbaden. 28 Oct. Composer;
        performed in German

517   Meyerowitz, Jan
        EASTWARD IN EDEN. Detroit. Wayne State Univer-
        sity. 16 Nov. Dorothy Gardner

518   Britten, Benjamin
        BILLY BUDD. London. 1 Dec. E. M. Forster and
        Eric Crozier

519   Wellesz, Egon
        INCOGNITA. Oxford, England. 5 Dec. Elisabeth
        Mackenzie

520   Menotti, Gian-Carlo
        AMAHL AND THE NIGHT VISITORS. New York. 24 Dec.
        Composer

1952

521   Wykes, Robert
      THE PRANKSTER. Bowling Green, Ohio. Bowling
      Green State University. 12 Jan. Composer

522   Verrall, John
      THE COWHERD AND THE SKY MAIDEN. Seattle. Uni-
      versity of Washington. 17 Jan. Esther Shephard

523   Weisgall, Hugo
      THE TENOR. Baltimore. Peabody Conservatory.
      11 Feb. Karl Shapiro and Ernst Lert

524   Kalmanoff, Martin
      THE EMPTY BOTTLE. New York. 11 Feb. Atra Bear;
      excerpts

525   Kaufmann, Walter
      A PARFAIT FOR IRENE. Bloomington, Indiana.
      Indiana University. 21 Feb.

526   Coates, Albert
      TAFELBERG SE KLEED. Capetown, South Africa.
      7 Mar.

527   Kubik, Gail
      BOSTON BAKED BEANS. New York. 9 Mar. Composer

528   Partch, Harry
      OEDIPUS. Oakland, California. Mills College
      14 Mar.

529   Franchetti, Arnold
      THE PRINCESS. Hartford, Connecticut. Hartt
      College. 16 Mar.

530   Rieti, Vittorio
      DON PERLIMPLIN. Urbana, Illinois. University of
      Illinois. 30 Mar. Composer

531   Bush, Alan Dudley
        WAT TYLER. East Berlin. 3 Apr.

532   Bryan, Charles F.
        SINGIN' BILLY. Nashville, Tennessee. Vanderbilt
        University. 23 Apr. Donald Davidson

533   Hamm, Charles Edward
        THE MONKEY'S PAW. Cincinnati. Cincinnati Con-
        servatory of Music. 2 May. Composer

534   Garland, Kathryn
        RUTH. Fredericksburg, Virginia. Mary Washington
        College. 4 May

535   Gaburo, Kenneth
        THE SNOW QUEEN. Lake Charles, Louisiana.
        McNeese State College. 5 May. Marjorie Wilson

536   Kahn, Emil
        THE RIBBON. Montclair, New Jersey. Hillside
        Junior High School. 8 May

537   Wilder, Alec
        THE LOWLAND SEA. Montclair, New Jersey. Mont-
        clair State College. 8 May. Arnold Sundgaard

538   Shaw, G.
        ALL AT SEA. London. 12 May. Margaret Dalmere
        and Sebastian Shaw

539   Garland, Charles
        IF MEN PLAYED CARDS AS WOMEN DO. Chicago.
        Chicago American Conservatory. 22 May

540   Bernstein, Leonard
        TROUBLE IN TAHITI. Waltham, Massachusetts.
        Brandeis University. 12 June. Composer

551   Miller, Frank
        THESPIS. New York. 16 Jan.

552   Giannini, Vittorio
        THE TAMING OF THE SHREW. Cincinnati. 31 Jan.
        Composer and Dorothy Fee

553   Berezowsky, Nicolai
        BABAR THE ELEPHANT. New York. 21 Feb. Randal
        Heyward

554   Ahlstrom, David
        THE OPEN WINDOW. Cincinnati. Cincinnati Con-
        servatory of Music. 1 Mar.

555   Ahlstrom, David
        THREE SISTERS WHO ARE NOT SISTERS. Cincinnati.
        Cincinnati Conservatory of Music.
        (Gertrude Stein play)

556   Hamm, Charles Edward
        THE CASK OF AMONTILLADO. Cincinnati. Cincinnati
        Conservatory of Music. 1 Mar.

557   Hammond, Tom
        RAPUNZEL. Colchester. 5 Mar. Composer

558   Fletcher, Grant
        THE CARRION CROW. Bloomington, Illinois. Illi-
        nois Wesleyan University. 20 Mar. Frances Wells
        Fletcher

559   Peter, Darrell
        THE PARROT. New York. 24 Mar. (The Parrot was
        the first television opera commissioned by a
        commercial sponsor)

560   Byrd, William Clifton
        THE SCANDAL AT MULFORD INN. Cincinnati. Cincin-
        nati College of Music. 1 Apr. Charlotte Shockley

561   Magnuson, Karl
        ADAM AND EVE AND THE DEVIL. Cincinnati. Cincin-
        nati College of Music. 1 Apr.

562   Williams, R. R.
        OLEANDER RED. Cincinnati. Cincinnati College
        of Music. 1 Apr.

563   Victory, Gerald
        AN FEAR A PHÓS BALBMIN. Dublin. 6 Apr. Per-
        formed in Gaelic

564   Ruger, Morris Hutchen
        THE FALL OF THE HOUSE OF USHER. Los Angeles.
        15 Apr. Francis Millington

565   Norden, Norris Lindsey
        NEBRAHAM. Philadelphia. 16 Apr.

566   Benjamin, Arthur
        A TALE OF TWO CITIES. London. 17 Apr. Cedric
        Cliffe

567   Schuman, William
        THE MIGHTY CASEY. Hartford, Connecticut. Hartt
        College. 4 May. Jeremy Gury

568   Delius, Frederick
        IRMELIN. Oxford, England. 4 May. Composer;
        completed in 1892

569   Westergaard, Peter
        CHARIVARI. Cambridge, Massachusetts. Harvard
        University. 13 May

570   Winslow, Richard
        SWEENEY AGONISTES. New York. Columbia Univer-
        sity. 20 May

First Performances   1953

571   Elkus, Jonathan
        TOM SAWYER. San Francisco. Everett Junior High
        School. 22 May

572   Wilder, Alec
        CUMBERLAND FAIR. Montclair, New Jersey. Mont-
        clair State Teachers College. 22 May. Arnold
        Sundgaard

573   Blitzstein, Marc
        THE HARPIES. New York. Manhattan School of
        Music. 25 May. Composer

574   "Vernon, Ashley" [Kurt Manschinger]
        THE BARBER OF NEW YORK. New York. Hunter
        College. 26 May. Greta Hartwig

575   Engel, A. Lehman
        BROTHER JOE. Cleveland. 28 May

576   Britten, Benjamin
        GLORIANA. London. 8 June. William Plomer
        (Gloriana was written for the coronation of
        Elizabeth II)

577   Kalmanoff, Martin
        BRANDY IS MY TRUE LOVE'S NAME. New York.
        17 June. Atra Bear

578   Kondorossy, Leslie
        A NIGHT IN THE PUSZTA. Cleveland. 28 June

579   Wilder, Alec
        SUNDAY EXCURSION. Interlochen, Michigan.
        18 July. Arnold Sundgaard

580   Antill, J.
        ENDYMION. Sydney. 22 July

581   Hamm, Charles Edward
        THE SECRET LIFE OF WALTER MITTY. Athens, Ohio.
        Ohio University. 30 July. Composer

582   Trogan, Ronald
        THE HAT MAN. Interlochen, Michigan. 1 Aug.

583   Mason, Wilton
        KINGDOM COME. Boone, North Carolina. Appala-
        chian State College. 17 Aug.

584   Meyerowitz, Jan
        BAD BOYS IN SCHOOL. Lenox, Massachusetts.
        17 Aug. Composer

585   Duke, John
        CAPTAIN LOVELOCK. Hudson Falls, New York.
        18 Aug. Composer

586   Geto, Alfred
        THE TREASURE. Pottersville, New York. 22 Aug.

587   Fragale, Frank D.
        DR. JEKYLL AND MR. HYDE. Berkeley, California.
        28 Aug.

588   Marais, Josef
        AFRICAN HEARTBEAT. Idyllwild, California.
        Idyllwild School. 28 Aug.

589   Schumann, Walter
        JOHN BROWN'S BODY. Los Angeles. 21 Sept.

590   Miller, Alma Grace
        THE WHIRLWIND. Arlington, Virginia. 24 Sept.

591   Gundry, Inglis
        THE TINNERS OF CORNWALL. London. 30 Sept.
        Composer

592   Metcalf, Clarence
        THE TOWN MUSICIANS OF BREMEN. Cleveland.
        ? Sept. Gilbert O. Ward

593   Chisholm, Erik
        THE INLAND WOMAN. Capetown, South Africa.
        21 Oct.

594   Hughes, Arwel
        MENNA. Cardiff. 7 Nov. Wyn Griffith

595   Bucci, Mark
        THE DRESS. New York. 8 Dec. Composer

596   ______.
        SWEET BETSY FROM PIKE. New York. 8 Dec.
        Composer

597   Wilder, Alec
        MISS CHICKEN LITTLE. New York. 27 Dec.

598   Bucci, Mark
        THIRTEEN CLOCKS. New York. 29 Dec.

                              1954

599   Laufer, Beatrice
        'ILE. New York. 14 Feb.

600   Siegmeister, Elie
        MY DARLING CORIE. Hempstead, Long Island.
        Hofstra University. 18 Feb. Lewis Allen

601   Mayer, Robert
        THE PORTER AT THE DOOR. Winston-Salem, North
        Carolina. 26 Feb.

602   Hunkins, Eusebia
        SMOKY MOUNTAIN. Monmouth, Illinois. Monmouth
        College. ? Feb. Composer

603   Middleton, Robert
        THE NIGHTINGALE IS GUILTY. Boston. 5 Mar.

604   Kreutz, Arthur
        THE UNIVERSITY GREYS. Clinton, Mississippi.
        University of Mississippi. 15 Mar. Zoe Lunde
        Schiller

605   Hollingsworth, Stanley
        THE MOTHER. Philadelphia. Curtis Institute.
        29 Mar. Composer and John Fandel

606   Groth, Howard
        PETRUCHIO. Conway, Arkansas. Arkansas State
        Teachers College. 29 Mar.

607   Copland, Aaron
        THE TENDER LAND. New York. 1 Apr. Horace
        Everett

608   Glanville-Hicks, Peggy
        THE TRANSPOSED HEADS. Louisville, Kentucky.
        University of Louisville. 8 Apr. Composer

609   Smith, Julia
        COCKCROW. Austin, Texas. 22 Apr. C. d'Arcy
        Mackay

610   Ahlstrom, David
        CHARLIE'S UNCLE. Columbus, Indiana. 23 Apr.
        Composer

611   Lamb, Dorothy
        THE NIGHTINGALE. Poughkeepsie, New York. Vassar.
        27 Apr.

612   Saminsky, Lazare
        THE VISION OF ARIEL. Chicago. University of
        Chicago. 9 May. Composer

613   Kondorossy, Leslie
        THE PUMPKIN. Cleveland. 15 May. Caroline
        Kulin

614   ______.
        THE VOICE. Cleveland. 15 May. Shawn Hall and
        Lenek

615   Gustafson, Dwight
        THE JAILER. Greenville, South Carolina. Bob
        Jones University. 27 May.

616   Engel, A. Lehman
        MALADY OF LOVE. New York. 27 May. Lewis Allen

617   Beeson, Jack
        HELLO OUT THERE. New York. 27 May. Composer

618   Norden, Norris Lindsay
        THROUGH A GLASS DARKLY. Philadelphia. ? May.

619   Kalmanoff, Martin
        A QUIET GAME OF CRIBBLE. New York. Greenwich
        House Music School. 8 June. Composer

620   Berkeley, Lennox
        A DINNER ENGAGEMENT. Aldeburgh. 17 June.
        Paul Dehn

621   Chisholm, Erik
        MURDER IN THREE KEYS. Greenwich Village.
        6 July. (Murder in Three Keys is a trilogy
        comprised of Black Roses, Dark Sonnet, and
        Simoon.)

1954   First Performances

622   Joubert, John
        ANTIGONE. London. 21 July

623   Forrest, Hamilton
        DAELIA. Interlochen, Michigan. 21 July

624   Goodman, Alfred Grant
        THE AUDITION. Athens, Ohio. Ohio University.
        27 July

625   Antheil, George
        THE BROTHERS. Denver. University of Denver.
        28 July. Composer

626   Clarke, Henry Leland
        THE LOAFER AND THE LOAF. Stockbridge,
        Massachusetts. ? July. Evelyn Sharp

627   Wilder, Alec
        KITTIWAKE ISLAND. Interlochen, Michigan. 7 Aug.
        Arnold Sundgaard

628   Forrest, Hamilton
        A MATINEE IDYLL. Interlochen, Michigan. 17 Aug.

629   Hamm, Charles E.
        THE SCENT OF SARSAPARILLA. San Francisco.
        5 Sept.

630   Britten, Benjamin
        THE TURN OF THE SCREW. Venice. 14 Sept.
        Myfanwy Piper

631   Berkeley, Lennox
        NELSON. London. 22 Sept. Alan Pryce-Jones

632   Argento, Dominick
        SICILIAN LIMES. New York. New School for Social
        Research. ? Oct.

First Performances   1954

633   Kassern, Tadeusz Z.
         SUN-UP. New York. 10·Nov.

634   Perry, Julia
         THE CASK OF AMONTILLADO. New York. Columbia
         University. 20 Nov. Composer and Virginia
         Card

635   Kechley, Gerald
         THE BECKONING FAIR ONE. Seattle. University
         of Washington. 30 Nov.

636   Walton, William
         TROILUS AND CRESSIDA. London. 3 Dec.
         Christopher Hassall

637   Mohaupt, Richard
         DOUBLE-TROUBLE. Louisville, Kentucky. 4 Dec.
         Roger Maren

638   Mopper, Irving
         THE DOOR. Newark, New Jersey. 5 Dec. Margaret
         Hordyke

639   Kleinsinger, George
         ARCHY AND MEHITABEL. New York. 6 Dec. Joe
         Darion

640   Byrd, William Clifton
         HOLD THAT NOTE. Philadelphia. 10 Dec.

641   Herrmann, Bernard
         A CHRISTMAS CAROL. New York. 23 Dec.

642   Broekman, David
         BARBARA ALLEN. New York. 26 Dec.

643   Menotti, Gian-Carlo
         THE SAINT OF BLEEKER STREET. New York. 27 Dec.
         Composer

1955

644   DeBanfield, Raffaello
        LORD BYRON'S LOVE LETTER. New Orleans. Tulane
        University. 17 Jan. Tennessee Williams

645   Tippett, Michael
        THE MIDSUMMER MARRIAGE. London. 27 Jan.
        Composer

646   DiGiovanni, Rocco
        MEDEA. New York. 13 Feb.

647   Fink, Myron
        THE BOOR. St. Louis. 14 Feb.

648   Albright, Lois
        HOPITY. New York. 16 Feb. M. W. Billingsley

649   Floyd, Carlisle
        SUSANNAH. Tallahassee, Florida. Florida State
        University. 24 Feb. Composer

650   Hamm, Charles Edward
        THE SALESGIRL. Bristol, Virginia. Virginia
        Intermont College. 1 Mar.

651   Kondorossy, Leslie
        THE MIDNIGHT DUEL. Cleveland. 8 Mar. Caroline
        Kulin

652   Sable, Daniel
        THE INFORMER. Columbus, Ohio. Ohio State
        University. 11 Mar.

653   Caldwell, Mary E.
        PEPITO'S GOLDEN FLOWER. Pasadena, California.
        13 Mar. Composer

654   Antheil, George
        THE WISH. Louisville, Kentucky. 2 Apr.
        Composer

655   Kondorossy, Leslie
        THE TWO IMPOSTERS. Cleveland. 10 Apr.

656   Burnham, Cardon V.
        ARIA DE CAPO. New Orleans. Tulane University.
        17 Apr.

657   Marcus, R.
        THE PRINCESS WHO TALKED BACKWARD. New York.
        Sarah Lawrence. 23 Apr.

658   Beckett, William Wheeler
        THE MAGIC MIRROR. Neward, New Jersey. 27 Apr.

659   Kalmanoff, Martin
        THE DELINQUENTS. Philadelphia. ? Apr. Composer

660   Virzi, Salvatore
        THE PRINCESS AND THE SPINDLE. New York. 6 May

661   Kondorossy, Leslie
        THE STRING QUARTET. Cleveland. 8 May

662   Chanler, Theodore
        THE POT OF FAT. Cambridge, Massachusetts. Longy
        School of Music. 9 May. Hester Pickman

663   Rogers, Bernard
        THE NIGHTINGALE. New York. 10 May. Composer

664   Rorem, Ned
        A CHILDHOOD MIRACLE. New York. 10 May.
        Elliot Stein

1955   First Performances

665   Stein, Leon
       THE FISHERMAN'S WIFE. Chicago. 12 May. Roslyn
       Rosen

666   Reed, Herbert Owen
       MICHIGAN DREAM. East Lansing, Michigan.
       Michigan State University. 13 May. John
       Jennings

667   Dello Joio, Norman
       THE RUBY. Bloomington, Indiana. Indiana
       University. 13 May. William Mass

668   Verrall, John
       THREE BLIND MICE. Seattle. University of
       Washington. 20 May

669   Doran, Matt
       THE COMMITTEE. Corpus Cristi, Texas. 25 May.
       Composer and Lawrence

670   Koutzen, Boris
       THE FATAL OATH. New York. Hunter College.
       26 May. Composer

671   Duffy, John
       THE EVE OF ADAM. Interlochen, Michigan.
       Stockbridge School. 1 June

672   Wilder, Alec
       THE LONG WAY. Nyack, New York. 3 June. Arnold
       Sundgaard

673   Kondorossy, Leslie
       MYSTIC FORTRESS. Cleveland. 12 June

674   "Vernon, Ashley" [Kurt Manschinger]
       GRAND SLAM. Stamford, Connecticut. 25 June.
       Greta Hartwig

First Performances   1955

675   Davis, Katherine
        THE DISAPPOINTED IMPRESARIO. Duxbury,
        Massachusetts. 15 July. Composer and Heddie
        Kent

676   Cohn, James
        THE FALL OF THE CITY. Athens, Ohio. Ohio
        University. 29 July

677   Davis, Allan
        THE SAILING OF THE NANCY BELLE. Duxbury,
        Massachusetts. 3 Aug.

678   Mennini, Louis
        THE ROPE. Lenox, Massachusetts. 8 Aug.
        Composer

679   Black, Arnold
        THE PRINCE AND THE PAUPER. Duxbury,
        Massachusetts. 26 Aug.

680   Low, James
        MOBY DICK. Idyllwild, California. Idyllwild
        School. 2 Sept. Brainerd Duffield

681   Meyerowitz, Jan
        THE MEETING. Falmouth, Massachusetts. 16 Sept.
        Dorothy Gardner

682   Goodman, J. F.
        THE PIZZA PUSHER. San Francisco. ? Sept.

683   Foss, Lukas
        GRIFFELKIN. New York. 6 Nov. Alastair Reid

684   Liebermann, Rolf
        THE SCHOOL FOR WIVES. Louisville, Kentucky.
        3 Dec. Heinrich Ströbel

1956   First Performances

685   Patacchi, Van
        THE SECRET. Columbia, Missouri. Stephens
        College. 5 Dec. William Ashbrook

686   Piket, Frederick
        ISAAC LEVI. White Plains, New York. 11 Dec.

687   Strassburg, Robert
        CHELM. White Plains, New York. 11 Dec.

688   Berkowitz, Ralph
        A TELEPHONE CALL. Rio de Janeiro. 15 Dec.

689   Kleinsinger, George
        A TREE THAT FOUND CHRISTMAS. New York. Hunter
        College. 17 Dec. Joe Darien

690   Raines, Vernon
        THE HAPPY PRINCE. Emporia, Kansas. Emporia
        College. ? Dec. McCaffery

1956

691   Townsend, Douglas
        LIMA BEANS. New York. 7 Jan.

692   Dvorkin, Judith
        CRESCENT EYEBROWS. New York. 8 Jan.

693   Schwartz, Paul
        THE EXPERIMENT. Gambier, Ohio. Kenyon College.
        27 Jan. Composer

694   Benjamin, Arthur
        MANANA. London. 1 Feb. Caryl Brahms

695   Bergsma, William
        THE WIFE OF MARTIN GUERRE. New York. Juilliard.
        15 Feb. Janet Lewis

First Performances   1956

696   Raphling, Sam
         DR. HEIDEGGER'S EXPERIMENT. New York. 18 Feb.

697   Cockshott, Gerald
         APOLLO AND PERSEPHONE. New York. 22 Feb.
         Composer

698   Kalmanoff, Martin
         OPERA, OPERA. New York. Finch College. 22 Feb.
         William Saroyan

699   Levine, Julius
         THE GOLDEN MEDAL. Fort Wayne, Indiana. 25 Feb.
         Max Levine

700   Franchetti, Arnold
         THE ANACHRONISM. Hartford, Connecticut. Hartt
         College of Music. 4 Mar.

701   Bohrnstedt, W. R.
         THE NECKLACE. Redlands, California. University
         of Redlands. 12 Mar. Lucille March

702   Burnham, Cardon V.
         THE NITECAP. New Orleans. Tulane University.
         14 Mar. Composer

703   Phillips, Roy
         TREVALLION. London. 21 Mar. Philip Phillips
         and Malcolm Morley

704   Hively, Wells
         JUNIPERO SERRA. Palma Majorca, Spain. 28 Mar.

705   Neeld, Peggy
         THE MAGIC FISH. New York. 2 Apr.

706   Zimbalist, Efrem
         LANDRA. Philadelphia. Curtis Institute.
         6 Apr. Bernice Kenyon

1956   First Performances

707   Dello, Joio, Norman
         THE TRIAL AT ROUEN. New York. 8 Apr. Composer
         (The Trial at Rouen is later considerably re-
         vised and produced under the title Joan of Arc)

708   Avshalom, Aaron
         THE GREAT WALL. New York. Columbia University.
         21 Apr.

709   Kerr, Walter
         SING OUT, SWEET LAND! Los Angeles. Occidental
         College. ? Apr.

710   Broekmann, David
         THE TOLEDO WAR. New York. 4 May

711   Franchetti, Arnold
         THE GAME OF CARDS. Hartford, Connecticut.
         Hartt College. 9 May

712   Siegmeister, Elie
         MIRANDA AND THE DARK YOUNG MAN. Hartford,
         Connecticut. Hartt College. 9 May. Edward
         Eager

713   Gross, Robert
         THE BALD SOPRANO. Los Angeles. Occidental
         College. 13 May. Composer and Donald Allen

714   Canning, Thomas
         BEYOND BELIEF. Rochester, New York. Eastman
         School of Music. 14 May

715   Nelson, Ron
         THE BIRTHDAY OF THE INFANTATA. Rochester, New
         York. Eastman School of Music. 14 May. Composer

716   Ward, Robert
         PANTALOON. New York. Columbia University.
         17 May. Bernard Stambler

717   Van Buskirk, Carl G.
        THE LAND BETWEEN THE RIVERS. Bloomington,
        Indiana. Indiana University. 18 May

718   DiJulio, Max
        BABY DOE. Loretto, California. Loretto Heights
        College. 24 May

719   Canning, Thomas
        ALBERT AND TIBERIUS. Williamsport, Pennsylvania.
        Lycoming College. ? May. Gratwick

720   Martin, Vernon
        LADIES VOICES. Norman, Oklahoma. University of
        Oklahoma. 3 June. Gertrude Stein

721   Kastle, Leonard
        THE SWING. New York. 11 June. Composer

722   Moore, Douglas
        THE BALLAD OF BABY DOE. Central City, Colorado.
        7 July. John Latouche

723   Bush, Geoffrey
        IF THE CAP FITS. Cheltenham, England. 10 July.
        Composer

724   Hopkins, Anthony
        TEN O'CLOCK CALL. Cheltenham, England. 11 July.
        Winiford Radford

725   Slates, Philip M.
        THE BARGAIN. Athens, Ohio. Ohio University.
        26 July

726   ______.
        THE CANDLE. Athens, Ohio. Ohio University.
        26 July

1956   First Performances

727   "Vernon, Ashley" (Kurt Manschinger)
       CUPID AND PSYCHE. Woodstock, New York. 27 July.
       Greta Hartwig

728   Barab, Seymour
       CHANTICLEER. Aspen, Colorado. 4 Aug. Mary
       Caroline Richards

729   Berkovitz, Sol
       FAT TUESDAY. Tamiment, Pennsylvania. 8 Aug.
       James Lipton

730   Gundry, Inglis
       THE LOGAN ROCK. Portchurno, England. 15 Aug.
       Composer

731   Burnand, N.
       PICKWICK. Eureka Springs, Arkansas. ? Aug.

732   Berkeley, Lennox
       RUTH. London. 2 Oct. Eric Crozier

733   Kondorossy, Leslie
       UNEXPECTED VISITOR. Cleveland. 21 Oct.

734   Menotti, Gian-Carlo
       THE UNICORN, THE GORGON AND THE MANTICORE, OR
       THE THREE SUNDAYS OF A POET. Washington, D.C.
       21 Oct. Composer

735   Joubert, John
       IN THE DROUGHT. Johannesburg. 22 Oct.

736   Bernstein, Leonard
       CANDIDE. Boston. 29 Oct. Lillian Hellman

737   Bush, Alan Dudley
       THE MEN OF BLACKMOOR. Weimar. 8 Nov. Nancy
       Bush; performed in a German translation

738   Helm, Everett
        DIE BELAGERUNG VON TOTENBURG.   Stuttgard.
        ? Nov.   Performed in German

739   Starer, Robert
        THE INTRUDER.   New York.   4 Dec.   Wolfsohn

740   Arnold, M.
        THE OPEN WINDOW.   London.   14 Dec.   Sidney
        Gilliatt

                          1957

741   Barab, Seymour
        A GAME OF CHANCE.   Rock Island, Illinois.
        Augustana College.   11 Jan.   Evelyn Mancher

742   Weiner, Lazar
        THE GOLEM.   White Plains, New York.   13 Jan.

743   Claflin, Avery
        LA GRANDE BRETECHE.   New York.   2 Feb.   George
        Mills

744   Lee, Dai-Keong
        SPEAKEASY.   New York.   8 Feb.

745   Hollingsworth, Stanley
        LA GRANDE BRETECHE.   New York.   10 Feb.   Harry
        Duncan

746   Leginska, Ethel
        THE ROSE AND THE RING.   Los Angeles.   23 Feb.
        E. E. Ohlson

747   Newbern, Kenneth
        THE ARMOR OF LIFE.   New York.   26 Feb.

1957   First Performances

748   Krenek, Ernest
        THE BELL-TOWER. Urbana, Illinois. University
        of Illinois. 17 Mar. Composer

749   Levy, Marvin David
        SOTOBA KOMACHI. New York. 7 Apr. Sam Houston
        Brock

750   Roy, Klaus G.
        STERLINGMAN. Boston. 18 Apr. Composer

751   Smith, Russell
        THE UNICORN IN THE GARDEN. Hartford, Connecticut.
        Hartt College. 2 May. Joseph Longstreth

752   Argento, Dominick
        THE BOOR. Rochester, New York. Eastman School
        of Music. 6 May. John Olon Scrymgeour

753   Pitman, Evelyn
        COUSIN ESTHER. Paris. 8 May

754   Chavez, Carlos
        PANFILO AND LAURETTE. New York. Columbia
        University. 9 May. Chester Kallman

755   Gillis, Don
        THE PARK AVENUE KIDS. Elkhart, Indiana. Elk-
        hart High School. 12 May. Composer

756   Meyerowitz, Jan.
        ESTHER. Urbana, Illinois. University of Illinois.
        17 May. Langston Hughes

757   Trimble, J.
        BLIND RAFTERY. London. 22 May. Cedric Cliffe

758   Antheil, George
        VENUS IN AFRICA. Denver. University of Denver.
        24 May. Michael Dyne

First Performances   1957

759   Gardner, John
       THE MOON AND SIXPENCE. London. 24 May. Patrick
       Terry

760   Kupferman, Meyer
       THE CURIOUS FERN. New York. Master Institute.
       5 June. Alastair Reid

761   ______.
       VOICES FOR A MIRROR. New York. Master Insti-
       tute. 5 June. Alastair Reid

762   Benjamin, Arthur
       A TALE OF TWO CITIES. London. 23 July. Cedric
       Cliffe; revised version

763   Laderman, Ezra
       JACOB AND THE INDIANS. Woodstock, New York.
       26 July. Ernest Kinoy

764   Rogers, Bernard
       THE MUSICIANS OF BREMEN. Rochester, New York.
       Eastman School of Music. ? July. Composer

765   Levy, Marvin David
       THE TOWER. Santa Fe, New Mexico. 2 Aug.
       Townsend Brewster

766   Bucci, Mark
       A TALE FOR A DEAF EAR. Lenox, Massachusetts.
       5 Aug. Composer

767   Gillis, Don
       PEP RALLY. Interlochen, Michigan. 15 Aug.
       Composer

768   Wolfe, Jacques
       THE TRYSTING PLACE. Coral Gables, Florida.
       University of Miami. 15 Aug.

1958   First Performances

769   Humphrey, Henry R.
        MAYERLING. Cincinnati. Cincinnati Conservatory
        of Music. 16 Nov.

770   Beeson, Jack
        THE SWEET BYE AND BYE. New York. Juilliard.
        22 Nov. Kenward Elmslie

771   Greenberg, Noah
        THE PLAY OF DANIEL. New York. ? Dec.
        Narration by W. H. Auden

1958

772   Barber, Samuel
        VANESSA. New York. 15 Jan. Gian-Carlo Menotti

773   Taylor, Deems
        THE DRAGON. New York. New York University.
        6 Feb. Composer

774   Beveridge, Thomas
        DIDO AND AENEAS. Boston. 14 Feb.

775   Kanitz, Ernest
        ROOM NO. 12. Los Angeles. U. C. L. A.
        26 Feb. Richard Thompson

776   ______.
        ROYAL AUCTION. Los Angeles. U. C. L. A.
        26 Feb. S. Shrager and A. Chorney

777   Arnell, R.
        LOVE IN TRANSIT. London. 27 Feb. Hal Burton

778   Johnson, Mary
        THIRTEEN CLOCKS. New York. 8 Mar. M. Morgan
        and N. Morgan

First Performances   1958

779   Gottlieb, Jacob
           SONATA ALLEGRO. Urbana, Illinois. University
           of Illinois. 9 Mar. Horace Everett

780   Moore, Douglas
           GALLANTRY. New York. 19 Mar. Arnold Sundgaard

781   Saunders, M.
           THE LITTLE BEGGARS. London. 20 Mar. Caryl
           Brahms

782   Patacchi, Van
           THE BANDIT. Columbia, Missouri. Stephens
           College. 7 Apr. William Ashbrook

783   Whiton, Peter
           THE BOTTLE IMP. Wilton, Connecticut. 10 Apr.

784   Rieti, Vittorio
           THE PET SHOP. New York. Mannes College.
           14 Apr. Composer and Claire Nichols

785   Rorem, Ned
           THE ROBBERS. New York. Mannes College. 14 Apr.

786   Nabokov, Nicholas
           THE HOLY DEVIL. Louisville, Kentucky. 16 Apr.
           Stephen Spender (The Holy Devil is later re-
           vised and re-titled Death of Gregory Rasputin)

787   Barab, Seymour
           THE RAJAH'S RUBY. New York. 19 Apr.

788   Davis, Allan
           OTHERWISE ENGAGED. New York. 23 Apr.

789   Holton, Robert
           A REAL STRANGE ONE. New York. 23 Apr.

1958   First Performances

790   Kurka, Robert
      THE GOOD SOLDIER SCHWEIK. New York. 23 Apr.
      Lewis Allen

791   Hokanson, Dorothy C.
      UNDINE. Seattle. University of Washington.
      2 May. Shepard and Conway

792   McKee, Jeanellen
      COLLECTOR'S PIECE. Chicago. 2 May

793   Levy, Marvin David
      ESCURIAL. New York. 4 May. Lionel Abel

794   Kupferman, Meyer
      DRAAGENFOOT GIRL. Bronxville, New York. Sarah
      Lawrence. 8 May. Composer

795   Kayden, Mildred
      MARDI GRAS. New York. 22 May

796   Alspach, Addison
      CALVARIO. Duluth, Minnesota. University of
      Minnesota. ? May. Composer

797   Kalmanoff, Martin
      VIDEOMANIA. Lincoln, Nebraska. 8 June.
      Composer

798   McClain, Floyd
      THE SNACK SHOP. Yankton, South Dakota. 12 June

799   Britten, Benjamin
      NOYE'S FLUDDE. Aldeburgh. 18 June. (The
      Chester Miracle Play)

800   Hoiby, Lee
      THE SCARF. Spoleto, Italy. 20 June. Harry
      Duncan

801   Honigman, Saul
      THE TICKET. Woodstock, New York. 11 July

802   Wilder, Alec
        THE IMPOSSIBLE FOREST. Westport, Connecticut,
        13 July

803   Floyd, Carlisle
        WUTHERING HEIGHTS. Santa Fe, New Mexico. 16
        July. Composer

804   Weigel, Eugene
        THE MOUNTAIN CHILD. Missoula, Montana. Univer-
        sity of Montana. 27 July

805   Duke, John
        THE SIRE DE MALEDROIT. Schroon Lake, New York.
        15 Aug. Dorothy Duke

806   Menotti, Gian-Carlo
        MARIA GOLOVIN. Brussels. 20 Aug. Composer

807   Levister, Alonzo
        BLUES IN THE SUBWAY. New York. 27 Sept.

808   Searle, Humphrey
        THE DIARY OF A MADMAN. West Berlin. 8 Oct.
        Composer; performed in a German translation by
        Hermann Scherchen

809   Fricker, Peter Racine
        A VISION OF JUDGEMENT. Leeds, England. 13 Oct.

810   Poples, Henry
        THE MASTER THIEF. Pittsburgh. Duquesne Univer-
        sity. 5 Nov. Dan Pociernicki

811   Humel, Gerald
        THE TRIANGLE. Oberlin, Ohio. Oberlin Conserva-
        tory. 14 Nov.

812   Engel, A. Lehman
        THE SOLDIER. Jackson, Mississippi. Millsaps
        College. 24 Nov. Lewis Allen

813   Laderman, Ezra
        SARAH. New York. 30 Nov. Clari Rascom

814   Marsh, Lucille Crews
        THE CONCERT. Redlands, California. University
        of Redlands. 5 Dec.

815   Duke, Vernon
        MISTRESS INTO MAID. Santa Barbara, California.
        University of California - Santa Barbara.
        12 Dec. Composer

816   Vaughan Williams, Ralph
        THE FIRST NOWELL. London. 19 Dec. Simona
        Pakenham (The instrumentation for The First
        Nowell was extended by Roy Douglas)

817   Dallapiccola, Luigi
        JOB. New York. 19 Dec.

                            1959

818   Kreutz, Arthur
        SOURWOOD MOUNTAIN. Clinton, Mississippi. Uni-
        versity of Mississippi. 8 Jan. Zoe Lunde
        Schiller

819   Ellstein, Abraham
        THE THIEF AND THE HANGMAN. Athens, Ohio. Ohio
        University. 17 Jan. Morton Wishengrad

820   Fine, Vivian
        A GUIDE TO THE LIFE EXPECTANCY OF THE ROSE.
        New York. 7 Feb. Composer

821   Wehner, George
        FRISCO BELLE, BALLAD OF THE OLD WEST. New York.
        12 Feb. Composer

822   Presser, W.
        THE WHISTLER. Hattiesburg, Mississippi. Southern
        Mississippi College. 14 Feb.

823   Warren, Raymond
        THE LADY OF EPHESUS. Belfast. 16 Feb.

824   Landau, Siegfried
        THE SONS OF AARON. Scarsdale, New York.
        Scarsdale Junior High School. 28 Feb. Composer

825   Beckwith, John
        NIGHT BLOOMING CEREUS. Toronto. 3 Mar. James
        Reaney

826   Kalmanoff, Martin
        LIZZIE STROTTER. Des Moines, Iowa. Drake
        University. 6 Mar. Composer

827   Milano, Robert L.
        THE HIRED HAND. New York. 23 Mar.

828   Hines, Jerome
        I AM THE WAY. South Orange, New Jersey. 24 Mar.

829   McKee, Jeanellen
        DREAM OF AN EMPIRE. Chicago. ? Mar.

830   Parmentier, Francis Gordon
        THE LITTLE PRINCE. San Francisco. 1 Apr.

831   Kilpatrick, Jack F.
        THE BLESSED WILDERNESS. Dallas, Texas. Southern
        Methodist University. 18 Apr.

832   Franchetti, Arnold
        PRELUDE AND FUGUE. Elmwood, Connecticut. Hartt
        College. 21 Apr.

833   Weisgall, Hugo
        SIX CHARACTERS IN SEARCH OF AN AUTHOR. New York.
        26 Apr. Dennis Johnston

1959   First Performances

834   Mailman, Martin
       THE HUNTED. Rochester, New York. Eastman School
       of Music. 27 Apr. Composer

835   Chapman, Harold
       THE ROSE AND THE RING. Hampton, Virginia.
       27 Apr. Composer and E. Chapman

836   Kechley, Gerald
       THE GOLDEN LION. Seattle. University of
       Washington. 28 Apr. Elwyn Kechley

837   Barab, Seymour
       PINK SIAMESE. Detroit. ? Apr. Susan Otto

838   Meyers, Emerson
       DOLCEDO. Washington, D.C. Catholic University.
       ? Apr. Dominic Rover

839   Arnell, Richard
       THE PETRIFIED PRINCESS. London. 5 May. Bryan
       Guinness

840   Morris, Franklin
       THE POSTPONEMENT. Syracuse, New York. Syracuse
       University. 7 May. Composer

841   Jones, George Thaddeus
       THE CAGE. New York. 10 May. Leo Brady

842   Graves, William
       THE JUGGLER. Washington, D.C. Catholic Univer-
       sity. 13 May

843   Glanville-Hicks, Peggy
       THE GLITTERING GATE. New York. 14 May.
       Composer

844   Harrison, Lou
       RAPUNZEL. New York. 14 May

First Performances   1959

845   Woolen, R.
       THE DECORATOR. New York. Catholic University.
       24 May. Mr. and Mrs. P. Getlein

846   McClain, Floyd
       THE PRINCESS AND THE FROG. Yankton, South
       Dakota. Yankton College. 13 June

847   Barber, Samuel
       A HAND OF BRIDGE. Spoleto, Italy. 17 June
       Gian-Carlo Menotti

848   Halahan, G.
       THE SPUR OF THE MOMENT. London. 17 June. Joe
       Mendoza

849   Wishart, Peter
       TWO IN A BUSH. Birmingham, Alabama. 23 June.
       Don J. Roberts

850   Muldoon, George
       ILLUSION FOR THREE. San Francisco. 1 July

851   Hopkins, Anthony
       HANDS ACROSS THE SKY. Cheltenham, England.
       8 July. Gordon Snell

852   Horovitz, J.
       GENTLEMAN'S ISLAND. Cheltenham, England.
       9 July. Gordon Snell

853   Novak, Lionel A.
       THE CLARKSTOWN WITCH. Piermont, New York.
       11 July

854   Grove, Isaac Van
       THE OTHER WISE MAN. Bentonville, Arkansas.
       14 July. Composer

855   Arnell, Richard
       MOONFLOWERS. Kent, England. 23 July. Composer

856   Bezanson, Philip
       WESTERN CHILD. Iowa City, Iowa. Iowa State
       University. 28 July. Paul S. Engle

857   Cockshott, Gerald
       A FAUN IN THE FOREST. Westport, Connecticut.
       9 Aug. Composer

858   Park, Stephen F.
       SALLY BACK AND FORTH. Tampa, Florida. Univer-
       sity of Tampa. 6 Oct.

859   ______.
       STORM GATHERING. Tampa, Florida. University
       of Tampa. 6 Oct.

860   Barlow, David
       DAVID AND BATHSHEBA. Newcastle-on-Tyne.
       15 Oct.

861   Hoiby, Lee
       BEATRICE. Louisville, Kentucky. 23 Oct.
       Marcia Nardia

862   Venth, Carl
       LA VIDA DE LA MISION. San Antonio, Texas.
       28 Oct.

863   Hunkins, Eusebia
       THE YOUNG LINCOLN. Galesburg, Illinois. Knox
       College. ? Oct.

864   Coke, R. S.
       THE CENCI. London. 5 Nov. Composer

First Performances

1960

865   Nobokov, Nicholas
DEATH OF GREGORY RASPUTIN. Cologne. 27 Nov.
Stephen Spender; performed in a German translation (The Death of Gregory Rasputin is a
considerably revised version of The Holy Devil)

866   Warren, Raymond
FINN AND THE BLACK HAG. Belfast. 11 Dec.

867   Hovhaness, Alan
BLUE FLAME. San Antonio, Texas. 13 Dec.
Composer

868   Maconchy, Elizabeth
THE SOFA. London. 13 Dec. Ursula Vaughan
Williams

869   Patacchi, Van
THE FOUNDLING. Columbia, Missouri. Stephens
College. ? Dec. William Ashbrook

1960

870   Eastwood, T.
CHRISTOPHER SLY. London. 24 Jan. Ronald
Duncan

871   Mayer, William
HELLO, WORLD! Hempstead, New York. Hofstra
University. ? Jan. Susan Otto

872   Gray, David
A CHRISTMAS CAROL. Nottingham, England. ? Jan.

873   Foss, Lukas
INTRODUCTIONS AND GOODBYES. Spoleto, Italy.
? Jan. Gian-Carlo Menotti

1960   First Performances

874   Krane, Sherman
        THE GIANT'S GARDEN. Norfolk, Virginia. College
        of William and Mary. 12 Mar. June Krane

875   Binder, Abraham Wolfe
        A GOAT IN CHELM. New York. 20 Mar.

876   Elkus, Jonathan
        THE OUTCASTS OF POKER FLAT. Bethlehem,
        Pennsylvania. Leigh University. 16 Apr.
        Robert G. Bander

877   Maxfield, Richard
        STACKED DECK. New York. 30 Apr. Dick Higgins

878   Prunty, William
        THE LOTUS TREE. Morgantown, West Virginia.
        13 May

879   Bliss, Sir Arthur
        TOBIAS AND THE ANGEL. London. 19 May.
        Christopher Hassall

880   Putsche, Thomas
        THE CAT AND THE MOOR. Hartford, Connecticut.
        22 May

881   Laderman, Ezra
        GOODBYE TO THE CLOWN. New York. 22 May. Ernest
        Kinoy

882   Gustafson, Dwight
        THE HUNTED. Greenville, South Carolina. Bob
        Jones University. 26 May

883   Taff, Anthony
        THE TEN VIRGINS. Albion, Michigan. Albion
        College. ? May

884   Burt, F.
          VOLPONE. Stuttgart. 2 June. Composer; per-
          formed in German

885   Britten, Benjamin
          MIDSUMMER NIGHT'S DREAM. Aldeburgh. 11 June.
          Composer and Peter Pears

886   Serulnikoff, John Laurence
          THIS EVENING. Bennington, Vermont. Bennington
          College. 20 June

887   Wishart, Peter
          THE CAPTIVE. Birmingham, Alabama. 29 June.
          Don Roberts

888   Tate, Phyllis
          THE LODGER. London. Royal Academy of Music.
          14 July. David Franklin

889   Hannay, Roger
          TWO TICKETS TO OMAHA (PERFIDY COMPOUNDED)
          Moorhead, Minnesota. Concordia College.
          21 July. Jerome Lamb

890   Hughes, S.
          SERCH YW'R DOCTOR. Cardiff. 1 Aug. Saunders
          Lewis

891   Meyerowitz, Jan
          PORT TOWN. Lenox, Massachusetts. 4 Aug.
          Langston Hughes

892   Brant, Henry
          GRAND UNIVERSAL CIRCUS. Piermont, New York.
          ? Aug. Patricia Brant

893   Haslam, Herbert
          POSTLOGUE. Piermont, New York. ? Aug. M.
          Heiner

1961   First Performances

894   Cole, Hugo
       THE TUNNEL. London. 24 Oct. Composer

895   Giannini, Vittorio
       THE MEDEAD. Atlanta, Georgia. ? Oct.

896   Piket, Frederick
       SATAN'S TRAP. New York. 26 Nov. Charles S.
       Levy

897   Esile, Joseph
       STILL DARK CLOUDS. Scottsdale, Arizona. ? Nov.
       Frank Langer

898   Beckler, Stanworth
       THE OUTCASTS OF POKER FLAT. Stockton,
       California. College of the Pacific. 2 Dec.
       Jon Pearce

899   Bezanson, Philip
       THE GOLDEN CHILD. New York. 18 Dec. Paul
       Engle

900   Gillis, Don
       THE LIBRETTO. Norman, Oklahoma. University of
       Oklahoma. ? Dec. Composer

                          1961

901   Kastle, Leonard
       DESERET. New York. 1 Jan. Anne Howard Bailey

902   Youse, Glad Robinson
       THE THIRTY-FOURTH STAR. Learned, Kansas.
       17 Jan.

903   Moross, Jerome
       SUSANNA AND THE ELDERS. Augusta, Georgia.
       21 Jan. John La Touche

904   Flanagan, William
        BARTLEBY. New York.   24 Jan.   Composer

905   Kondorossy, Leslie
        THE FOX. Cleveland.   28 Jan.   Caroline Kulin
        and Shawn Hall

906   Hamm, Charles Edward
        THE BOX. New Orleans.   Tulane University.
        4 Feb.   Composer

907   Gesensway, Louis
        THE GREAT BUFFO AND HIS TALKING DOG.   Philadelphia.
        Academy of Vocal Arts. 7 Feb.   Christopher Davis

908   Beadell, Robert
        THE SWEETWATER AFFAIR. Lincoln, Nebraska.   Uni-
        versity of Nebraska.   8 Feb.

909   Bradley, Ruth
        THE BARREN PINES. New York.   12 Feb.   Dorothy
        Dix Lawrence

910   Weisgall, Hugo
        PURGATORY. Washington, D.C.   17 Feb.   (The
        complete text of William Butler Yeat's Purgatory)

911   Flagello, Nicholas
        THE SISTERS. New York.   22 Feb.   Manhattan
        School of Music.   Dean Mundy

912   Gaburo, Kenneth
        THE WIDOW. Urbana, Illinois.   University of
        Illinois.   26 Feb.   Composer

913   Hoag, Charles
        LONELY GAME. Iowa City, Iowa.   Iowa State Uni-
        versity.   11 Mar.

914   Fiore, Ronald Michael
        LINDA. Philadelphia. 13 Mar.

915   Stevens, Noel Scott
        THE ENCHANTED CANARY. Bemidji, Minnesota.
        Bemidji State College. 18 Mar. Andrew Oerke

916   Laderman, Ezra.
        THE HUNTING OF THE SNARK. New York. Hunter
        College. 25 Mar. Composer

917   Faberman, Harold
        MEDEA. Boston, Massachusetts. Boston University.
        26 Mar.

918   Robb, Willard
        THE TWILIGHT SAINT. Norfolk, Virginia. ? Mar.

919   Solomon, R.
        DAVID AND GOLIATH. Cleveland. ? Mar.

920   Partch, Harry
        REVELATIONS IN THE COURTHOUSE PARK. Champaign,
        Illinois. University of Illinois. 11 Apr.

921   Kanitz, Ernest
        PERPETUAL. Los Angeles. 26 Apr. Ellen Terry

922   Head, Michael
        BACHELOR MOUSE. Charleston, Pennsylvania.
        Charleston Conservatory. ? Apr.

923   Kaufmann, Walter
        THE SCARLET LETTER. Bloomington, Indiana.
        Indiana University. 6 May

924   Straus, John L.
        THE ACCUSED. New York. 7 May. Shepherd Kerman

First Performances   1961

925   Joubert, John
       SILAS MARNER. Cape Town, South Africa. Univer-
       sity of Cape Town. 20 May. Rackel Trickett

926   Henze, Hans Werner
       ELEGIE FÜR JUNGE LIEBENDE. Schwetzinger. 20 May.
       W. H. Auden and Chester Kallman; performed in a
       German translation

927   Meyerowitz, Jan
       GODFATHER DEATH. New York. Brooklyn College.
       1 June. John P. Stevens

928   Britain, Radie
       KUTHARA. Los Angeles. Mount St. Mary's College.
       24 June

929   Wehner, George
       SO SINGS THE BELL. New York. 24 June. Composer

930   Moss, Lawrence
       THE BRUTE. Norfolk, Connecticut. 15 July.
       Eric Bentley

931   Wehner, George
       THE WILD SWAN. New York. 18 July

932   _____.
       THE AMIABLE BEAST. New York. 25 July. Composer

933   Lockwood, Normand
       EARLY DAWN. Denver. University of Denver.
       7 Aug. R. Russell Porter

934   Glanville-Hicks, Peggy
       NAUSICAA. Athens. 19 Aug. Robert Graves and
       Alastair Reid

1961   First Performances

935   Wehner, George
        STAR IN THE NIGHT. New York. 22 Aug. Composer

936   Bennett, Richard Rodney
        THE LEDGE. London. 11 Sept. Adrian Mitchell

937   Dello Joio, Norman
        BLOOD MOON. San Francisco. 18 Sept. Composer
        and Gale Hoffman

938   Moore, Douglas
        THE WINGS OF THE DOVE. New York. 12 Oct.
        Ethan Ayer

939   Ward, Robert
        THE CRUCIBLE. New York. 26 Oct. Bernard
        Stambler

940   Sokoloff, Noel
        THE FRANKLIN'S TALE. Baton Rouge, Louisiana.
        Louisiana State University. 10 Nov. Ted Hart

941   Middleton, Robert
        COMMAND PERFORMANCE. Poughkeepsie, New York.
        Vassar College. 11 Nov. Harold W. Smith

942   Giannini, Vittorio
        THE HARVEST. Chicago. 25 Nov. Karl Flaster

943   Caldwell, Mary E.
        THE GIFT OF SONG. Pasadena, California. 3 Dec.
        Composer

944   Sheldon, Robert
        A FIFTH FOR BRIDGE. San Francisco. San Fran-
        cisco Conservatory of Music. 3 Dec. Hitchcock

945   Apivor, Denis
        YERMA. London. 17 Dec. Montague Slater

946   Hindemith, Paul
        THE LONG CHRISTMAS DINNER. Mannheim. 17 Dec.
        Thornton Wilder; performed in German

947   La Montaine, John
        NOVELLIS, NOVELLIS. Washington, D.C. 24 Dec.
        Composer

948   Brandt, William
        NO NEUTRAL GROUND. Pullman, Washington. Wash-
        ington State University. ? Dec.

949   Kaufmann, Walter
        SGNARELLE. New York. ? Dec.

                            1962

950   Kay, Ulysses
        THE JUGGLER OF OUR LADY. New Orleans. Xavier
        University. 3 Feb. Alexander King

951   Giannini, Vittorio
        REHEARSAL CALL. New York. Juilliard. 15 Feb.
        Robert A. Simon and Francis Swan

952   Reed, Herbert Owen
        EARTH-TRAPPED. East Lansing, Michigan. Michigan
        State University. 24 Feb. Composer

953   White, John D.
        LEGEND OF SLEEPY HOLLOW. Kent, Ohio. Kent
        State University. 28 Feb. Martin Nurmi

954   Mullins, Hugh
        THE JADE GODDESS. Los Angeles. Los Angeles
        State College. ? Feb.

                                  First Performances

955   Talma, Louise
THE ALCESTIAD. Frankfurt. 1 Mar. Thornton
Wilder

956   Fisher, William J.
THE HAPPY PRINCE. Iowa City, Iowa. Iowa State
University. 10 Mar. John Gutman

957   Ellstein, Abraham
THE GOLEM. New York. 22 Mar. Composer and
Sylvia Regan

958   Weisgall, Hugo
ATHALIA. New York. 9 Apr. Richard Goldman

959   Gury, Louis
HITHER AND THITHER OF DANNY DITHER. Cleveland,
Ohio. ? Apr.

960   Siegmeister, Elie
THE MERMAID IN LOCK NUMBER SEVEN. Hempstead,
New York. Hofstra University. 4 May. Edward
Mabley

961   Richmond, Gordon
THE WILD BEASTS. New York. Juilliard. 17 May

962   Fink, Myron
JEREMIAH. Binghampton, New York. 25 May.
P. Fink and E. Hawley

963   Tippett, Michael
KING PRIAM. Coventry. 29 May. Composer

964   Still, William Grant
THE PEACEFUL LAND. Coral Gables, Florida. University of Miami. ? May

965   Adler, Samuel
        THE OUTCASTS OF POKER FLAT. Denton, Texas.
        North Texas State University. 8 June. Judith
        Stampfer

966   Stravinsky, Igor
        THE FLOOD. New York. 14 June. Robert Craft

967   Tate, Phyllis
        DARK PILGRIMAGE. London. 5 July. David
        Franklin

968   Novak, Lionel A.
        KATYDIDS. Piermont, New York. 26 July.

969   Lockwood, Normand
        THE WIZARDS OF BALIZAR. Denver. University of
        Denver. 1 Aug. R. Russell Porter

970   Duke, John
        THE YANKEE PEDLAR. Schroon Lake, New York.
        17 Aug. Dorothy Duke

971   Davis, Carl
        PUBCRAWL. New Haven, Connecticut. Yale Uni-
        versity. ? Aug.

972   Floyd, Carlisle
        THE PASSION OF JONATHAN WADE. New York. 11 Oct.
        Composer

973   Moss, Lawrence
        THE QUEEN AND THE REBEL. New York. N. Y. U.
        1 Nov. Composer

974   Dougherty, Celius
        MANY MOONS. Poughkeepsie, New York. Vassar.
        3 Nov. Composer

1962   First Performances

975   Kagen, Sergius
         HAMLET. Baltimore. Peabody Conservatory.
         9 Nov. Composer

976   Mayer, William
         ONE CHRISTMAS LONG AGO. Muncie, Indiana. Ball
         State University. 9 Nov. Composer

977   Burge, David
         INTERVALS. Evanston, Illinois. Northwestern
         University. 13 Nov.

978   Britain, Radie
         NISAN. Detroit. ? Nov.

979   Moore, Douglas
         THE GREENFIELD CHRISTMAS TREE. Baltimore.
         Peabody Conservatory. 8 Dec. Arnold Sundgaard

980   Kalmanoff, Martin
         THE BALD PRIMA DONNA. New York. 15 Dec.

981   Maconchy, Elizabeth
         THE DEPARTURE. London. 16 Dec. Anne Ridler

982   Orr, Baxton
         THE WAGER. London. 16 Dec. Hamilton Johnson

983   Coleman, Edwin
         A CHRISTMAS CAROL. London. 24 Dec. Margaret
         Burns Harris

984   Hughes, Langston
         BLACK NATIVITY. New York. 23 Dec.

1963

985   Taff, Anthony
       NOAH. Albion, Michigan. Albion College.
       10 Feb. Composer

986   Hovhaness, Alan
       SPIRIT OF THE VALANCHE. Tokyo. 15 Feb.
       Composer

987   Heiden, Bernard
       THE DARKENED CITY. Bloomington, Indiana.
       Indiana University. 23 Feb. Robert Kelly

988   Menotti, Gian-Carlo
       LABYRINTH. New York. 3 Mar. Composer

989   Searle, Humphrey
       THE PHOTO OF THE COLONEL. London. 8 Mar.

990   Menotti, Gian-Carlo
       THE LAST SAVAGE. Paris. 2 Apr. Composer

991   Parnell, Raymond
       ARIA DA CAPO. Toronto. 5 Apr.

992   Lenel, Ludwig
       YOUNG GOODMAN BROWN. Allentown, Pennsylvania.
       Muhlenberg College. 25 Apr.

993   Gilbert, John
       A MOTHER'S REQUIEM. Lubbock, Texas. Texas
       Technical College. 30 Apr.

994   Jones, Robert
       THE GARDEN. San Bernadino, California. ? Apr.

995   Mullins, Hugh
       THE STONE OF HEAVEN. Los Angeles. Los Angeles
       State College. ? Apr.

1963   First Performances

996   Neumann, Alfred
         AN OPERA FOR EASTER. Silver Springs, Maryland
         ? Apr.

997   Kalmanoff, Martin
         YOUNG TOM EDISON. New York. ? Apr. Robert K.
         Adams

998   Still, William Grant
         HIGHWAY NO. 1. Coral Gables, Florida. Univer-
         sity of Miami. 11 May. Verna Avery

999   Siegmeister, Elie
         THE PLOUGH AND THE STARS. St. Louis. Washing-
         ton University. 15 May. Edward Mabley

1000   DuPage, Florence
         TRIAL UNIVERSELLE. Westbury, New York. Advent
         Tuller School. 17 May. Sister Jean

1001   Kalmanoff, Martin
         HALF MAGIC IN KING ARTHUR'S COURT. New York.
         17 May. Edward Eager

1002   Menotti, Gian-Carlo
         THE DEATH OF BISHOP BRINDSI. Cincinnati. 18 May.
         Composer

1003   Chavez, Carlos
         THE VISITORS. Mexico City. 21 May. Chester
         Kallman

1004   Kagel, Maurice
         ANAGRAM. Ojai, California. 24 May

1005   Griffis, Robert
         PORT OF PLEASURE. Los Angeles. Immaculate
         Heart College. 29 June

First Performances   1963

1006   Overton, Hall
          PIETRO'S PETARD. New York. ? June. Robert
          de Maria

1007   Williamson, Malcolm
          OUR MAN IN HAVANA. London. 2 July. Sidney
          Gilliat

1008   Wagner, Thomas
          THE CROCODILE. New York. New York University.
          ? Sept.

1009   Miller, Michael
          A SUNNY MORNING. New York. N. Y. U. ? Sept.

1010   Moross, Jerome
          GENTLEMEN, BE SEATED! New York. 10 Oct.
          Composer and Edward Eager

1011   Neumann, Alfred
          AN OPERA FOR EVERYONE. Silver Springs, Maryland.
          3 Nov.

1012   Warren, Raymond
          GRADUATION ODE. Belfast. 17 Nov.

1013   Williams, Guy Bevier
          THE MASTER THIEF. Pasadena, California. 28 Nov.

1014   Mullins, Hugh
          THE KISS. Los Angeles. Los Angeles State Col-
          lege. ? Nov.

1015   Floyd, Carlisle
          THE SOJOURNER AND MOLLIE SINCLAIR. Raleigh,
          North Carolina. East Carolina State College.
          2 Dec. Composer

1964   First Performances

1016   Jones, Daniel
        THE KNIFE. London. 2 Dec. Composer

1017   Greenberg, Noah
        THE PLAY OF HEROD. New York. 10 Dec. Narra-
        tion by W. H. Auden

1018   Bolcom, William
        DYNAMITE TONIGHT. New York. 21 Dec. Arnold
        Weinstein

1019   Clark, Roger
        TI YETTE. Detroit. Celeste College. 28 Dec.

1020   Strilko, Anthony
        THE LAST PUPPET. New York. ? Dec. Harry
        Duncan

1964

1021   Argento, Dominick
        THE MASQUE OF ANGELS. Minneapolis. 1 Jan.
        John Olon Scrymgeour

1022   Blatt, Joseph
        MOSES ON MOUNT SINAI. Ann Arbor, Michigan.
        University of Michigan. 22 Jan.

1023   Haskins, Robert
        CASSANDRA SOUTHWICK. Springfield, Ohio. 24 Jan.
        Allen J. Koppenhave

1024   Winslow, Richard
        ALICE. Hartford, Connecticut. ? Jan. Susan
        McAllester

1025   Le Mon, Melvin
        DOWN, DOWN, DOWN. Rockville Center, New York.
        Southside Senior High School. 6 Feb.

First Performances   1964

1026   Kanitz, Ernest
        VISIONS AT MIDNIGHT. Los Angeles. U. C. L. A.
        26 Feb.

1027   Shore, William
        WHARF'S EDGE. New York. Barnard College.
        28 Feb. Kenneth James

1028   Hannay, Roger
        THE FORTUNE OF ST. MACABRE. Moorhead, Minnesota.
        Concordia College. 21 Mar.

1029   Hurd, Michael
        LITTLE BILLY. Newnham-on-Severn. Brightlands
        Prep School. 25 Mar. Composer

1030   Lockwood, Normand
        THE HANGING JUDGE. Denver. Denver University.
        ? Mar. R. Russell Porter

1031   Feliciano, Richard
        SIR GAWAIN AND THE GREEN KNIGHT. San Francisco.
        Lone Mountain College. 4 Apr. Robert Fahrner

1032   Fletcher, Grant
        THE SACK OF CALABASAS. Phoenix, Arizona. 6 Apr.
        John Meyers

1033   Magney, Ruth Taylor
        THE GIFT OF THE MAGI. Minneapolis. 16 Apr.
        Composer

1034   Edelman, David
        THE CURE. Lexington, Massachusetts. William
        Diamond Junior High School. 17 Apr.

1035   Papale, Henry
        THE ONLY GREEN PLANET. Philadelphia. 19 Apr.

Twentieth Century Opera

1036   Sessions, Roger
          MONTEZUMA. West Berlin. 19 Apr. Antonio
          Borghese

1037   Gilbert, John
          IF THIS BE MADNESS. Lubbock, Texas. Texas
          Technical College. 21 Apr.

1038   Liggett, Lonnie
          THE HERMITS. Syracuse, New York. Syracuse University. 23 Apr.

1039   Rescia, R. R.
          PORTRAIT. Amherst, Massachusetts. 25 Apr.

1040   Lasker, Henry
          JACK AND THE BEANSTALK. Boston. 25 Apr.

1041   Dupage, Florence
          WHITHER. Westbury, New York. Advent Tuller
          School. 15 May. Sister Jean

1042   Leoni, Eva
          MR. CUPID, AMERICAN AMBASSADOR. New York.
          16 May

1043   Krenek, Ernst
          WHAT PRICE CONFIDENCE? Zurich. 25 May
          Composer

1044   Menotti, Gian-Carlo
          MARTIN'S LIE. Bath. 3 June. Composer

1045   Taff, Anthony
          THE SUMMONS. Albion, Michigan. Albion College.
          7 June. James Brock

1046   Williamson, Malcolm
          ENGLISH ECCENTRICS. Aldeburgh. 11 June.
          Geoffrey Dunn

1047   Britten, Benjamin
          CURLEW RIVER. Aldeburgh. 13 June. William
          Plomer

1048   Wehner, George
          INTO THE SILENCE. New York. 18 July

1049   Cannon, Philip
          MORVOREN. London. 15 July. Maisie Radford

1050   Reiners, Ann
          CINDY. Eureka Springs, Arkansas. 27 July

1051   Grove, Isaac Van
          THE SHINING CHALICE. Eureka Springs, Arkansas.
          30 July. Janice Lovood

1052   Ward, Robert
          THE LADY FROM COLORADO. Central City, Colorado.
          3 Aug. Bernard Stambler

1053   Swift, Richard
          THE TRAIL OF TENDER O'SHEA. Davis, California.
          University of California–Davis. 12 Aug.

1054   Hovhaness, Alan
          WIND DRUM. Gatlinburg, Tennessee. Union Col-
          lege. 23 Aug. Composer

1055   ______.
          THE BURNING HOUSE. Gatlinburg, Tennessee.
          Union College. 23 Aug. Composer

1056   Hoiby, Lee
          NATALIA PETROVNA. New York. 8 Oct. William
          Ball

1057   Zador, Eugene
          THE VIRGIN AND THE FAWN. Los Angeles.
          U. C. L. A. 24 Oct.

1964   First Performances

1058   Morrison, Donald
        THE MERCHANT'S MOON. Sioux City, Iowa. Morning-
        side College. 29 Oct. Mrs. Donald Morrison

1059   Young, LaMonte
        THE TORTOISE DRONING SELECTED PITCHES FROM THE
        HOLY NUMBERS FOR THE TWO BLACK TIGERS, THE GREEN
        TIGER, AND THE HERMIT. New York. 30 Oct.

1060   Aschaffenburg, Walter
        BARTELBY. Oberlin, Ohio. Oberlin College.
        12 Nov. Jay Leyda

1061   Maw, Nicholas
        ONE-MAN SHOW. London. 12 Nov. Arthur Jacobs

1062   Lockwood, Normand
        REQUIEM FOR A RICH YOUNG MAN. Denver. Univer-
        sity of Denver. 24 Nov. Donald Sutherland

1063   Benjamin, Arthur
        TARTUFFE. London. 30 Nov. Cedric Cliffe

1064   Owen, Richard
        A MOMENT OF WAR. Buenos Aires. ? Nov. Composer

1065   Lees, Benjamin
        THE GILDED CAGE. New York. ? Nov.

1066   Imbrie, Andrew
        THREE AGAINST CHRISTMAS. Berkeley, California.
        University of California-Berkeley. 3 Dec.
        Richard Wincor

1067   Gibbs, Cecil Armstrong
        THE THREE KINGS. New Haven, Connecticut.
        Prospect Hill School. 5 Dec.

1068   Young, LaMonte
         THE TORTOISE RECALLING THE DRONE OF THE HOLY
         NUMBERS AS THEY WERE REVEALED IN THE DREAMS OF
         THE WHIRLWIND AND THE OBSIDIAN GONG, ILLUMINATED
         BY THE SAWMILL, THE GREEN SAWTOOTH OCELOT, AND
         THE HIGH TENSION LINE STEPDOWN TRANSFORMER. New
         York. 12 Dec.

                              1965

1069   Foss, Lukas
         ECHOI ECHOI. New York. Hunter College. 25 Jan.

1070   Wright, Morris
         THE LEGEND. Muncie, Indiana. Ball State Uni-
         versity. 28 Jan.

1071   Gundry, Inglis
         THE PRINCE OF THE COXCOMBS. London. Morley
         College. 3 Feb. 1965. Composer

1072   Brush, Ruth
         THE STREET SINGERS OF MARKET STREET. Borger,
         Texas. 16 Feb.

1073   LaMothe, Susan
         THE KITCHEN SINK. Buffalo, New York. State
         University of New York at Buffalo. 19 Feb.
         David Posner

1074   Robb, John Donald
         DONTARO. San Francisco. 20 Feb. Composer

1075   Bennett, Richard Rodney
         THE MINES OF SULPHUR. London. 24 Feb. Beverly
         Cross

1965   First Performances

1076   Donato, Anthony
        THE WALKER-THROUGH-WALLS. Evanston, Illinois.
        Northwestern University. 26 Feb. Composer

1077   Wagner, Joseph
        NEW ENGLAND SAMPLER. Los Angeles. Pepperdine
        College. 26 Feb. Jean Karasavina

1078   Lauridsen, Cora
        JOB. Los Angeles. Occidental College. 28 Feb.

1079   Brush, Ruth
        THE FAIR. Bartleville, Ohio. ? Feb.

1080   Baurer, Harold Gene
        LAZARUS. Lake Forest, Illinois. 5 Mar.

1081   Owen, Richard
        A FISHERMAN CALLED PETER. Carmel, New York.
        14 Mar. Composer

1082   Reynolds, Roger
        THE EMPEROR OF ICE CREAM. New York. 19 Mar.

1083   Fuchs, Peter Paul
        SERENADE AT NOON. Baton Rouge, Louisiana.
        Louisiana State University. 22 Mar. Ann Vermel

1084   Beeson, Jack
        LIZZIE BORDEN. New York. 25 Mar. Kenward
        Elmslie

1085   Kagel, Maurice
        SUR SCENE. Buffalo, New York. State University
        of New York at Buffalo. ? Mar.

1086   Gross, Eric
        THE AMOROUS JUDGE. Sydney. 2 Apr. L. McGlashan

First Performances   1965

1087   Jenni, Donald
        THE EMPEROR CLOTHED ANEW. Chicago. De Paul
        University. 2 Apr. Composer

1088   Hundley, Richard
        EMMA IMMACULATE LIES. New York. 2 Apr.

1089   Yellin, Victor
        ABAYLER. New York. 2 Apr.

1090   Halpern, Sidney
        MACBETH. New York. 4 Apr.

1091   ______.
        THE MONKEY'S PAW. New York. 4 Apr. Composer

1092   Wright, Kenneth
        WING OF EXPECTATION. Lexington, Kentucky. Uni-
        versity of Kentucky. 7 Apr. Composer

1093   Amram, David
        THE FINAL INGREDIENT. New York. 11 Apr.

1094   Stewart, Robert
        THE CURL. Lexington, Virginia. Washington and
        Lee University. 27 Apr. J. Shillington and
        J. Cravens

1095   Burgstahler, Elton
        HAT SPAT. Springfield, Missouri. Southwest
        Missouri State College. 2 May

1096   Martirano, Salvatore
        UNDER WORLD. New York. 8 May

1097   Gibbs, Geoffrey
        DOLPHIN OFF HIPPO. Rochester, New York. East-
        man School of Music. 9 May. Alonzo Gibbs

1965   First Performances

1098   Lenel, Ludwig
        THE BOSS. Allentown, Pennsylvania. Muhlenberg
        College. 13 May

1099   Williams, Jack Eric
        THE HINGE TUNE. Interlochen, Michigan. 13 May

1100   DeBanfield, Raffaelo
        ALISSA. Geneva, Switzerland. 15 May. Richard
        Miller

1101   Freed, Arnold
        ZODIAC. Rochester, Minnesota. John Marshall
        High School. 19 May

1102   Fisher, Truman
        THE WASPS. Los Angeles. Occidental College.
        21 May

1103   Williamson, Malcolm
        THE HAPPY PRINCE. Farnham, England. 22 May.
        Composer

1104   McDowell, John H.
        OKLAHOMA DANGER REMARK. New York. 25 May

1105   Dickinson, Peter
        THE JUDAS TREE. London. 27 May

1106   Davis, Carl
        THE ARRANGEMENT. London. 30 May. Leo Lehman

1107   Dupage, Florence
        A NEW WORLD FOR NELLIE. Westbury, New York.
        Advent Tuller College. 11 June. Composer

1108   Wehner, George
        THREE DAYS AFTER. New York. 18 June. Composer

1109   Mayer, Lutz
          REFUGE. Cortland,.New York. State University
          of New York at Cortland. 20 July. Edward Devany

1110   Hunkins, Eusebia
          CHILD OF PROMISE. Eureka Springs, Arkansas.
          25 July

1111   Sitsky, Larry
          THE FALL OF THE HOUSE OF USHER. Hobart,
          Australia. ? July. G. Harwood

1112   Sutherland, M.
          THE YOUNG KABARI. Hobart, Australia. ? July.
          M. Casey

1113   Penberthy, J.
          OPHELIA OF THE NINE MILE BEACH. Hobart,
          Australia. ? July

1114   Pasatieri, Thomas
          THE WOMEN. Aspen, Colorado. 20 Aug. Composer

1115   Kont, Paul
          INZWISCHEN (FOR THE TIME BEING). Salzburg.
          ? Aug. W. H. Auden

1116   Zaninelli, Luigi
          FRESHMAN DANCE. Delaware Gap, Pennsylvania.
          17 Sept. Composer

1117   Bucci, Mark
          THE HERO. Boston. 24 Sept. David Rogers

1118   Fetler, Paul
          STURGE MACLEAN. St. Paul, Minnesota. Hardin
          High School. 11 Oct. Loyce Houlton

1965   First Performances

1119   Coe, Kenton
        SUD. Marseilles. 14 Oct. Julien Green

1120   Rorem, Ned
        MISS JULIE. New York. 4 Nov. Kenward Elmslie

1121   Cox, David Harold
        THE CHILDREN IN THE FOREST. Birmingham, England.
        4 Nov.

1122   Schwartz, Ira
        ALL IN BLACK MY LOVE WENT RIDING. Minot, North
        Dakota. Minot State College. 11 Nov. Gary
        Luckert

1123   White, Raymond Wilding
        THE SELFISH GIANT. Cleveland. 30 Nov.

1124   Caldwell, Mary E.
        NIGHT OF THE STAR. Pasadena, California. 5 Dec.
        Composer

1125   Meyerowitz, Jan
        I RABBINI. Rome. 5 Dec. Fidele d'Amico

1126   Whelen, Christopher
        THE CANCELLING DARK. London. 5 Dec. Vernon
        Scannell

1127   Gillis, Don
        THE GIFT OF THE MAGI. Fort Worth, Texas. Texas
        Wesleyan University. 7 Dec.

1128   Hastie, John
        MARA. Croydon, England. 14 Dec.

1129   Dubbioso, S.
        THE PIED PIPER. New York. ? Dec.

1130   Mount-Burke, William
          THE LEGEND OF THE MERRYFEATHER. New York.
          ? Dec.

                              1966

1131   Williamson, Malcolm
          JULIUS CAESAR JONES. London. 4 Jan. Geoffrey
          Dunn

1132   Kent, Charles
          A ROOM IN TIME. Baltimore. 9 Jan. Composer

1133   Schaefer, Murray
          LOVING (TOI). Montreal. 3 Feb.

1134   Gordon, David
          DAMASK DRUM. Kansas City, Missouri. 5 Feb.

1135   Polifrone, Jon J.
          THE KENTUCKY STORY. Barbourville, Kentucky.
          Union College. ? Feb.

1136   ______.
          THE WICKED SAM AND THE DEVIL. Evanston, Illinois.
          ? Feb.

1137   Johnson, Carl
          ESCORIAL. Iowa City, Iowa. University of Iowa.
          17 Mar.

1138   Parrott, Ian
          THE BLACK RAM. Aberystwyth, Wales. 9 Mar.
          H. Idis Bell and H. Parry-Williams

1139   Pasatieri, Thomas
          LA DIVINA. New York. Juilliard. 16 Mar.
          Composer

1966   First Performances

1140   Flagello, Nicholas
        JUDGEMENT OF ST. FRANCIS. New York. Manhattan
        School of Music, 18 Mar. Armand Aulicino

1141   Westergaard, Peter
        MR. AND MRS. DISCOBBOLOS. New York. Columbia
        University. 21 Mar. Composer

1142   Six, Herbert
        WITHOUT MEMORIAL BANNERS. Kansas City, Missouri.
        24 Mar. Dan Jaffe

1143   Floyd, Carlisle
        MARKHEIM. New Orleans. 31 Mar. Composer

1144   Van Buskirk, Carl G.
        CHRISTMAS DOLL. Bloomington, Indiana. Indiana
        University. ? Mar.

1145   Schramm, Harold
        SHILAPPADIKARAM (THE ANKLE BRACELET). New York.
        13 Apr. Alain Danielou

1146   Eakin, Charles
        THE BOX. Norman, Oklahoma. University of Okla-
        homa. 15 Apr. Composer

1147   Chajes, Julius
        OUT OF THE DESERT. Detroit. 17 Apr.

1148   Blisa, Alice
        THE MUSIC CLUB. Atlanta, Georgia. 22 Apr.

1149   Moore, Douglas
        CARRIE NATION. Lawrence, Kansas. University of
        Kansas. 28 Apr. William North Jayne

1150   Williams, Grace
        THE PARLOUR. Cardiff. 5 May. Composer

First Performances   1966

1151   Zador, Eugene
          THE MAGIC CHAIR. Baton Rouge, Louisiana.
          Louisiana State University. 14 May. George
          Jellinek

1152   Beadell, Robert
          A NUMBER OF FOOLS. Evanston, Illinois. North-
          western University. 14 May

1153   Reif, Paul
          PORTRAIT IN BROWNSTONE. New York. 15 May.
          Henry Butler

1154   Gordon, Philip
          A TALE FROM CHAUCER. Trenton, New Jersey.
          Trenton College. ? May

1155   Britten, Benjamin
          THE BURNING FIERY FURNACE. Orford Church,
          Suffolk, England. 9 June. William Plomer

1156   Vollrath, Carl
          THE QUEST. Tallahassee, Florida. Florida State
          University. 10 June. Composer

1157   McGraw, Charles B.
          THE ANNUNCIATION. New York. 21 June

1158   ______
          TRISTA. New York. 21 June

1159   Hovhaness, Alan
          PILATE. Los Angeles. Pepperdine College.
          26 June. Composer

1160   Kelly, Robert
          THE WHITE GODS. Urbana, Illinois. University
          of Illinois. 3 July. Composer and Chester
          Israel

1966   First Performances

1161   Crosse, Gordon
        PURGATORY. Cheltenham, England. 7 July. (The
        complete text of William Butler Yeats' Purgatory)

1162   Tate, Phyllis
        THE WHAT D'YE CALL IT. Cheltenham, England.
        7 July. V. C. Clinton-Bradley

1163   Grove, Isaac Van
        RUTH. Eureka Springs, Arkansas. 22 July.
        Janice Lovood

1164   Kaufmann, Walter
        A HOOSIER TALE. Bloomington, Indiana. Indiana
        University. 30 July. Composer

1165   Henze, Hans Werner
        DIE BASSARIDEN. Salzburg. 6 Aug. W. H. Auden
        and Chester Kallman; performed in a German
        translation

1166   Barber, Samuel
        ANTONY AND CLEOPATRA. New York. 16 Sept.
        Composer and Franco Zefferelli

1167   Schiller, Gunther
        THE VISITATION. Hamburg. 12 Oct. Composer

1168   Kalmanoff, Martin
        HUCK FINN AND TOM SAWYER. New York. 15 Oct.
        Thomas and Lebowitz

1169   Franchetti, Arnold
        AS A CONDUCTOR DREAMS, OR NOTTURNO IN LA. Hart-
        ford, Connecticut. Trinity College. 20 Oct.
        Louis Berrone

1170   House, Margueritte
        THE TOURISTS. Interlochen, Michigan. ? Oct.

First Performances   1967

1171   Lubin, Ernest
          THE PARDONER'S TALE. Denver. 19 Nov. Ted Hart

1172   Fink, Harold
          THE BRIDEGROOM. Cleveland. 26 Nov.

1173   Williamson, Malcolm
          THE VIOLINS OF ST. JACQUES. London. 29 Nov.

1174   Kalmanoff, Martin
          MR. SCROOGE. New York. 3 Dec.

1175   Bush, Alan Dudley
          THE SUGAR REAPERS. Leipzig. 11 Dec. Nancy
          Bush; performed in a German translation by
          Reinhard Geilert and Hans Michael Richter

1176   Brunswick, Mark
          THE MASTERBUILDER. New York. C. C. N. Y.
          16 Dec.

1177   Chappell, Herbert
          MAK THE SHEEP STEALER. London. 25 Dec. Don
          Taylor

1178   Smith, Julia
          THE SHEPHERDESS AND THE CHIMNEY SWEEP. Fort
          Worth, Texas. 28 Déc. C. d'Arcy Mackay

1179   Mathewson, Ramona B.
          OTHER YEARS, OTHER CHRISTMASES. Los Angeles.
          ? Dec.

                         1967

1180   Berio, Luciano
          PASSAGIO. New York. Juilliard. 9 Jan.
          Composer and Eduardo Sanguineti

1181   Ehlen, Christopher
        SOME PLACE OF DARKNESS. London. Johns
        Hopkins. 23 Jan.

1182   Mack, Gordon
        NORA. Shreveport, Louisiana. 23 Jan. Composer

1183   Meyerowitz, Jan
        DIE DOPPELGANGERIN. Hanover. 29 Jan.

1184   Taff, Anthony
        LILITH. Albion, Michigan. Albion College.
        26 Feb.

1185   Adler, Marvin
        BROCK'S PLACE. New York. 6 Feb. Charles Levy

1186   Gardiner, John
        ALICE THROUGH THE LOOKING GLASS. Essex, England.
        ? Feb.

1187   Goehr, Alexander
        ARDEN MUSS STERBEN. Hamburg. 4 Mar. Erich
        Fried; performed in German

1188   Giannini, Vittorio
        THE SERVANT OF TWO MASTERS. New York. 9 Mar.
        Bernard Stambler

1189   Austin, John
        ORPHEUS. Chicago. 10 Mar. Composer

1190   Kalmanoff, Martin
        CANTERVILLE GHOST. New York. 11 Mar.

1191   Levy, Marvin David
        MOURNING BECOMES ELECTRA. New York. 16 Mar.
        Henry Butler

First Performances   1967

1192   Lopatnikoff, Nicolai
         DANTON. Pittsburgh. 25 Mar.

1193   Marek, Robert
         ARABESQUE. Vermillion, South Dakota. University
         of South Dakota. 4 Apr. Wayne Knutson

1194   Barthelson, Joyce
         CHANTICLEER. New York. 15 Apr. Composer

1195   Strouse, Charles
         THE FAMILY. New York. 15 Apr.

1196   Stubbs, Thomas
         LES HAUTS DE HURLEVANT. Rouen. 16 Apr.
         P. Heriat; performed in French

1197   Hovhaness, Alan
         THE TRAVELLERS. Los Altos Hills, California.
         Foothill College. 22 Apr. Composer

1198   Williamson, Malcolm
         THE MOONRAKERS. Brighton. 22 Apr. Composer

1199   McKay, Neil
         RING AROUND HARLEQUIN. Honolulu. Hawaii Uni-
         versity. 24 Apr.

1200   Elliott, William
         DANIEL BOONE. New York. 6 May

1201   Williamson, Malcolm
         DUNSTAN AND THE DEVIL. London. 10 May.
         Geoffrey Dunn

1202   Sacco, Peter
         MR. VINEGAR. Redding, California. Shasta Col-
         lege. 12 May

1967   First Performances

1203   Laderman, Ezra
        GALILEO GALILEI. New York. 14 May. Joe Darien

1204   Piket, Frederick
        TRILBY. New York. 15 May

1205   Major, Douglas
        THE LOYALIST. St. John, New Brunswick. 18 May.
        E. Parkhill and J. Holmes

1206   Rorem, Ned
        THE LAST DAY. New York. New School for Social
        Research. 22 May. Jay S. Harrison

1207   Mayer, William
        BRIEF CANDLE. New York. New School for Social
        Research. 22 May. Milton Feist

1208   Marsh, John
        ENTR'ACTE. New York. New School for Social
        Research. 22 May

1209   Marsh, John
        SOUND STUDIO. New York. New School for Social
        Research. 22 May

1210   Davis, John
        THE PARDONER'S TALE. Tucson, Arizona. University
        of Arizona. 23 May. Ted Hart

1211   Kondorossy, Leslie
        THE POOREST SUITOR. Cleveland. 24 May. Shawn
        Hall

1212   Adaskin, Murray
        GRANT, WARDEN OF THE PLAINS. Winnipeg, Manitoba.
        31 May

1213   Argento, Dominick
         CHRISTOPHER SLY, OR THE TAMING OF THE SHREW.
         Minneapolis. University of Minnesota. 31 May.
         John Manlove

1214   ______.
         SHOEMAKER'S HOLIDAY. Minneapolis. 1 June.
         John Olon Scrymgeour

1215   Berkeley, Lennox
         CASTAWAY. Aldeburgh. 3 June. Paul Dehn

1216   Walton, William
         THE BEAR. Aldeburgh. 3 June. Paul Dehn

1217   Anderson, John Stuart
         TYNDALE. Norfolk, England. 4 June

1218   Stoker, Richard
         JOHNSON PRESERV'D. London. 5 June. Jill Watt

1219   Laderman, Ezra
         MAGIC PRISON. New York. 12 June

1220   Jones, Kelsey
         SAM SLICK. Toronto. 4 July. Mrs. Jones

1221   Straight, William
         TOYON OF ALASKA. Anchorage, Alaska. 7 July.
         Frank Brink

1222   Blakeslee, Samuel Earle
         RED CLOUD. Los Angeles. U. C. L. A. ? July

1223   Britten, Benjamin
         THE GOLDEN VANITY. Aldeburgh. ? July. Colin
         Graham

1967   First Performances

1224   Doblin, Samuel
        CASINO. Stratford, Ontario. ? July. Ronald
        Hambleton

1225   Berney, William
        DARK OF THE MOON. Gatlinburg, Tennessee. Uni-
        versity of Tennessee. ? July. Howard
        Richardson

1226   Noble, Harold
        THE LAKE OF MENTEITH. London. 13 Aug. David
        Harris

1227   Pannell, Raymond
        THE LUCK OF GINGER COFFEY. Toronto. 15 Sept.
        Ronald Hambleton

1228   Somers, Harry
        LOUIS RIEL. Toronto. 23 Sept. M. Moore and
        J. Languirand

1229   Finn, Ben
        LITTLE WOMEN. New York. 11 Oct.

1230   Garwood, Margaret
        THE TROJAN WOMEN. Chester, Pennsylvania.
        22 Oct. Howard Wiley

1231   Elkus, Jonathan
        THE MANDARIAN. New York. 26 Oct. Richard
        Franko Goldman

1232   Bennett, Richard Rodney
        A PENNY FOR A SONG. London. 31 Oct. Colin
        Graham

1233   ....
        JUSTICE PREVAILS. Hartford, Connecticut. East-
        ern Connecticut State College. ? Oct. (Composed
        and performed by 17 children)

1234   Somers, Harry
        WILLIAM LYON MACKENZIE. Toronto. ? Oct.
        William Kilbourn

1235   Bruce, Neeley
        PYRAMUS AND THISBE. University, Alabama. Uni-
        versity of Alabama. 14 Nov.

1236   Pasatieri, Thomas
        PADREVIA. New York. Brooklyn College. 18 Nov.
        Composer

1237   Bentz, Cecil
        WINDOW GAMES. New York. 18 Nov.

1238   Musgrave, Thea
        THE DECISION. London. 30 Nov. Maurice Lindsay

1239   Jones, Trevor
        SCOTTISH LANDING. Halifax, Nova Scotia. ? Nov.

1240   Johnson, Dee Strickland
        MACLEOD O'DUNATORE. Tucson, Arizona. University
        of Arizona. 2 Dec.

1241   Johnson, Henry
        THE MOUNTAIN. Tucson, Arizona. University of
        Arizona. 12 Dec. David Grozier

1242   Booth, Thomas
        GENTLEMEN IN WAITING. New York. 20 Dec.

1243   LaMontaine, John
        THE MAGI. Washington, D.C. 27 Dec.

1244   ______.
        THE SHEPHERDES PLAY. Washington, D.C. ? Dec.

1968

1245   Gundry, Inglis
        THE THREE WISE MEN. London. 11 Jan.

1246   Bush, Geoffrey
        THE EQUATION (X = O). London. 11 Jan.

1247   Behrens, Jack
        THE LAY OF THRYME. Saskatoon. University of
        Saskatchewan. 24 Jan. Keith Cockburn

1248   Baska, Robert
        ARIA DA CAPO. New York. 6 Feb. Composer

1249   Siegmeister, Elie
        DICK WHITTINGTON AND HIS CAT. Philadelphia.
        10 Feb.

1250   Morgenstern, Sam
        THE BLACK BOX. New York. 13 Feb. Francis
        Steegmuller

1251   Avril, Lloyd
        HEADS OR TAILS. Glassboro, New Jersey. Glass-
        boro State College. 23 Feb.

1252   Gates, Keith
        MIGLE AND THE BOYS. Winston-Salem, North Caro-
        lina. North Carolina School of the Arts. ? Feb.

1253   Searle, Humphrey
        HAMLET. Hamburg. 5 Mar. Composer; performed
        in a translation by Hans Keller

1254   Cardew, Cornelius
        SCHOOLTIME COMPOSITIONS. London. 11 Mar.

First Performances   1968

1255   Vallerand, Jean
        LE MAGICIEN. Montreal. McGill University.
        15 Mar.

1256   Humphrey, Henry
        JOAN OF ARC AT RHEIMS. Cincinnati. 17 Mar.

1257   Kay, Ulysses
        THE BOOR. Louisville, Kentucky. University of
        Kentucky. 3 Apr. Composer

1258   Orr, Robin
        FULL CIRCLE. Perth, Scotland. 10 Apr. Sidney
        Goodsir Smith

1259   Williamson, Malcolm
        KNIGHTS IN SHINING ARMOUR. Brighton. 19 Apr.
        Composer

1260   Kosteck, Gregory
        MAURYA. Greenville, South Carolina. East
        Carolina State College. 24 Apr. Composer

1261   Provenzano, V.
        THE CASK OF AMONTILLADO. Rochester, New York.
        Eastman School of Music. 26 Apr.

1262   Castiglione, Niccolo
        SILENCE. San Diego, California. University of
        California-San Diego. 28 Apr.

1263   Combs, Ronald
        THE THREE WISHES. Evanston, Illinois. North-
        western University. 30 Apr.

1264   Williamson, Malcolm
        THE SNOW WOLF. Brighton. 30 Apr.

1968   First Performances

1265   Goodman, Alfred Grant
        THE ACTOR. Pforzheim, Germany. ? Apr.

1266   White, Michael
        METAMORPHOSIS. Philadelphia. 3 May. Milton
        Goldberg

1267   Arnatt, Ronald
        THE BOY WITH A CART. St. Louis. 8 May

1268   Buhrman, Bur
        THE BALD KNOBBERS. Point Lookout, Missouri.
        School of the Ozarks. 12 May. Karl Bratton

1269   Henze, Hans Werner
        MORALITIES. Cincinnati. 18 May. W. H. Auden

1270   Kay, Norman
        THE ROSE AFFAIR. London. 19 May. Composer

1271   Mayer, Lutz
        THE PARANOID PARAKEET. Cortland, New York.
        State University of New York at Cortland. 24 May.
        Edward Devany

1272   Searle, Humphrey
        THE OWL AND THE PUSSYCAT. New York. 26 May

1273   Brumby, Colin J.
        THE WISE SHOEMAKER. Brisbane. ? May. Composer

1274   Brumby, Colin J.
        RITA AND DITA. Brisbane. ? May. Composer

1275   Birtwistle, Harrison
        PUNCH AND JUDY. Aldeburgh. 3 June. Stephen
        Pruslin

First Performances1968

1276   Maconchy, Elizabeth
THE THREE STRANGERS. Herts, England. Bishop
Stortford College for Boys. 5 June. Composer

1277   ______.
THE BIRDS. Herts, England. Bishop Stortford
College for Boys. 5 June. Composer

1278   Britten, Benjamin
THE PRODIGAL SON. Aldeburgh. 10 June. William
Plomer

1279   Goehr, Alexander
NABOTH'S VINEYARD. London. 16 July. Composer

1280   Amram, David
TWELFTH NIGHT. Glen Falls, New York. 20 July.
Joseph Papp

1281   Effinger, Cecil
CYRANO DE BERGERAC. Boulder, Colorado. University of Colorado. 21 July. Donald Sutherland

1282   Horacek, Leo
THE TELL-TALE HEART. Morgantown, West Virginia.
West Virginia University. 7 Aug. Joseph Golz

1283   Silverman, Stanley
ELEPHANT STEPS. Lenox, Massachusetts. 7 Aug.
Richard Foreman

1284   Williamson, Malcolm
THE GROWING CASTLE. Llandeilo, Wales. 13 Aug.
Composer

1285   Kalmanoff, Martin
THE AUDITION. Pittsburgh. Chatham College.
21 Aug.

1968   First Performances

1286   Castiglione, Niccolo
        THREE MYSTERIES. Rome. 2 Oct.

1287   Weisgall, Hugo
        NINE RIVERS FROM JORDAN. New York. 9 Oct.
        Dennis Johnston

1288   Eaton, John
        HERACLES. Turin, Italy. 10 Oct. Michael Fried

1289   Zador, Eugene
        THE SCARLET MILL. Brooklyn, New York. Brooklyn
        College. 26 Oct. George Jellinek

1290   Travis, Roy
        THE PASSION OF OEDIPUS. Los Angeles. U. C. L. A.
        8 Nov. Composer

1291   Bethea, Kay
        THE LITTLE PRINCESS. Lawrence, Kansas. Univer-
        sity of Kansas. 12 Nov.

1292   Kalmanoff, Martin
        THE VICTORY AT MASADA. Detroit. 14 Nov.
        Composer

1293   ______.
        THE GREAT STONE FACE. Muncie, Indiana. Ball
        State University. 14 Nov.

1294   Najern, Edmund
        THE FREEWAY OPERA. Los Angeles. Immaculate
        Heart College. 12 Nov.

1295   Horvit, Michael
        TOMO. Houston. University of Houston. 21 Nov.

1296   Camillieri, Charles
        MELITA, OR, A CUP FULL OF TEARS. Belfast.
        28 Nov. Ursula Vaughan Williams

1297   Bottje, Will Gay
        REVILED PATRIOT. Carbondale, Illinois. South-
        ern Illinois University. ? Nov.

1298   Nixon, Roger A.
        THE BRIDE COMES TO YELLOW SKY. Charleston,
        Illinois. Eastern Illinois University. ? Nov.
        Ray B. West, Jr.

1299   Victory, Gerald
        MUSIC HATH MISCHIEF. Dublin. 2 Dec.

1300   Menotti, Gian-Carlo
        HELP! HELP! THE GLOBOLINKS! Hamburg. 19 Dec.
        Composer

1969

1301   Dorward, David
        TONIGHT MRS. MORRISON. London. 15 Jan. George
        Bruce

1302   Gillis, Don
        THE LEGEND OF THE STAR VALLEY JUNCTION. New
        York. 7 Jan. Partial performance

1303   Liota, A.
        ROMEO AND JULIET. New York. 7 Jan.

1304   Pouhé, Joseph Frank
        PANTOMIME. New York. 7 Jan.

1305   Partch, Harry
        DELUSION OF THE FURY. Los Angeles. U. C. L. A.
        9 Jan.

1306   Miller, Martin
        THE FLYING MACHINE. Redlands, California. Uni-
        versity of Redlands. 23 Jan.

1969

1307   "Vernon, Ashley" [Kurt Manschinger]
        THE TRIUMPH OF PUNCH. Brooklyn, New York. Brook-
        lyn Academy of Music. 25 Jan. Greta Hartwig

1308   Stokes, Eric
        HORSPFAL. Minneapolis. 15 Feb. Alvin
        Greenberg

1309   Bohlen, Donald
        ISMENE. Warrensburg, Missouri. Central Missouri
        State College. 17 Feb. Robert Jones

1310   Brumby, Colin J.
        THE PRINCE WHO COULDN'T LAUGH. Brisbane. ? Feb.
        Composer

1311   Haslam, Herbert
        CARNIVAL OF EDEN. New Delhi. University of New
        Delhi. ? Feb.

1312   Laird, Bruce
        THE PARTISANS. Wilmington, Delaware. ? Feb.

1313   Turner, Thomas
        $4000. Iowa City, Iowa. University of Iowa.
        6 Mar. Vance Bourjaily

1314   Bottje, Will Gay
        ALTGELD. Carbondale, Illinois. Southern Illi-
        nois University. 7 Mar.

1315   Aria, Pietro
        JERICHO ROAD. Philadelphia. 12 Mar.

1316   Wilson, Thomas
        THE CHARCOAL BURNER. Edinburgh. 16 Mar. Edwin
        Morgan

First Performances   1969

1317   Salzman, Eric
          THE NUDE PAPER SERMON. New York. Hunter College.
          21 Mar.

1318   Chadabe, Joel
          STREET SCENE. New York. 25 Mar.

1319   Bennett, Richard Rodney
          ALL THE KING'S MEN. Coventry. Coventry Tech-
          nical College. 28 Mar. Beverley Cross

1320   Colby, ?
          RUMPELSTILTSKIN. Detroit. ? Mar.

1321   Eastwood, Thomas
          THE REBEL. London. 4 Apr. Ronald Duncan

1322   Ramsier, Paul
          THE MAN ON THE BEARSKIN RUG. Aberdeen, South
          Dakota. Northern State Teachers College.
          13 Apr. James Elward

1323   Moran, Robert Leonard
          LET'S BUILD A NUT HOUSE. San Jose, California.
          San Jose State College. 19 Apr.

1324   Davies, Peter Maxwell
          EIGHT SONGS FOR A MAD KING. London. 22 Apr.
          Randolph Stow

1325   Kondorossy, Leslie
          SHIZUKA'S DANCE. Cleveland. 22 Apr. Shawn
          Hall

1326   Barnard, Francis
          THE MASQUE OF MASKA. New York. 26 Apr.

1327   Arnell, Richard
          COMBAT ZONE. Hempstead, New York. Hofstra Col-
          lege. 27 Apr. Composer

1969

1328   McCabe, John
       THE LION, THE WITCH, AND THE WARDROBE. Man-
       chester, England. 29 Apr.

1329   Miller, Edward
       THE YOUNG GOD. Hartford, Connecticut. Hartt
       College. 30 Apr.

1330   Morgenstern, Sam
       THE HAIRCUT. New York. 2 May. Jan Henry

1331   Birtwistle, Harrison
       DOWN BY THE GREENWOOD SIDE. Brighton. 8 May.
       Michael Nyman

1332   Mead, George
       THE BROKER'S OPERA. New York. 8 May

1333   Leginska, Ethel
       JOAN OF ARC. Los Angeles. 10 May

1334   Goldberg, Theo
       GALATEA ELETTRONICA. Bellingham, Washington.
       Western Washington State University. 14 May.
       Composer

1335   Neumann, Alfred
       THE RITES OF MAN. Silver Springs, Maryland.
       18 May

1336   Phillips, Peter
       MANTRA. Seattle. 18 May

1337   Britten, Benjamin
       CHILDREN'S CRUSADE. London. 19 May

1338   Wilder, Alec
       THE OPENING. Boston. 19 May. Arnold Sundgaard

1339   Turner, Charles and ten students from the
               Wykeham Rise School
          THE BALLAD OF BARNABY. Washington, Connecticut.
          Wykeham Rise School. 23 May. W. H. Auden

1340   Whelen, Christopher
          INCIDENT AT OWL CREEK. London. 26 May.
          Composer

1341   Wigglesworth, Frank
          THE WILLOWDALE HANDCAR OR THE RETURN OF THE
          BLACK DOLL. New York. New School for Social
          Research. 28 May. Edward Gorey

1342   Joubert, John
          UNDER WESTERN EYES. Camden, England. 29 May.
          Cedric Cliffe

1343   Hahn, Thomas
          THE WALL. Prince Edward Island, Canada. Prince
          Edward Island University. ? May

1344   Mennin, Peter
          PIED PIPER. Cincinnati. ? May

1345   Crosse, Gordon
          THE GRACE OF TODD. Aldeburgh. 7 June. David
          Rudkin

1346   Silverman, Stanley
          THE SATYRICON. Stratford, Ontario. 4 July.
          Peter Raby

1347   Bennett, Richard Rodney
          VICTORY. Aldeburgh. ? July. Beverley Cross

1348   Penberthy, J.
          DALGERIE. Perth, Scotland. ? Aug.

1349 Kalmanoff, Martin
AESOP, THE FABULOUS FABELIST. Camp Pemigewasset,
New Hampshire. ? Aug.

1350 Purser, John
THE UNDERTAKER. Edinburgh. 1 Sept. Composer

1351 Detweiler, Alan
DAVID AND GOLIATH. London. 25 Sept.

1352 Kalmanoff, Martin
KING DAVID AND DAVID KING. New York. 12 Oct.

1353 Hopkins, Anthony
RICH MAN, POOR MAN, BEGGAR MAN, SAINT. Stroud,
England. 18 Oct. G. David Nixon

1354 Dreyfus, George
THE TAKEOVER. Camberra. ? Oct. F. Kellaway

1355 Long, Newell and Eleanor Newell
THE MUSIC HATER. Aberdeen, South Dakota. North-
ern State College. ? Oct.

1356 Wilson, James
TWELFTH NIGHT. Wexford, England. 1 Nov.

1357 Drummond, John
THE HAWKEYE'S SENTINEL. Birmingham, Alabama.
4 Nov. Composer

1358 Cox, David Harold
DISAPPEARING ACT. Birmingham, England. University of Birmingham. 4 Nov.

1359 Swann, Donald
PERELANDRA. Bryn Mawr, Pennsylvania. Bryn Mawr
and Haverford College. 21 Nov. David Marsh

1360   Morris, Richard
          AGAMMENON. Oxford. Oxford University. 25 Nov.
          Anthony Holden

1361   Marshall, Yale
          OEDIPUS AND THE SPHINX. Minneapolis. 29 Nov.
          Wesley Balk

1362   Burt, Francis
          BARNSTABLE (OR SOMEONE IN THE ATTIC). Stuttgart.
          30 Nov. James Saunders

1363   Carrier, Loran
          GAME OPERA. Washington, D.C. 12 Dec.

1364   Williamson, Malcolm
          LUCKY PETER'S JOURNEY. London. 18 Dec. Edmund
          Tracy

1365   Leginska, Ethel
          GALE THE HUNTING. Los Angeles. 19 Dec.

1366   Barthelson, Joyce
          GREENWICH VILLAGE 1910. Scarsdale, New York.
          Scarsdale Junior High School. 20 Dec.

1367   Burtch, Mervyn
          THE SELFISH GIANT. Wales. 25 Dec.

1368   LaMontaine, John
          ERODE THE GREAT. Washington, D.C. 31 Dec.

1369   Poynter, Arthur
          THE BIRTH OF OUR LORD. Toronto. ? Dec.

1970

1370   Tulane University Students
       SHORT NIGHT'S JOURNEY INTO DAY. Tulsa, Oklahoma.
       Tulsa University. 2 Jan.

1371   Floyd, Carlisle
       OF MICE AND MEN. Seattle. 22 Jan. Composer

1373   Berger, Jean
       THE PIED PIPER. Dayton, Ohio. ? Jan.

1374   Austin, Larry
       AGAPE. Buffalo, New York. 25 Feb.

1375   Boesing, Paul and Martha Boesing
       THE WANDERER: A BALLAD OF NOW. Minneapolis.
       28 Feb.

1376   Miller, Lewis
       IMAGINARY INVALID. Hays, Kansas. Fort Hays
       Kansas State College. ? Feb. Patrick Goeser

1377   Beeson, Jack
       MY HEART'S IN THE HIGHLANDS. New York. 18 Mar.

1378   Lavry, Marc
       TAMAR AND JUDAH. New York. 22 Mar. **Rabbi**
       Newman

1379   Crawford, John
       THE TRAGICOMEDY OF DON CHRISTOBEL AND ROSITA.
       Wellesley, Massachusetts. Wellesley College.
       22 Mar. Composer

1380   Crabtree, Ray
       THE FOOL. New York. 29 Mar.

First Performances   1970

1381   Phillips, Harry
        THE PRINCESS AND THE FROG PRINCE. University,
        Alabama. University of Alabama. ? Mar.

1382   Wade, James
        THE MARTYRED. Seoul. 8 Apr. Composer

1383   Flagello, Nicholas
        THE PIED PIPER OF HAMLIN. New York. Manhattan
        School of Music. 18 Apr.

1384   Kosteck, Gregory
        THE STRONGER. Greenville, South Carolina. East
        Carolina State College. 30 Apr.

1385   Cabena, Barrie
        THE SELFISH GIANT. London, Ontario. ? Apr.
        Composer

1386   Gilbert, Anthony
        JUGENDOPER. Cassel, Germany. 1 May

1387   Lee, Bill
        THE DEPOT. New York. 8 May

1388   Schuller, Gunther
        THE FISHERMAN AND HIS WIFE. Boston. 8 May.
        John Updike

1389   McKay, Neil
        PLANTING A PEAR TREE. Honolulu. University of
        Honolulu. 17 May

1390   Josephs, Wilfred
        MORTALES. Cincinnati. 23 May

1391   Kohs, Ellis B.
        AMERIKA. ?, California. 27 May

1970   First Performances

1392   Mason, Derrick
        MAMMON. London. Morley College. 5 June.
        C. Dandy

1393   Rowland, David
        TRIQUETRA. London. 25 June

1394   Goehr, Alexander
        SHADOWPLAY 2. London. 8 July. Kenneth Cavander

1395   Maw, Nicholas
        THE RISING OF THE MOON. Glyndebourne. 19 July.
        Beverley Cross

1396   Mellers, Wilfrid
        THE ANCIENT WOUND. Victoria, British Columbia.
        University of Victoria. 27 July. Peter Garvie

1397   Berio, Luciano
        OPERA. Sante Fe, New Mexico. 12 Aug. Composer

1398   Hammond, Tom
        NO TIME FOR FUNERALS. Meiford, England. Meiford
        Institute. 18 Aug. Composer

1399   Bush, Alan Dudley
        JOE HILL. East Berlin. 29 Sept.

1400   Macochy, Elizabeth
        THE JESSE TREE. Dorchester Abbey. 7 Oct. Anne
        Ridler

1401   Seymour, John L.
        RAMONA. Provo, Utah. Brigham Young University.
        11 Nov. Composer

1402   Elkus, Jonathan
        MEDEA. Milwaukee. University of Wisconsin-
        Milwaukee. 13 Nov. Composer

First Performances   1970

1403   Elkus, Jonathan
          HELEN IN EGYPT. Milwaukee. University of
          Wisconsin-Milwaukee. 13 Nov. Jere Knight

1404   Tippett, Michael
          THE KNOT GARDEN. London. 2 Dec. Composer

1405   Cohen, Joseph
          A CHRISTMAS CAROL. West de Père, Wisconsin.
          St. Norbert College. 5 Dec. Composer

1406   Ashley, Robert
          THAT MORNING THING   Oakland, California. Mills
          College. 8 Dec.

1407   Marshall, Yale
          CHRISTMAS MUMMERIES. Minneapolis. 12 Dec.
          Wesley Balk

1408   LoPresti, Ronald
          PLAYBACK. Tucson, Arizona. University of
          Arizona. 18 Dec. Joy Harvey

1409   Siegel, Norman
          WHO STOLE THE CROWN JEWELS? New York. ? Dec.
          Jean Reavey

                           1971

1410   Kelly Robert
          TOD'S GAL. Norfolk, Virginia. Old Dominion
          University. 8 Jan. Composer

1411   Brooks, Richard
          RAPUNZEL. Binghampton, New York. 22 Jan.
          Harold Mason

1412   DeBanfield, Rafaello
          TANGO POUR UNE FEMME SEULE. Marseille. 23 Jan.
          Performed in French

1971   First Performances

1413   Stewart, Robert
          MORALS A LA MODE. Surrey, England. 27 Jan.
          David Gardiner

1414   Gessner, John
          FAUST COUNTER FAUST. Minneapolis. 30 Jan.
          Wesley Balk

1415   Barab, Seymour
          WHO AM I? Tempe, Arizona. Arizona State Univer-
          sity. 5 Feb.

1416   Leichtling, Alan
          A WHITE BUTTERFLY. New York. Juilliard.
          18 Feb. Gabrielle Roepke

1417   Seager, Gerald
          THE MARRIAGE OF THE GROCER OF SEVILLE. Columbus,
          Ohio. Ohio State University. ? Feb.

1418   Ziskin, Victor and Joan Javits
          YOUNG ABE LINCOLN. New York. ? Feb. Richard
          Bernstein and John Allen

1419   Menotti, Gian-Carlo
          THE MOST IMPORTANT MAN IN THE WORLD. New York.
          7 Mar. Composer

1420   Kay, Ulysses
          THE CAPITOLINE VENUS. Quincy, Illinois. Uni-
          versity of Illinois. 12 Mar. Judith Dvorkin

1421   Valenti, R.
          THE PLEDGE. New York. 25 Mar.

1422   Faberman, Harold
          THE LOSERS. New York. Juilliard. 26 Mar.
          Barbara Fried

First Performances   1971

1423   Ridout, Alan
          THE PARDONER'S TALE. Canterbury. 1 Apr.
          Norman Platt

1424   Gilbert, Anthony
          THE SCENE MACHINE. Cassel, Germany. 4 Apr.
          George Macbeth

1425   Berio, Luciano
          PRAYER. New York. 5 Apr.

1426   Pasatieri, Thomas
          CALVARY. Seattle. 7 Apr. (The full text of
          William Butler Yeat's play)

1427   Moross, Jerome
          THE ECCENTRICITIES OF DAVY CROCKETT. Wilkes-
          Barre, Pennsylvania. Wilkes College. 16 Apr.
          John Latouche

1428   Beversdorf, Thomas
          VISION OF CHRIST. Lewisburg, Pennsylvania.
          Bucknell University. 1 May

1429   McDowell, John H.
          A DOG'S LIFE. New York. 9 May

1430   Wilson, Charles
          PHRASES FROM ORPHEUS. Guelph Spring, Ontario.
          10 May

1431   Overton, Hall
          HUCKLEBERRY FINN. New York. Juilliard. 20 May.
          Judith Stampfer

1432   Rorem, Ned
          FABLES. Martin, Tennessee. University of Ten-
          nessee. 21 May

1971   First Performances

1433   Six, Herbert
        ALL CATS TURN GREY WHEN THE SUN GOES DOWN. New
        York. Henry Street Settlement Music School.
        21 May. Dan Jaffe

1434   Kupferman, Meyer
        VISIONS AND GAMES. New York. Sarah Lawrence.
        24 May. Composer

1435   Britten, Benjamin
        OWEN WINGRAVE. London. ? May

1436   El-Dabh, Halim
        OPERA FLIES. Washington, D.C. Hawthorne School.
        ? May. Composer

1437   Yannatos, James
        THE ROCKET'S RED BLARE. Cambridge, Massachusetts.
        Harvard University. ? May

1438   Wishart, Peter
        THE CLANDESTINE MARRIAGE. Cambridge, England.
        1 June. Don Roberts

1439   Zador, Eugene
        REVISOR (THE INSPECTOR GENERAL). Torrance,
        California. El Camino College. 11 June

1440   Hoiby, Lee
        SUMMER AND SMOKE. St. Paul, Minnesota. 19 June.
        Lanford Wilson

1441   Kalmanoff, Martin
        PHOTOGRAPH--1920. Lake Placid, New York.
        27 July

1442   Schwartz, Marvin
        LOOK AND LONG. Lake Placid, New York. 27 July.
        Gertrude Stein

First Performances   1971

1443   Cole, Hugo
        THE FAIR TRADERS. Shawford, England. 29 July

1444   Rorem, Ned
        THREE SISTERS WHO WERE NOT SISTERS. Lake Placid,
        New York. ? July

1445   Williams, Jack Eric
        ALEXANDER THE GREAT. Columbia, South Carolina.
        University of South Carolina. 8 Aug.

1446   ______.
        WE GAVE HIM PIANO LESSONS. Myrtle Beach, South
        Carolina. University of South Carolina. 8 Aug.
        Elizabeth Williams

1447   Silverman, Stanley
        DREAM TANTRAS FOR WESTERN MASSACUSETTS. Lenox,
        Massachusetts. 12 Aug. Richard Foreman

1448   Harrison, Lou
        YOUNG CAESAR. Aptos, California. 21 Aug.

1449   Bernstein, Leonard
        MASS. Washington, D.C. 8 Sept. Composer and
        Stephen Schwartz

1450   Murdoch, Elaine
        TAMBURLAINE. Liverpool. University of Liver-
        pool. 9 Sept. John Murdoch

1451   Roberts, Edwin
        THE HUNTING OF THE SNARK. New York. 9 Sept.
        Bill Tchakirides

1452   Kondorossy, Leslie
        KALAMONA AND THE FOUR WINDS. Cleveland.
        12 Sept. Shawn Hall

1971   First Performances

1453   Williamson, Malcolm
        THE STONE WALL. London. 18 Sept.

1454   Espinoza, Felipe
        MACIAS. New York. ? Sept.

1455   Argento, Dominick
        POSTCARD FROM MOROCCO. Minneapolis. 14 Oct.
        John Donahue

1456   Bird, Herbert
        THE POWERFUL POTION OF DR. DEE. Palm Desert,
        California. College of the Desert. 24 Oct.

1457   Moran, Robert
        DIVERTISSEMENT, NO. 3, A LUNCH BAG OPERA.
        London. 31 Oct.

1458   Hurd, Michael
        WIDOW OF EPHESUS. Stroud, England. ? Oct.

1459   Webber, Andrew Lloyd
        JOSEPH AND HIS TECHNICOLOR DREAMCOAT. Detroit.
        5 Nov. Tim Rice

1460   Carmines, Al
        JOAN. New York. 21 Nov. Composer

1461   Ashley, Robert
        IN MEMORIAM...KIT CARSON. Oakland, California.
        Mills College. 10 Dec.

1462   Argento, Dominick
        COLONEL JONATHAN THE SAINT. Denver. 31 Dec.
        Composer

1463   Faith, Richard
        SLEEPING BEAUTY. Tucson, Arizona. University
        of Arizona. ? Dec.

First Performances   1972

1464   Campbell, Norman
         ANNE OF GREEN GABLES. New York. ? Dec. Donald
         Harron

                              1972

1465   Horovitz, Joseph
         THE DUMB WIFE. Antwerp. 10 Jan.

1466   Cole, Bruce
         HARLEQUINADE. London. 16 Jan.

1467   Joplin, Scott
         TREEMONISHA. Atlanta. 27 Jan.

1468   Cole, Bruce
         PANTOMIMES. London. 12 Feb.

1469   Wood, Russell
         THE EMPEROR'S NEW CLOTHES. Chicago. 12 Feb.

1470   Pasatieri, Thomas
         THE TRIAL OF MARY TODD LINCOLN. Boston. 14 Feb.
         Anne Howard Bailey

1471   Hiller, Lejaren
         A RAGE OVER THE LOST BEETHOVEN. Buffalo, New
         York. State University of New York at Buffalo.
         19 Feb. Frank Parman

1472   Lutyens, Elizabeth
         TIME OFF. London. 1 Mar. Composer

1473   Pasatieri, Thomas
         BLACK WIDOW. Seattle. 2 Mar. Composer

1474   Eakin, Charles
         BEING OF SOUND MIND. Boulder, Colorado. Uni-
         versity of Colorado. 3 Mar.

                                          First Performances

1475   Duncan, John
         GIDEON AND ELIZA. New Orleans. Xavier Univer-
         sity. 22 Mar.

1476   Babcock, Jeffrey
         MIRRORS. Santa Barbara, California. 6 Apr.
         Carl Zytowsky

1477   Thomson, Virgil
         BYRON. New York. Juilliard. 13 Apr. Jack
         Larson

1478   Fussell, Charles
         JULIAN. Winston-Salem, North Carolina. Salem
         College. 15 Apr.

1479   Reif, Paul
         THE ARTIST. New York. 17 Apr. Kenneth Koch

1480   Crumb, George
         ANCIENT VOICES OF CHILDREN. Millbrook, New York.
         Bennett College. 20 Apr.

1481   Jarrett, Jack
         CYRANO DE BERGERAC. Greensboro, North Carolina.
         University of North Carolina at Greensboro.
         27 Apr.

1482   Crawford, Dawn
         THE PEARL. Houston. Dominican College. ? Apr.
         Composer

1483   Kalmanoff, Martin
         MOD TRAVIATA. Philadelphia. 4 May

1484   Kirk, Theron
         THE LIB: 393 B.C. San Antonio, Texas. San
         Antonio College. 5 May. Composer

First Performances

1972

1485   Slater, Neil
    AGAIN D.J. Bridgeport, Connecticut. University
    of Connecticut. 5 May. Nick Rossi

1486   Berger, Jean
    YIPHTAH AND HIS DAUGHTER. Upper Montclair, New
    Jersey. Montclair State College. 11 May. Per-
    formed in Hebrew, Latin, Spanish and English

1487   Barthelson, Joyce
    FEATHERTOP. New York. 12 May

1488   Martel, Tom
    HARD JOB BEING GOD. New York. 14 May. Composer

1489   Floyd, Carlisle
    FLOWER AND HAWK. Jacksonville, Florida. 16 May.
    Composer

1490   Johnson, Tom
    THE FOUR NOTE OPERA. New York. 16 May.
    Composer

1491   Mandelbaum, B.
    THE DYBBUK. New York. C. U. N. Y. 24 May

1492   Gorelli, Olga
    BETWEEN THE SHADOW AND THE DREAM. Princeton.
    28 May

1493   Davies, Peter Maxwell
    BLIND MAN'S BLUFF. London. 29 May

1494   Ogden, Mark
    SNEEZES. Ogden, Utah. Weber State University.
    ? May

1495   Moss, William
    CONCERT FOR ELEVEN. London. Morley College.
    ? May

1972   First Performances

1496   Gardner, John
        THE VISITORS. Aldeburgh. 7 June. John Green

1497   LeFanu, Nicola
        ANTI-WORLD. London. 29 June

1498   Davies, Peter Maxwell
        TAVERNER. London. 12 July. Composer

1499   Whelen, Christopher
        THE FINDINGS. London. 16 July. Composer

1500   Roberts, Edwin
        THE SONG OF HIAWATHA. New York. ? July. Bill
        Tchakirides

1501   Selig, Robert
        CHOCORUA. Lenox, Massachusetts. 6 Aug. Richard
        Moore

1502   Silverman, Stanley
        DOCTOR SELAVEY'S MAGIC THEATER. Lenox, Massa-
        chusetts. 12 Aug. Richard Foreman

1503   Schaefer, Murray
        PATRIA II: REQUIEM FOR A PARTY GIRL. Stratford,
        Ontario. 23 Aug.

1504   Laing, Alan
        PINOCCHIO. Stratford, Ontario. ? Aug. Collodi

1505   Hammond, Terence
        THE FRIEND. New York. 16 Sept.

1506   Higgs, Timothy
        THOMAS BULLEN. East Grimsted, England. 21 Oct.

1507   Alexander, William
        THE MONKEY'S PAW. Edinboro, Pennsylvania. Edin-
        boro State College. 13 Nov.

First Performances   1972

1508   Oliver, Stephen
         THE DUCHESS OF MALFI. Oxford, England. Oxford
         University. 23 Nov.

1509   Henderson, Alva
         MEDEA. San Diego, California. 29 Nov.

1510   Maesch, LaVahn
         THE GRANDMOTHER AND THE WITCH. Appleton, Wis-
         consin. ? Nov. Karl Bratton

1511   Silverman, Stanley
         OEDIPUS THE KING. Minneapolis. ? Nov.
         Anthony Burgess

1512   Bush, Geoffrey
         LORD ARTHUR SAVILE'S CRIME. London. Guildhall
         School of Music. 5 Dec.

1513   Burnham, Cardon V.
         CEREMONY OF STRANGERS. Minot, North Dakota.
         Minot State College. 14 Dec.

1514   Barnett, David and Josephine Barnett
         INNER VOICES. New York. 17 Dec.

1515   Frankenpohl, S.
         DOMESTIC RELATIONS. Potsdam, New York. State
         University of New York at Potsdam. 17 Dec.

1516   Zito, Vincent
         SGANARELLE. New York. N. Y. U. 17 Dec.

1517   Cage, John
         THEATRE PIECE. Kiel, Germany. ? Dec.

1973
First Performances

1973

1518 DiChiera, David
   RUMPELSTILTSKIN. Detroit. ? Jan. Karen
   DiChera

1519 Murray, Jeremiah
   MARRIAGE PROPOSAL. New York. 1 Feb.

1520 Franchetti, Arnold
   THE SUNCATCHER. Hartford, Connecticut. University of Hartford. 8 Feb. Barbara Sargeant

1521 Barthelson, Joyce
   THE KING'S BREAKFAST. New York. 26 Feb.

1522 Beadell, Robert
   NAPOLEON. Lincoln, Nebraska. University of Nebraska. ? Feb. Dean Tschetter and William Wallis

1523 Nabokov, Nicolai
   LOVE'S LABOR LOST. Brussels. ? Feb. W. H. Auden and Chester Kallman

1524 Clark, Garry E.
   WESTCHESTER LIMITED. Chesterton, Maryland. Washington College. 23 Mar. Norman James

1525 Harlow, Larry
   HOMMY. New York. 30 Mar.

1526 Hackett, Charles F.
   DONA ROSITA. Ithaca, New York. Ithaca College. 6 Apr. Composer and William Oliver

1527 Wilson Charles
   THE SUMMONING OF EVERYMAN. Halifax, Nova Scotia. Dalhousie University. 6 Apr. Eugene Benson

First Performances   1973

1528   Starer, Robert
         PANTAGLEIZE. New York. Brooklyn College.
         7 Apr.

1529   Davis, Mary
         COLUMBINE. Boulder, Colorado. 12 Apr. Joanna
         Sampson

1530   Grant, Bruce
         THE WOMEN OF TROY. Bloomington, Indiana.
         Indiana University. 12 Apr.

1531   Garza, W.
         THE BLUE ANGEL. Tucson, Arizona. University of
         Arizona. 13 Apr.

1532   Persichetti, Vincent
         THE CREATION. Fredonia, New York. State Uni-
         versity of New York at Fredonia. 13 Apr.

1533   Luytens, Elizabeth
         INFIDELIO. London. 17 Apr.

1534   Eaton, John
         MYSHKIN. Bloomington, Indiana. 23 Apr.
         Composer

1535   Isaacs, Gregory
         THE DEATH OF TINTAGILES. Indianola, Iowa.
         Simpson College. 4 May

1536   Susa, Conrad
         TRANSFORMATIONS. Minneapolis. 5 May. Anne
         Sexton

1537   Bush, Gordon
         THE HERMIT. Brooklyn, New York. 12 May.
         Robert Lallamant

1973   First Performances

1538   Vincent John
        PRIMEVAL VOID. Vienna. 14 May

1539   Rae, John
        THE PRISONER'S PLAY. Toronto. University of
        Toronto. 22 May. Paul Woodruff

1540   Conte, Michael
        BALLADE. Ottawa. 22 May. Arthur Samuels

1541   Crosse, Gordon
        WHEEL OF THE WORLD. Aldeburgh. 5 June. (The
        original short version of Wheel of the World was
        performed in Oct., 1970)

1542   Larsen, Elizabeth
        SOME PIG. Minneapolis. University of Minnesota.
        6 June

1543   Britten, Benjamin
        DEATH IN VENICE. Aldeburgh. 16 June. Myfanwy
        Piper

1544   Rivers, Sam
        SOLOMON AND SHEBA. New York. ? June

1545   Braswell, John
        INTERIOR CASTLE. Lenox, Massachusetts. 19 July.
        Barbara Benary

1546   McDowell, John H.
        AFTER THE BALL. New York. 19 July

1547   Conyngham, Barry
        EDWARD JOHN EYRE. Sydney. University of New
        South Wales. ? July

1548   Pannell, Raymond
        EXILES. Stratford, Ontario. 15 Aug. Beverly
        Pannell

First Performances   1973

1549   Menotti, Gian-Carlo
          TAMU-TAMU. Chicago. 5 Sept. Composer

1550   Wilson, Charles
          HELOISE AND ABELARD. Toronto. 8 Sept.

1551   Owen, Richard
          MARY DYER. Boston. 21 Sept.

1552   Wilder, Alec
          THE TRUTH ABOUT WINDMILLS. Avon, New York.
          12 Oct. Arnold Sundgaard

1553   Garwood, Margaret
          THE NIGHTINGALE AND THE ROSE. Chester, Pennsyl-
          vania. 21 Oct.

1554   Smith, Julia
          DAISY. Miami, Florida. 3 Nov. Bertita Harding

1555   Rorem, Ned
          BERTHA. New York. 26 Nov. (The complete text
          of Kenneth Koch's play)

1556   Hodkinson, S. P.
          VOX POPULOUS, VOX CRAPULOUS. St. Paul, Minnesota.
          1 Dec. Lee Devin

1557   Trogen, Stanley
          THE WANDERING SCHOLAR. Portland, Oregon. 4 Dec.
          Hans Sachs

1558   Corcoran, William
          GAMES OF CARDS. Cincinnati. 6 Dec.

1559   Wilson, Charles
          THE SELFISH GIANT. Toronto. 20 Dec.

1974   First Performances

1560   Lloyd, Alan
        THE LIFE AND TIMES OF JOSEPH STALIN. Brooklyn,
        New York. Brooklyn Academy of Music. ? Dec.
        Robert Wilson

                            1974

1561   Wishart, Peter
        CLYTEMNESTRA. London. London University.
        13 Feb. Don Roberts

1562   Salzman, Eric
        LAZARUS. New York. 16 Feb.

1563   Combs, Ronald
        THE MONKEY'S PAW. Stevens Point, Wisconsin.
        University of Wisconsin. ? Feb. Composer

1564   Pasatieri, Thomas
        THE SEAGULL. Houston. 5 Mar. Kenward Elmslie

1565   Bach, Jan
        THE SYSTEM. New York. Mannes College. 5 Mar.

1566   Stewart, Frank
        TO LET THE CAPTIVE GO. New York. Mannes Col-
        lege. 5 Mar. John R. Hubsky

1567   Argento, Dominick
        JONAH AND THE WHALE. Minneapolis. 9 Mar.

1568   Crosse, Gordon
        STORY OF VASCO. London. 13 Mar. Composer and
        Ted Hughes

1569   Sitsky, Larry
        LENZ. Sydney. 14 Mar.

First Performances   1974

1570   Werder, Felix
         THE AFFAIR. Sydney. 14 Mar. Leonard Radic

1571   Hamilton, Iain
         THE CATILINE CONSPIRACY. Stirling, Scotland.
         16 Mar. Composer

1572   North, ?
         AGONY OF KINGS. London. Morley College.
         25 Mar.

1573   Hoddinott, Alun
         BEACH OF FALSEA. Cardiff. 26 Mar. Glyn Jones

1574   Carmines, Al
         THE DUEL. Brooklyn, New York. 22 Apr. Composer

1575   Depue, Wallace E.
         DOCTOR JEKYLL AND MR. HYDE. Bowling Green, Ohio.
         Bowling Green State University. 25 Apr.

1576   Kondorossy, Leslie
         RUTH AND NAOMI. Cleveland. 28 Apr. Shawn Hall

1577   Levin, Gregory
         THE TEMPLE OF LOVE. Brunswick, Maine. Bowdoin
         College. 28 Apr.

1578   Love, Loretta
         THE STONE PRINCESS. Phoenix, Arizona. 29 Apr.
         Karl Bratton

1579   Underwood, William
         A MEDICINE FOR MELANCHOLY. Arkadelphia, Arkan-
         sas. Henderson State College. 30 Apr.

1580   Eakin, Thomas
         PASTICCIO. Cedar Falls, Iowa. University of
         Northern Iowa. 2 May

1974   First Performances

1581   Murray, Jeremiah
         THE BEAUTY AND THE BEAST. New York. 8 May

1582   Reif, Paul
         THE CURSE OF MAUVAIS-AIR. New York. 9 May.
         Composer

1583   Erb, Donald
         NEW ENGLAND'S PROSPECT. Cincinnati. 17 May

1584   Balk, Wesley
         THE NEWEST OPERA IN THE WORLD. Minneapolis.
         ? May. Philip Brunelle

1585   Davies, Peter Maxwell
         MISS DONNETHORNE'S MAGGOT. Adelaide, Australia.
         ? May

1586   Gonzalez, Manuel B.
         NELA. Bronx, New York. Hostos College. ? May

1587   Lees, Benjamin
         MEDEA IN CORINTH. New York. ? May

1588   Huston, Scott
         THE GIGGLING GOBLIN. Cincinnati. University of
         Cincinnati. 2 June. Karl Bratton

1589   Musgrave, Thea
         THE VOICE OF ARIADNE. Aldeburgh. 11 June.
         Amalia Elguera

1590   Lloyd, Alan
         A LETTER FOR QUEEN VICTORIA. Spoleto, Italy.
         15 June. Robert Wilson

1591   McDaniel, William J.
         THE GREEN TINT. Eureka Springs, Arkansas.
         7 July

First Performances   1974

1592   Barab, Seymour
        PHILIP MARSHAL OR TENDER MERCLES. Chautauqua,
        New York. 12 July. Composer

1593   Wuorinen, Charles
        PROFILE OF A COMPOSER. Wheatleigh, Massachu-
        setts. 26 July

1594   Pasatieri, Thomas
        SIGNOR DELUSO. Greenway, Virginia. ? July

1595   Lehrman, Leonard
        KARLA. Ithaca, New York. 3 Aug.

1596   ______.
        NOTES FROM A LADY AT A DINNER PARTY. Ithaca,
        New York. 3 Aug.

1597   Pasatieri, Thomas
        THE PENITENTES. Aspen, Colorado. 3 Aug. Anne
        Howard Bailey

1598   Bernardo, José Paul
        THE CHILD. Albany, New York. State University
        of New York at Albany. 8 Aug.

1599   Silverman, Stanley
        HOTEL FOR CRIMINALS. Lenox, Massachusetts.
        14 Aug. Richard Foreman

1600   Anderson, Beth
        JOAN. Cabrillo, California. 22 Aug.

1601   Barrett-Ayres, Reginald
        HUGH MILLER. Edinburgh. ? Aug. Colin Maclean

1602   Russo, William
        PEDROLINO'S REVENGE. New York. 11 Sept.
        Jonathan Arbabanel

1974   First Performances

1603   ______.
        ISABELLA'S FORTUNE. New York. 11 Sept. Albert
        Williams

1604   Baska, Robert
        RED CARNATIONS. New York. 24 Oct.

1605   Freund, Donald
        THE BISHOP'S GHOST. Memphis, Tennessee. 31 Oct.
        Hall Peyton

1606   Gross, Robert
        PROJECT 1521. Los Angeles. 1 Nov. Composer

1607   Winslow, Richard
        ENDGAME. Kingston, Rhode Island. University of
        Rhode Island. 6 Nov.

1608   Still, William Grant
        BAYOU LEGEND. Jackson, Mississippi. 15 Nov.
        Verna Avery

1609   Guy, Barry
        D. London. 25 Nov.

1610   Kavanaugh, Patrick
        JACK AND THE BEANSTALK. Washington, D.C. 24 Nov.

1611   Samuel, Douglas
        A CHRISTMAS CAROL. Columbia, South Carolina.
        University of South Carolina. 8 Dec.

1612   Zador, Eugene
        YEHU. Los Angeles. 21 Dec. Anna Egyud

II. ADDITIONAL OPERAS LACKING COMPLETE
PERFORMANCE INFORMATION

     This section is an alphabetical listing by
composer of operas for which there is incomplete
information. The style is the same as Section I.

1613   Adair, James
         ISOLDE OF THE SHORTSTOP. Thomas K. Baker

1614   Adams, Carrie Bell
         THE NATIONAL FLOWER. Composer

1615   Addinsell, Richard
         ADAM'S OPERA. London. 1928. Clemence Dane

1616   Adler, Samuel
         THE WRESTLER. Dallas, Texas. 1972. Judah
         Stampfer

1617   Aleksis, A.
         UZ TEVYNE (FOR THE NATIVE LAND). Waterbury,
         Connecticut. 1919. Performed in Lithuanian

1618   Alford, Harry L.
         SUNNY OF SUNNYSIDE. Beatrice Marie Casey

1619   Allen, Paul Hastings
         CLEOPATRA.

1620   ______.
         I FIORI

Additional Operas

1621   Allen, Paul Hastings
        LA PICCOLA FIGARO. Golisciani

1622   ______.
        THE MONASTERY. Florence. 1912. Performed in
        Italian

1623   ______.
        THE LOVE POTION

1624   Alter, Martha
        GROCERIES AND NOTIONS

1625   Antheil, George
        FLIGHT. 1930

1626   Armour, Eugene
        WE'RE BACK

1627   Arnold, Maurice
        THE LAST KING

1628   Arundell, Dennis
        GHOST OF ABEL

1629   ______.
        A MIDSUMMER'S MARRIAGE

1630   Aston, Peter
        SACRAPANT THE SORCERER. Paul Morgan

1631   Avshalom, Aaron
        THE TWILIGHT HOUR OF YANG-KUEI-FEI.
        A. E. Grantham

1632   Bacon, Ernest
        A. LINCOLN. Paul Horgan

Additional Operas

1633   _____.
        TAKE YOUR CHOICE

1634   Balk, Wesley
        THE MAGIC ABDUCTION AND COSI MARRIAGE OF TUTTI
        GIOVANNI. Aspen, Colorado. 1972

1635   Bantock, Granville
        CAEDMAR

1636   Barab, Seymour
        DEATH IN DECEMBER. Composer

1637   _____.
        HOW FAR TO BETHLEHEM?

1638   _____.
        JONAH. Paul Goodman

1639   _____.
        LITTLE RED RIDING HOOD

1640   _____.
        THE MALATROIT DOOR. New York. 1959

1641   _____.
        REBA. Martha England

1642   Barati, George
        NOELANI. 1971

1643   Barlow, Betty
        THE CASE OF THE MISSING PART OF SPEECH--A MELO-
        GRAMMAR. Composer and Janet Hutchinson

1644   _____.
        THE RABBIT WHO WANTED RED WINGS

Additional Operas

1645   Barlow, Samuel
        AMANDA. 1936

1646   ______.
        EUGÉNIE

1647   Barr, Al
        THE COAT OF MANY COLORS. Martin Barr

1648   Barri, Richard
        WUTHERING HEIGHTS

1649   Barth, Hans
        MIRAGIA. 1928

1650   Bartlett, Homer Newton
        HINOTITO

1651   ______.
        LA VALLIÈRE

1652   Barton, Andrew
        THE DISAPPOINTMENT, OR THE FORCE OF CREDULITY

1653   Bath, Hubert
        SPANISH STUDENT

1654   ______.
        YOUNG ENGLAND. 1915

1655   Beach, John
        JORINDA AND JORINDEL

1656   Beaton, Isabella
        ANACOANA

1657   Becker, John J.
        DEIDRE OF THE SORROWS. Chicago. 1956.
        Composer

1658 ______.
STAGE WORK NO. 5C: PRIVILEGE AND PRIVATION

1659 Bell, William Henry
HIPPOLYTUS

1660 ______.
ISABEAU

1661 Benedict, Allan
ROBIN HOOD, INC. Frederick H. Martens

1662 Bennett, Ken
THE SINGING FRESHMAN

1663 Bennett, Richard Rodney
THE MIDNIGHT THIEF

1664 Bennett, Robert Russell
AN HOUR OF DELUSION. 1928

1665 ______.
ENDIMION. 1927

1666 Bergh, Arthur
IN ARCADY. David Stevens

1667 ______.
NIORADA

1668 ______.
THE PIED PIPER OF HAMELIN

1669 ______.
THE RAVEN

1670 ______.
THE UNNAMED CITY

Additional Operas

1671   Berio, Luciano
        CIRCLES

1672   ______.
        LABORINTUS II

1673   ______.
        RECITAL FOR CATHY

1674   ______.
        TRACES. Milan. 1969. Susan Oyama

1675   Bermar, H. and B. Katz
        A GOAT'S TALE. Detroit. 1968

1676   Berwald, William
        UTOPIA. 1936

1677   Betts, Lorne M.
        RIDERS TO THE SEA. 1955

1678   ______.
        THE WOODCARVER'S WIFE. 1961

1679   Bezanson, Philip
        STRANGER IN EDEN. John Reardon

1680   Bimboni, Alberto
        CALANDRINO. 1903

1681   ______.
        KARINA. Minneapolis. 1928. Charles Wharton
        Stork

1682   Binder, Abraham Wolfe
        THE ROAD TO PEACE. 1936

1683   Bingham, Seth
        LA CHARELZENN. 1917

Additional Operas

1684 Birtwistle, Harrison
THE MARK OF THE GOAT. Milwaukee. University of
Wisconsin. 1971

1685 Bissell, Keith
HIS MAJESTY'S PIE

1686 Blank, Allen
ARIA DA CAPO

1687 ______.
EXCITEMENT AT THE CIRCUS. Irving Leitner

1688 Blatch, Herbert
RIP VAN WINKLE, JR. Charles Willmore Emlyn

1689 Bliss, Pearl
THE FEAST OF THE RED CORN. Milwaukee. 1955

1690 Blitzstein, Marc
IDIOTS FIRST

1691 ______.
THE MAGIC BARREL

1692 ______.
PARABOLA AND CIRCULA

1693 ______.
REUBEN REUBEN

1694 ______.
SACCO AND VANZETTI

1695 Bliza, Alica
THE SCHOOL BOARD

1696 Blumenfeld, Harold
AMPHITRYON 4. Composer

Additional Operas

1697   Blumenfeld, Harold
         THE ROAD TO SALEM

1698   Bonner, Eugene MacDonald
         BARBARA FRITCHIE. 1921

1699   ______.
         CELUI QUI EPOUSA UNE FEMME. 1923

1700   ______.
         FRANKIE AND JOHNNIE. 1945

1701   ______.
         THE GODS OF THE MOUNTAIN. 1935

1702   ______.
         THE VENETIAN GLASS NEPHEW. 1927

1703   Bornschein, Franz
         THE WILLOW PLATE. 1932

1704   Borowski, Felix
         FERNANDO DEL NONSENTISCO. 1935

1705   Boughton, Rutland
         AVALON. Composer

1706   ______.
         GALAHAD. Composer

1707   Bowers, Robert Hood
         THE ANNIVERSARY

1708   ______.
         LISTEN IN. 1929

1709   ______.
         OLD ENGLISH. 1924

1710   ______.
        OLD ERNEST. 1927

1711   ______.
        THE RED ROSE. New York. 1911

1712   Bowles, Paul Frederic
        DENMARK VESEY. 1937

1713   ______.
        THE WILD REMAINS. 1943

1714   Braine, Robert
        DIANA. 1929

1715   ______.
        THE ETERNAL LIGHT. 1924

1716   ______.
        VIRGINIA. 1926

1717   Brand, Max
        MACHINIST HOPKINS. 1928

1718   ______.
        STORMY INTERLUDE. 1955. Composer

1719   Brandorff, Carl
        THE GYPSY QUEEN

1720   ______.
        JESUS CHRIST

1721   ______.
        NOAH

1722   Brandt, Noah
        A CHINESE NEW YEAR

Additional Operas

1723   Brandt, Noah
            DANIEL

1724   ______.
            LEONA

1725   ______.
            WING WONG

1726   Branscombe, Gena
            THE BELLS OF CIRCUMSTANCE

1727   Brant, Henry
            ALIASUNDE

1728   ______.
            MISS O'GRADY. 1936

1729   Breil, Joseph Carl
            PROFESSOR TATTLE

1730   ______.
            THE SEVENTH CORD. 1913

1731   Brent-Smith, Alexander
            THE CAPTAIN'S PARROT

1732   Bridge, Frank
            THE CHRISTMAS ROSE

1733   Briggs, Mary Elizabeth
            OUR NIGHT OUT

1734   Brindle, Reginald Smith
            THE DEATH OF ANTIGONE

1735   Brisman, Heskel
            WHIRLIGIG   Jerome Greenfield

Additional Operas

1736   Britain, Radie
        BROTHERS OF THE CLOUDS

1737   ______.
        ETERNAL SPIRIT

1738   ______.
        HAPPYLAND. 1946

1739   ______.
        RAIN

1740   ______.
        THE STAR AND THE CHILD

1741   ______.
        UBIQUITY. 1937

1742   Broekhoven, John A. Van
        CAMARALZAMAN

1743   ______.
        A COLONIAL WEDDING. Cincinnati. 1905

1744   Brumby, Colin
        THE SEVEN DEADLY SINS. T. W. Shapcott

1745   Brumleu, Ernest
        THE PIED PIPER. Milwaukee. 1955

1746   Brunswick, Mark
        THE MASTER BUILDER

1747   Bryan, Charles Faulkner
        KINGDOM OF SORROW. 1934

1748   ______.
        REBEL ACADEMY. 1939

Additional Operas

1749   Bucci, Mark
         THE ADAMSES

1750   ______.
         THE CAUCASIAN CHALK CIRCLE

1751   ______.
         ELMER AND LILY

1752   ______.
         TRIAD. Ogden, Utah. Weber State College.
         1970-71

1753   Bullock, W. H.
         THE COUNT OF COMO, OR, A BANDIT'S BRIDE
         F. R. Bell and Harold Ellis

1754   Burroughs, Bob
         DAVID. 1968. Sarah Miller

1755   ______.
         NOW HEAR IT AGAIN!

1756   Bush, Alan Dudley
         THE FERRYMAN'S DAUGHTER

1757   ______.
         THE SPELL UNBOUND

1758   Bush, Geoffrey
         THE BLIND BEGGAR'S DAUGHTER

1759   ______.
         THE SPANISH RIVALS. Brighton. 1948

1760   Butler, Eugene S.
         SAMUEL. William N. McElrath

Additional Operas

1761   Cadman, Charles Wakefield
        BELLE OF HAVANA. G. M. Brown

1762   ______.
        BELLS OF CAPISTRANO. Roos

1763   ______.
        THE GHOST OF LOLLYPOP BAY

1764   ______.
        THE GOLDEN TRAIL

1765   ______.
        THE HOLLYWOOD EXTRA

1766   ______.
        THE LAND OF MISTY WATER. Nelle Richmond
        Eberhart

1767   ______.
        LELWALA, MAID OF NIAGRA. G. M. Brown

1768   ______.
        MEET ARIZONA

1769   ______.
        NURANOKA

1770   ______.
        SOUTH IN SONORA. Roos

1771   ______.
        RAMALA

1772   Campbell, C. M.
        OSCEOLA. Los Angeles. 1944

1773   Cannon, Philip
        THE MAIN FROM VENUS. Jacqueline Laidlow Cannon

1774   Carbonara, Gerard
        ARMAND

Additional Operas

1775   Carlson, Charles Frederick
        THE COURTSHIP OF MILES STANDISH. Composer

1776   ______.
        HESTER, OR THE SCARLET LETTER. Composer

1777   ______.
        THE MERCHANT OF VENICE. Composer

1778   ______.
        PHELIAS

1779   Carmines, Al
        THE JOURNEY OF SNOW WHITE. New York. 1971

1780   Carpenter, John A.
        KRAZY CAT

1781   Carr, Arthur
        CAPTAIN JUPITER. 1939

1782   Carr, Howard
        MASTER WAYFARER

1783   ______.
        UNDER THE GREENWOOD TREE

1784   Carroll, Peter
        MARGARET IN FAIRYLAND. Milwaukee. 1955

1785   Carter, Elliot Cook, Jr.
        TOM AND LILY. 1934

1786   Caryll, Ivan
        THE CHERRY GIRL. Hicks and Hopwood

1787   Castelnuovo-Tedesco, Mario
        ALL'S WELL THAT ENDS WELL. 1959

1788   ______.
        THE IMPORTANCE OF BEING EARNEST. 1962.
        Composer

1789   ______.
        THE MERCHANT OF VENICE

1790   ______.
        SAUL. 1960. Composer

1791   Castiglione, Niccolo
        SWEET. 1967. Composer

1792   Chadwick, George Whitefield
        THE PADRONE. 1915

1793   Chapin, Frederic
        THE FORBIDDEN LAND. Guy F. Steely

1794   Chignell, Robert
        AUCASSIN AND NICOLETTE

1795   ______.
        HERODE

1796   ______.
        ROMEO AND JULIET

1797   Chisholm, Erik
        THE FEAST OF SAMHAIN. 1941

1798   Chorbajian, John
        ANTIGONE. 1959

1799   Churchill, Beatrice
        THE CHRISTMAS SECRET. Gracia Caines

1800   Claflin, Avery
        THE FALL OF THE HOUSE OF USHER. 1921

Additional Operas

1801   Claflin, Avery
        UNCLE TOM'S CABIN. New York

1802   Clapp, Philip Greeley
        THE FLAMING BRAND

1803   Clark, Palmer John
        CARRIE COMES TO COLLEGE, OR, CAMPUS DAZE.
        Composer and Estelle Merrymon Clark

1804   Clark, Philip
        NO GAME FOR KIDS. Tougaloo, Mississippi.
        Tougaloo College. 1970-1971

1805   Clark, Rosemary
        THE CAT AND THE MOON

1806   Clarke, Henry Leland
        THE LIAR

1807   ______.
        LYSISTRATA

1808   Clokey, Joseph W.
        BUILDERS

1809   ______.
        THE EMPERORER'S CLOTHES

1810   ______.
        IN GRANDMOTHER'S GARDEN. Alfred H. Upham

1811   ______.
        WHEN THE CHRIST CHILD CAME

1812   Closson, David M.
        TWELVE DANCING PRINCESSES

1813   Clutsam, George H.
        AFTER A THOUSAND YEARS

Additional Operas

1814   ______.
            KONIG HARLEKIN. Berlin. 1912

1815   ______.
            THE QUEEN'S JESTER. 1905

1816   Coates, Albert
            ASSURBANIPAL

1817   ______.
            SARDANAPALUS. 1916

1818   Coerne, Louis Adolphe
            THE BELLS OF BEAUJOLAIS. David Stevens

1819   ______.
            THE MAIDEN QUEENS

1820   ______.
            SAKUNTALA. 1904

1821   Cole, Hugo
            ASSES' EAR

1822   ______.
            JONAH

1823   ______.
            PERSEPHONE

1824   ______.
            A STATUE FOR THE MAJOR

1825   Coleridge-Taylor, Samuel
            DREAM LOVERS

1826   ______.
            THE GITANOS

Additional Operas

1827   Coleridge-Taylor, Samuel
        THELMA

1828   Collison, William Alexander
        THE IRISH GIRL. Percy French

1829   Converse, Frederick S.
        THE IMMIGRANTS. Percy Mackaye

1830   ______.
        SINBAD THE SAILOR. Percy Mackaye

1831   Corder, Frederick
        OSSIAN. 1905

1832   Corder, Paul
        GRETTIR THE STRONG

1833   ______.
        RAPUNZEL

1834   Cowell, Henry
        O'HIGGINS CHILE. 1949

1835   Crews, Lucille
        ARIADNE AND DIONYSUS. 1935

1836   ______.
        THE CALL OF JEANNE D'ARC

1837   ______.
        EIGHT HUNDRED RUBLES. John G. Neidhardt

1838   Crosse, Gordon
        AHMET THE WOODSELLER. London. 1965

1839   Cumberworth, Starling
        HOME BURIAL. 1955

Additional Operas

1840   Cumming, Richard
        THE PICNIC. Henry Butler

1841   Curtis, Elizabeth
        CHRISTMAS EVE

1842   Curtis, Louis Woodsen
        BRIAR ROSE. Agnes Emilie Paterson

1843   Daiken, Melanie
        MAYAKOVSKY AND THE SUN. Edinburgh. 1972

1844   Dalton, Jane
        ONCE UPON A TIME. Composer

1845   Damrosch, Walter
        ELEPHANTS IN CONGRESS. 1944

1846   Daniels, Mabel
        THE LEGEND OF MARIETTA. 1909

1847   Davidson, Charles
        GIMPEL THE FOOL. Paul Kresh

1848   Davies, Sir Henry Walford
        WHAT LUCK!

1849   Davies, Vic
        CELEBRATION. Winnipeg, Manitoba. 1969

1850   ______.
        LET US PAY TRIBUTE TO LORD GORDON GORDON.
        Goldie Weatherhead

1851   Davis, Allan
        THE ORDEAL OF OSBERT. Duxbury, Massachusetts.
        1949

Additional Operas

1852   Davis, John David
        THE ZAPOROGUES. Birmingham, England. 1903.
        Lawrence Levy

1853   Davis, Katherine
        CINDERELLA

1854   ______.
        THE UNMUSICAL IMPRESSARIO. Composer and Heddie
        Root Kent

1855   Deems, James Monroe
        ESTHER

1856   DeFilippi, Amedeo
        THE GREEN COCATOO. 1927

1857   ______.
        MALVOLIO. 1937

1858   DeKoven, Reginald
        THE BEAUTY SPOT. New York. 1909

1859   ______.
        THE GOLDEN BUTTERFLY. New York. 1907

1860   ______.
        HAPPYLAND, OR, THE KING OF ELYSIA. New York.
        1905. Frederic Ranken

1861   ______.
        HER LITTLE HIGHNESS. New York. 1913

1862   ______.
        RED FEATHER. New York. 1913. Charles Emerson
        Clark

1863   ______.
        THE STUDENT KING. New York. 1906. Frederic
        Ranken and Stanislaus Stange

Additional Operas

1864 _____.
THE WEDDING TRIP. New York. 1911. Fred
DeGresac and Harry B. Smith

1865 DeLara, Isidore
LE RÉVEIL DE BOUDDHA. 1902

1866 DeLeone, Francesco B.
CAVE MAN STUFF

1867 _____.
DAVID

1868 _____.
THE GOLDEN CALF

1869 _____.
PERGOLESE. Nicolo Buonpare; performed in
Italian

1870 _____.
PRINCESS TING-AH-LING

1871 _____.
THE PRODIGAL SON

1872 _____.
RUTH

1873 DeLisa, Victor V.
MOSES, PRINCE OF EGYPT

1874 Delius, Frederick
MARGOT LA ROUGE. Mme. Rosenval

1875 Dibden, Charles
THE WATERMAN

Additional Operas

1876   Dodge, Cynthia
        COLLEGE DAYS. Composer

1877   ______.
        CYNTHIA'S TRAGEDY. Composer

1878   ______.
        EL BANDIDO. Composer

1879   ______.
        HULDA OF HOLLAND. Composer

1880   ______.
        IN OLD LOUISIANA. Composer

1881   ______.
        THE MAN WITH THE CROOKED NOSE

1882   ______.
        MISS CHERRYBLOSSOM

1883   ______.
        OLD CROSSPATCH. Composer

1884   ______.
        STEPHEN FOSTER. Composer

1885   ______.
        THE TALL TREES

1886   ______.
        WHAT'S THE MATTER WITH SALLY?

1887   ______.
        THE WISHING WELL. Composer

1888   Dodgson, Stephen
        CADILLY. David Reynolds

Additional Operas

1889   Doran, Matt
        THE LITTLE HAND SO OBSTINATE. 1970. Sonia
        Brown

1890   Drake, Earl R.
        THE MITE AND THE MIGHTY. Chicago. 1915

1891   Dreyfus, George
        GARNI SANDS. 1965. F. Kellaway

1892   ______.
        SONG OF MAYPOLE. Canberra. 1967. F. Kéllaway

1893   Dunhill, Thomas Frederick
        THE ENCHANTED GARDEN. London. 1927

1894   Dunlap, Fern
        EASTERTIME IS HAPPY TIME

1895   DuPage, Florence
        ALICE IN WONDERLAND

1896   Eames, Henry Purmont
        PRISCILLA

1897   ______.
        THE SACRED TREE OF THE OMAHA. Lincoln,
        Nebraska. University of Nebraska. 1917

1898*   Easdale, Brian
        RAPUNZEL. 1927

1899   Eaton, John
        ANDROCLES AND THE LION. Cincinnati. 1973

1900   ______.
        MA BARKER. 1957

1901   Edwards, Julian
        DOLLY VARDEN. Stanislaus Stange

Additional Operas

1902   Edwards, Julian
        THE GAY MUSICIAN. Edward Siedle and Charles J.
        Campbell

1903   ______.
        LOVE'S LOTTERY. Stanislaus Stange

1904   ______.
        THE PRINCESS CHIC. Kirke LaShelle

1905   Effinger, Cecil
        PANDORA'S BOX. Boulder, Colorado. University
        of Colorado. 1962. Sally Monsour

1906   Elgar, Edward
        THE SPANISH LADY. Composer and Barry Jackson.
        (180 fragments of The Spanish Lady, edited by
        Percy Young, were broadcast by B.B.C. on
        December 15, 1969)

1907   Elkus, Jonathan
        TREASURE ISLAND

1908   Elliot, Clinton
        POPE JOAN

1909   Elliott, Marjorie
        THE HAPPY SCARECROW

1910   Elmore, Robert
        THE INCARNATE WORD

1911   Elton, Antony
        THE MINISTER OF JUSTICE

1912   Engel, Carl
        WAY DOWN SOUTH IN DIXIE

1913   Engel, Lehman
        THE GOLDEN LADDER

Additional Operas

1914   _____.
          MEDEA.   1935

1915   Engels, Peter Joseph
          ADELGUNDE.   Composer; original libretto in
          German

1916   Engländer, Ludwig
          A MADCAP PRINCESS. Harry B. Smith

1917   _____
          THE OFFICE BOY.   Harry B. Smith

1918   _____.
          THE TWO ROSES.   Stanislaus Stange

1919   Errolle, Ralph
          BONDRI

1920   _____.
          ELMAR.   Composer

1921   Esile, Joseph
          SARA.   Scottsdale, Arizona. 1960.   Frank Langer

1922   Faberman, Harold
          IF MUSIC BE...

1923   Fanciulli, Francesco
          GABRIEL DI MONTGOMERY.   In Italian

1924   _____.
          THE INTERPRETER

1925   _____.
          THE MAID OF PARADISE

1926   _____.
          MALINCHE

Additional Operas

1927   Farmer, John
        THE PIED PIPER. A. O'D. Bartholeyns

1928   Farwell, Arthur
        THE EVERGREEN TREE

1929   Fennimore, J.
        EVENTIDE

1930   Ferris, William
        LITTLE MOON OF ALBAN

1931   Fink, Harold
        GOODMAN BROWN

1932   Fink, Myron
        CAUCASIAN CHALK CIRCLE

1933   Fitelberg, Jerry
        HENNY PENNY

1934   Flagello, Nicholas
        MIRRA. 1953

1935   ______.
        RIP VAN WINKLE. 1957

1936   ______.
        THE WIG. 1953. Composer

1937   Ford, Clifford
        HYPNOS. K. Peglar

1938   Forrest, Hamilton
        YZDRA. 1925

1939   Forsblad, Leland
        THE BOY WHO CRIED "WOLF!"

Additional Operas

1940   Forsyth, Cecil
        CINDERELLA

1941   ______.
        WESTWARD HO!

1942   Foster, Arnold
        LORD BATEMAN

1943   Franchetti, Arnold
        THE DOWSER

1944   Frank, Charles
        THE CAPTAIN AND THE COWBOY

1945   Fraser-Simpson, Harold
        BONITA. Wadham Peacock

1946   Freed, Isadore
        HOMO SUM. 1930

1947   Freeman, Harry Lawrence
        AMERICAN ROMANCE. 1927

1948   ______.
        ATHALIA. 1916

1949   ______.
        THE FLAPPER

1950   ______.
        LEAH KLESCHNA. 1930

1951   ______.
        THE OCTOROON. M. E. Braddon

1952   ______.
        THE PLANTATION. 1914

1953   ______.
        THE PROPHECY

Additional Operas

1954   Freeman, Harry Lawrence
        THE TRYST. New York. 1911

1955   ______.
        UZZIAH. 1931. Florence Lewis Speare

1956   ______.
        ZULUKI. Composer

1957   ______.
        ZULULAND.   (Zululand is composed of the shorter
        operas The Zulu King; Nada, the Lily; and Allah)

1958   Freer, Eleanor Everest
        THE CHILKOOT MAIDEN. Composer

1959   ______.
        JOAN OF ARC

1960   ______.
        THE MASQUE OF PANDORA. Composer

1961   ______.
        PRECIOSA

1962   Fricker, Peter Racine
        THE DEATH OF VIVIEN. 1956

1963   Friml, Rudolf
        GLORIANA

1964   ______.
        SOMETIME

1965   ______.
        TUMBLE IN

1966   ______.
        YOU'RE IN LOVE. Stamford, Connecticut. 1916

Twentieth Century Opera

1967 Fuleihan, Anis
   VASCO. 1960

1968 Gatty, Alfred
   RUMPELSTIZCHEN. Milwaukee. 1954

1969 Gatty, Nicholas Comyn
   MACBETH

1970 German, Sir Edward
   EMERALD ISLE

1971 ______.
   FALLEN FAIRIES

1972 ______.
   A PRINCESS OF KENSINGTON. 1903

1973 ______.
   THE RIVAL POETS. 1901

1974 Gerrish-Jones, Abbie
   THE ANADLUSIANS. Percy Friars Valentine

1975 ______.
   THE AZTEC PRINCESS

1976 ______.
   TWO ROSES. Composer

1977 Giannini, Vittorio
   CHRISTUS

1978 ______.
   FLORA

1979 Gideon, Miriam
   FORTUNATO. A. Quintero and J. Quintero

Additional Operas

1980   Gilbert, Henry F.
        FANTASY IN DELFT. 1915

1981   Gingold, Norbert
        A DATE WITH SANTA. San Francisco. Heddy Gingold

1982   ______.
        CINDERELLA. San Francisco. Heddy Gingold

1983   ______.
        THE EMPEROR'S NEW CLOTHES. San Francisco. Heddy
        Gingold

1984   ______.
        GOLDILOCKS BECOMES QUEEN. Heddy Gingold

1985   ______.
        JOHNNY APPLESEED. San Francisco. Heddy Gingold

1986   ______.
        LITTLE RED RIDING HOOD. San Francisco. Heddy
        Gingold

1987   ______.
        MAGIC LAMP. San Francisco. Heddy Gingold

1988   ______.
        PRINCESS HONEY BECOMES QUEEN. San Francisco.
        Heddy Gingold

1989   ______.
        PUSS 'N BOOTS. San Francisco. Heddy Gingold

1990   ______.
        SANTA CLAUS' BEARD. San Francisco. Heddy
        Gingold

1991   ______.
        SINBAD THE SAILOR. San Francisco. Heddy Gingold

Additional Operas

1992   ______.
        SLEEPING BEAUTY. San Francisco. Heddy Gingold

1993   ______.
        SNOW WHITE AND THE SEVEN DWARFS. San Francisco.
        Heddy Gingold

1994   ______.
        SONG OF HAPPINESS. San Francisco. Heddy
        Gingold

1995   ______.
        THREE LITTLE JITTERBUGS. San Francisco. Heddy
        Gingold

1996   Gladstein, Richard
        THE LOCKOUT

1997   Glanville-Hicks, Peggy
        CAEDMON

1998   ______.
        CARLOS AMONG THE CANDLES

1999   ______.
        SAPPHO. Lawrence Durrell

2000   Gleason, Frederick Grant
        MONTEZUMA

2001   Goehr, Alexander
        SONATA ABOUT JERUSALEM

2002   ______.
        TRIPTYCH

2003   Goldstein, William
        A BULLET FOR BILLY THE KID. 1965. Marvin Shofer

Additional Operas

2004   Goldstein, William
        THE PEDDLER. Marvin Shofer

2005   ______.
        A TOTAL SWEET SUCCESS. Marvin Shofer

2006   Gomer, Llywellyn
        THE DIVINE MYSTERY

2007   Goodman, Alfred Grant
        THE STATUES OF TURTLE BAY

2008   Goosens, Eugene
        GAINSBOROUGH

2009   Gordon, Philip
        THE SHOE OF LITTLE NOBY

2010   Graham, Jack
        ARANEA

2011   Gray, Cecil
        THE TEMPTATION OF ST ANTHONY. Composer

2012   Green, Lydia
        EXIT THE VILLAIN. Harriet Lyons

2013   Grey, Julian
        BEAUTIFUL DREAMER

2014   Griffis, Elliot
        THE BLUE SCARAB. 1934

2015   Griffiths, Philip
        MY DAUGHTER COPPELIA. Composer and Eric Shaw

2016   Gross, Eric
        THE BROKEN PITCHER. Sydney. 1965

Additional Operas

2017   Grossmith, Leslie
        UNCLE TOM'S CABIN

2018   Gruenberg, Louis
        ANTONY AND CLEOPATRA

2019   ______.
        THE BRIDE OF THE GODS

2020   ______.
        THE DUMB WIFE

2021   ______.
        HELEN'S HUSBAND

2022   ______.
        THE MIRACLE OF FLANDERS.   1950

2023   ______.
        QUEEN HELENA.   1936.   Philip Moeller

2024   ______.
        VOLPONE.   1945

2025   ______.
        THE WITCH OF BROCKEN.   E. Malkowsky

2024   Gruendler, Hermann Frederick
        LA CARTOUCHE, OR, KING OF THE BAREFOOTS.   P. J.
        Dugan

2027   Gulesian, Grace Warner
        CAPE COD ANNE

2028   Gundry, Inglis
        NAAMAN.   1938

2029   ______.
        THE RETURN OF ODYSSEUS.   1941

Additional Operas

2030   Gyring, Elizabeth
        NIGHT AT SEA AND DAY IN COURT. Composer

2031   Hadley, Henry
        HAPPY JACK. Samuel F. Batchelder

2032   ________.
        NANCY BROWN

2033   Hagemann, Virginia
        THE BIRD'S CHRISTMAS CAROL. Eleanor Jones

2034   ________.
        A CHRISTMAS CAROL. Composer and Eleanor Jones

2035   Hahn, Thomas
        RASPUTIN

2036   Haile, Eugene
        VIOLA D'AMORE

2037   Hamill, Roseann
        THE BLESSED EVENT. Diane Ward

2038   Hamilton, Iain
        AGAMEMNON. Composer

2039   ________.
        PHARSALIA. Edinburgh. 1969. Composer

2040   ________.
        THE ROYAL HUNT OF THE SUN. Composer

2041   Hamilton, Marcia
        TO PLEASE MR. PLUMJOY. Pittsburgh. Duquesne
        University. 1957

2042   Hand, Colin
        THE KING OF THE GOLDEN RIVER

Additional Operas

2043   Harling, W. Franke
       THE SUNKEN BELL

2044   Harman, Carter
       CHARMS FOR THE SAVAGE

2045   Harnick, Sheldon
       FRUSTRATION

2046   Harris, Russell G.
       THE ONLY JEALOUSY OF EMER

2047   Harris, Theodore
       THE FIRST PRESIDENT. Rutherford, New Jersey.
       Fairleigh Dickinson University. 1964. William
       Carlos Williams

2048   Harrison, Julius Allen Greenway
       CANTERBURY PILGRIMS

2049   Hart, Frederic Patton
       POISON

2050   ______.
       THE ROMANCE OF ROBOT. New York. 1937

2051   ______.
       THE WHEEL OF FORTUNE. 1937

2052   Hart, Peter
       A CHRISTMAS CAROL

2053   Hatch, Owen A.
       ONCE UPON A CHRISTMAS. M. Rettke

2054   Haubiel, Charles
       BERTA

2055   ______.
       BRIGANDS REFERRED

Additional Operas

2056   Haubiel, Charles
        THE WITCHES' CURSE

2057   Haufrecht, Herbert
        A POT OF BROTH. New York. 1964

2058   _____.
        THE STORY OF FERDINAND. Rochester, New York.
        1964

2059   _____.
        WE'VE COME FROM THE CITY

2060   Haverson, Leslie
        SUZANNAH WITH THE BELL

2061   Haydon, Claude M.
        PAOLO AND FRANCESCA

2062   Hazlehurst, Cecil
        THE DREAM

2063   _____.
        THE PRINCE ELECT

2064   Hector, Chastey
        THE GOLDEN ARGOSY. Stanley C. West

2064a   Heller, Alfred
        SISTER CARRIE. Bloomington, Indiana. Indiana
        University. 1969-1970

2065   Henderson, Alva
        THE UNFORGIVEN

2066   Henekker, David
        JORROCKS

2067   Herbert, Muriel
        CANDY FLOSS. Composer

Additional Operas

2068   ______.
          COME TO THE ZOO. Composer

2069   ______.
          CHRISTMAS EVE'S DREAM. Composer

2070   Herrmann, Bernard
          WUTHERING HEIGHTS. 1950. Lucille Fletcher

2071   Heywood, Percival Meredith
          THE BATSMAN'S BRIDE

2072   Higgins, Richard C.
          LAVENDER BLUE. 1963

2073   ______.
          PEACEABLE KINGDOM. 1961

2074   Hill, Alfred
          THE WEIRD FLUTE

2075   Hill, Mabel Wood
          THE JOLLY BEGGARS

2076   ______.
          THE ROSE AND THE RING

2077   Hinton, Arthur
          THE DISAGREEABLE PRINCESS

2078   ______.
          ST. ELIZABETH'S ROSE

2079   Hively, Wells
          THE DISCREET CADIGA

2080   Hoiby, Lee
          THE WITCH. 1956

Additional Operas

2081   Holbrooke, Josef
        THE ENCHANTER

2082   _____.
        THE SNOB

2083   _____.
        THE WIZARD

2084   Holden, Bernice
        THE TRAVELLING MUSICIAN. Cleveland. Josephine
        F. Royle

2085   Holloway, Robin
        CLARISSA. 1971

2086   Holst, Gustav
        THE YOUTH'S CHOICE. 1902

2087   _____.
        SITA. Composer

2088   Hopkins, Anthony
        CROWN OF GOLD

2089   _____.
        DOCTOR MUSICUS

2090   _____.
        THREE'S COMPANY. Michael Flanders

2091   _____.
        A TRIP TO ITALY. Canterbury. 1951. Christopher
        Hassall

2092   Hopkins, Edwin
        CROSSTOWN STROLL

2093   Hosmer, Lucius
        THE ROSE OF THE ALAHAMBRA. Rochester. 1905

2094   ______.
            THE WALKING DELEGATE. (Revised title of The
            Walking Delegate is The Koreans)

2095   Hovhaness, Alan
            AFTON WATER

2096   ______.
            THE LEPER KING. Composer

2097   ______.
            THE TRAVELLERS. Composer

2098   Howell, Alice
            CHRISTMAS IN COVENTRY

2099   Hugo, John Adam
            THE HERO OF BYZANZ

2100   ______.
            THE SUN GOD. Bartlett B. James

2101   Humel, Gerald
            THE PROPOSAL. Roger Brucker

2102   Hunkins, Eusebia
            MICE IN COUNCIL

2103   ______.
            THE SPIRIT OWL

2104   ______.
            WONDROUS LOVE

2105   Hurd, Michael
            MR. PUNCH. Composer

2106   Hyde, Herbert
            THE KITCHEN CLOCK. 1927   Florence C. Comfort

Additional Operas

2107   Iscove, Rob
        JACK. Montreal. 1974

2108   Jarrett, Jack
        CINDERELLA. Gainesville, Florida. University
        of Florida. 1956. Composer

2109   Jerome, Benjamin
        THE ROYAL CHIEF, OR THE MYTHICAL ISLE OF OOLONG.
        George E. Stoddard and Charles S. Taylor

2110   Johnson, David
        ALL THERE WAS BETWEEN THEM. Jack Ronder

2111   Johnson, Harriet
        PETS OF THE MET. Don Freeman and Lydia Freeman

2112   Johnson, James Weldon
        THE CZAR OF ZANI

2113   Johnston, Edward F.
        THE DRUM-MAJOR. Maude Elizabeth Inch

2114   Johnstone, Alexander
        FIDDLERS THREE. William Cary Duncan

2115   Jones, George
        BREAK OF DAY

2116   Jones, Sidney
        THE GIRL FROM UTAH. London. 1903

2117   ______.
        THE HAPPY DAY. London. 1916

2118   ______.
        THE KING OF CADONIA. London. 1908

2119   ______.
        THE MEDAL AND THE MAID. London. 1903

Additional Operas

2120   ______.
        MY LADY MOLLY. London. 1903

2121.   ______.
        THE PERSIAN PRINCESS. London. 1909

2122   ______.
        SEE SEE. London. 1906

2123   ______.
        SPRING MAID. London. 1911

2124   Joplin, Scott
        A GUEST OF HONOR

2125   Jordan, Jules
        NISIEA. Composer

2126   Joubert, John
        THE QUARRY. David Holbrook

2127   Kalmanoff, Martin
        THE GHOST OF THE MOUNTAIN. G. Regney and N.
        Regney

2128   ______.
        GODIVA. Atra Bear

2129   ______.
        THE INSECT COMEDY. Lewis Allen

2130   ______.
        THE MAGIC LAND OF OPERA

2131   Kanitz, Ernest
        KUMANA. 1953. Jane Marshall

2132   ______.
        THE LUCKY DOLLAR. Los Angeles. U. C. L. A.
        1958. Ann Stanford

Additional Operas

2133   Kaufmann, Walter
        THE RESEARCH. Tallahassee, Florida. Florida
        State University. 1963

2134   Kay, Sidney
        STRATEGY

2135   Kayden, Mildred
        SOLOMON

2136   Kechley, Gerald
        ROBIN GOODFELLOW

2137   Kellam, Ian
        THE JOURNEY

2138   Keller, Walter
        THE CRUMPLED ISLE

2139   Kelly, Brian
        HEROD, DO YOUR WORST

2140   _____.
        THE SPIDER MONKEY. London. 1971. John Fuller

2141   Kent, Richard
        ARNO

2142   Kirchner, Leon
        RAPPACINI'S DAUGHTER

2143   _____.
        SCENES FOR AN OPERA

2144   Klauss, Kenneth
        THE FALL OF THE HOUSE OF USHER

2145   Kleinsinger, George
        TOMMY PITCHER. Stockbridge, Massachusetts.
        1952. Paul Tripp

Additional Operas

2146   Knight, Morris
        A LEGEND

2147   Knollner, Jacob
        ESTHER.   Composer

2148   Knowlton, E. Bruce
        MONTANA.   Composer

2149   Kohs, Ellis B.
        LORD OF THE ASCENDENT

2150   _____.
        RHINOCEROS

2151   Kondorossy, Leslie
        THE BAKIS

2152   _____.
        NATHAN THE WISE

2153   Korn, Clara Anna
        THEIR LAST WAR

2154   Korn, Peter
        HEIDI

2155   Kraft, Leo
        THE CALIPH'S CLOCK

2156   Kupferman, Meyer
        DOCTOR FAUSTUS LIGHTS THE LIGHTS.   Gertrude
        Stein

2157   Laderman, Ezra
        AIR RAID

2158   _____.
        SHADOWS AMONG US.   Normal Rosten

Additional Operas

2159   LaMonaca, Joseph
        THE FESTIVAL OF GUARI.   Francesco Cubiciotti

2160   Landgrave, J. Philip
        LIVING IN THE SPIRIT.   Composer

2161   LaViolette, Wesley
        THE ENLIGHTENED ONE.   1955

2162   Lasker, Henry
        BEAUTY AND THE BEAST

2163   Laukandt, Renato and L. M. Hluse.
        THE STOCKINGS WERE HUNG

2164   Lawergen, Bo
        THREE ACTS

2165   Lee, Dai-Keong
        NIGHT PEOPLE.   Robert Healey

2166   ______.
        OPEN THE GATES

2167   ______.
        PHINEAS AND THE NIGHTINGALE

2168   Lees, Benjamin
        THE ORACLE

2169   LeFleming, Christopher Kaye
        SQUIRREL NUTKIN

2170   Leichtling, Alan
        THE TEMPEST.   Gabriella Roepke

2171   Lester, William
        MANABOZO

Additional Operas

2172   ______.
        SE-A-WAN-A.   Frederick H. Martens

2173   Levy, Marvin David
        THE BALCONY

2174   Lewis, Carrie
        THE QUEEN OF THE GARDEN.   Frederick H. Martens

2175   Lewis, Leo Rich
        OLD FORTUNATIS

2176   Liebling, George
        CHULA.   Alice Liebling

2177   Linstead, George Frederick
        AGAMEMNON.   1924

2178   Lloyd, Caroline
        DONA BARBARA.   Caracas, Venezuela.   1967

2179   Loeffler, Charles Martin
        LIFE IS BUT A DREAM

2180   Lombord, Benjamin
        WOODSTOCK

2181   Lombardo, Robert
        THE DODO.   Kathleen Lombardo

2182   Loomis, Clarence
        THE CAPTIVE WOMAN.   1953

2183   ______.
        CASTLE OF GOLD

2184   ______.
        DAVID.   Cole Young Rice

Additional Operas

2185   Loomis, Clarence
        DUN AN OIR. Howard McKent Barnes; written in
        Gaelic

2186   ______.
        SUSANNAH DON'T YOU CRY. New York. 1939. Ethel
        Ferguson

2187   ______.
        THE WHITE CLOUD. 1935

2188   Lora, Antonio
        THE LEGEND OF SLEEPY HOLLOW. Morton Bowe

2189   ______.
        SHOES AND SHIPS. Caroline Raney

2190   ______.
        VIOLANTE. Composer and Harry Kemp

2191   Lord, David
        THE SEA JOURNEY. Farnham, England. 1968.
        Michael Dennis Browne

2192   Lourie, Arthur.
        THE BLACKAMOOR OF PETER THE GREAT. 1961

2193   Luders, Gustav
        WOODLAND. Frank Pixley

2194   Lutyens, Elisabeth
        THE NUMBERED

2195   Lybbert, Donald
        SCARLET LETTER

2196   MacDermott, Galt
        CRESSIDA. Joseph Papp

Additional Operas

2197   Maganini, Quinto
        THE ARGONAUTS

2198   Mainville, Denise
        THE JIG IS UP

2199   Mamorsky, Morris
        TWELVE DANCING PRINCESSES

2200   Mann, Robert W.
        SCARLET LETTER

2201   Manning, Kathleen Lockhart
        FOR THE SOUL OF RAFAEL

2202   ______.
        MR. WU

2203   Marshall, Nicholas.
        ARION AND THE DOLPHINS.   Dulce Rapaport

2204   Maryon, Edward
        THE CYCLE OF LIFE.   (The Cycle of Life is a
        heptalogy comprised of Lucifer, Cain, Krishna,
        Magdalen, Sangraal, Psyche, and Nirvana)

2205   ______.
        THE FEATHER ROBE

2206   ______.
        GREATER LOVE

2207   ______.
        PAOLO AND FRANCESCA

2208   ______.
        THE PRODIGAL SON

Additional Operas

2209   Maryon, Edward
        REMBRANDT

2210   ______.
        LA ROBE DE PLUME

2211   ______.
        THE SMELTING POT

2212   ______.
        WEREWOLF

2213   Marzo, Eduardo
        SANTA CLAUS, JUNIOR.   Margaret E. Lacey

2214   Mathias, William
        CULWCH AC OLWEN, DIFYRRWCH.   Gwyn Thomas; writ-
        ten in Welsh

2215   Matteson, Maurice
        SOUTHRONS ALL

2216   Mayer, William
        THE GREATEST SOUND AROUND.   1954

2217   McCollin, Francis
        KING CHRISTMAS.   1926.   Composer

2218   McKee, Jeanellen
        THE DEPOT

2219   ______.
        THE FIRE WARDEN

2220   ______.
        MONETTE

2221   ______.
        REUNION

Additional Operas

2222   McLeod, Jenny
        EARTH AND SKY. Wellington, New Zealand. Uni-
        versity of Wellington. 1971

2223   _____.
        UNDER THE SUN. Wellington, New Zealand. Uni-
        versity of Wellington. 1971

2224   Mellers, Wilfred Howard
        THE TRAGICAL HISTORY OF CHRISTOPHER MARLOWE.
        1952

2225   Meredith, Ola
        GOLDILOCKS AND THE THREE BEARS

2226   _____.
        PETER RABBIT

2227   _____.
        THE THREE LITTLE PIGS

2228   Mildenberg, Albert
        LOVE'S LOCKSMITH. New York. 1912. Composer

2229   _____.
        MICHAEL ANGELO

2230   _____.
        RAFAELLO. Naples. 1910. Composer; performed
        in Italian

2231   Miles, Philip Napier
        DEMETER

2232   _____.
        GOOD FRIDAY

2232   _____.
        QUEEN ROSAMOND

Additional Operas

2234   Minetti, Carlo
        EDANE THE FAIR

2235   Moe, Daniel
        COVENTRY NATIVITY

2236   Mokrejs, John
        THE MAYFLOWER

2237   ______.
        SOHRAB AND RUSTUM

2238   ______.
        WHEN WASHINGTON WAS YOUNG

2239   Mollicone, Henry
        YOUNG GOODMAN BROWN

2240   Montgomery, Bruce
        JOHN BARLEYCORN

2241   Moore, Daniel
        BLISS APOCALYPSE. San Francisco. 1969

2242   ______.
        THE WALLS ARE RUNNING BLOOD

2243   Moore, Douglas
        PUSS 'N BOOTS

2244   Moore, Homer
        THE ELFWIFE

2245   ______.
        THE FALL OF ROME

2246   ______.
        THE PURITANS

2247   Moore, Mary Carr
       THE COST OF EMPIRE.   Composer

2248   ______.
       LEOPARD

2249   ______.
       LOVE AND THE SORCERER.   Eleanor Flaig

2250   Mopper, Irving
       GEORGE

2251   Moross, Jerome
       WILLIE THE WEEPER

2252   Morris, Heyward
       IN PARADISE.   New York.   Manhattan School of
       Music

2253   Mullins, Hugh
       ROMEO AND JULIET

2254   ______.
       THE SCARLET LETTER

2255   Murrill, Herbert Henry John
       MAN IN CAGE.   London.   1930

2256   Musgrave, Thea
       THE ABBOT OF DRIMROCK.   London.   1955

2257   Negri, Guido
       CLEOPATRA.   Iginio Squassoni

2258   ______.
       KING PHILIP.   Iginio Squassoni

2259   Nelhybel, Vaclav
       FOUR READINGS FROM MARLOWE'S "DOCTOR FAUSTUS"

Additional Operas

2260   Neumann, Alfred
        AN OPERA FOR CHRISTMAS. Composer

2261   Newlin, Dika
        FEATHERTOP

2262   Niebel, Mildred
        FRIENDSHIP ON PARADE

2263   Noble, Thomas
        KILLIBEGS. 1911

2264   Norden, Norris Lindsey
        THE LITTLE MATCH GIRL

2265   Nordoff, Paul
        THE CHILDREN'S CHRISTMAS PLAY. Clive Robbins

2266   ______.
        MR. FORTUNE. 1937

2267   ______.
        THE THREE BEARS. Clive Robbins

2268   Norman, Ruth and Hardy Wieder
        THE GYPSIES' REWARD

2269   Nunn, Edward Cuthbert
        THE FAIRY SLIPPER

2270   ______.
        THE GARDEN OF PARADISE

2271   ______.
        KAMAR-AL-ZAMAN

2272   ______.
        THE SHEPHERDESS

2273   ______.
         THE WOODEN BOWL

2274   Obenchain, Virginia
         UNCLE BILLY'S CANDY SHOP

2275   Oberndorfer, Marx E.
         THE MAGIC MIRROR. Grace Hoffman White

2276   Odam, George
         ST. GEORGE AND THE DRAGON. Composer and Steuart
         Allin

2277   O'Gorman, Denis
         THE SHEPHERD'S STORY. Composer

2278   O'Hara, Geoffrey
         THE COUNT AND THE CO-ED

2279   ______.
         HARMONY HALL. Harry B. Smith

2280   ______.
         LITTLE WOMEN. John Ravold and Frederick Howard

2281   ______.
         PEGGY AND THE PIRATE. Geoffrey F. Morgan

2282   ______.
         THE PRINCESS RUNS AWAY. Harry B. Smith

2283   ______.
         RIDING DOWN THE SKY

2284   ______.
         THE SMILING SIXPENCE

2285   Oldham, Arthur
         THE LAND OF THE GREEN GINGER

Additional Operas

2286   Oldham, Arthur
        LOVE IN A VILLAGE. Aldeburgh. 1952

2287   Ostransky, Leroy
        THE MELTING OF MOLLY. 1974

2288   Owen, Richard
        DISMISSED WITHOUT PREJUDICE

2289   ______.
        THAT'S CULTURE. Ulm, Germany. 1969

2290   Papale, Henry
        THE BALLOON

2291   ______.
        THE NOSE

2292   ______.
        THE SHOVEL-TOOTHED WITCH

2293   Parris, Robert
        MAD SCENE. Composer

2294   Pascal, Floram
        IN WONDERLAND. Edith Wheeler

2295   Patterson, Franklin
        BEGGAR'S LOVE. 1918

2296   ______.
        CAPRICE

2297   ______.
        THE FOREST DWELLERS

2298   ______.
        MOUNTAIN BLOOD. 1925

2299   ______.
         THROUGH THE NARROW GATE

2300   Patterson, Pat
         THE DANDY LION.   Composer and Dodi Robb

2301   ______.
         THE POPCORN MAN.   Composer and Dodi Robb

2302   ______.
         RED RIDING HOOD.   Composer and Dodi Robb

2303   Paynter, John
         THE SPACE DRAGON OF GALATAR

2304   Penn, Arthur
         CAPTAIN CROSSBONES, OR THE PIRATES BRIDE.
         Composer

2305   ______.
         LADIES AID.   Milwaukee.   1955

2306   ______.
         THE LASS OF LIMERICK TOWN

2307   ______.
         MAM'ZELLE TAPS, OR, THE SILVER BUGLER.   Composer

2308   ______.
         YOKOHAMA MAID.   Composer

2309   "Penniless, David Michael"   [David Ayerst,
              Michael Tippett, and Ruth Pennyman]
         ROBIN HOOD.   1934

2310   Perry, Julia
         THE SELFISH GIANT.   Composer

Additional Operas

2311   Phillips, Burrill
         A LION BY THE TAIL

2312   Phillipus, Christian Louis
         NOTRE DAME.   Composer

2313   ______.
         RICHELIEU.   Composer

2314   Pickhardt, Ione
         MOIRA.   Philadelphia.   George Gibbs, Jr.

2315   Pimsleur, Solomon
         DIARY OF ANNE FRANK

2316   ______.
         REIGN OF TERROR

2317   Pinkham, Daniel
         THE GARDEN OF ARTEMIS, OR, APOLLO'S REVELS.
         Cambridge, Massachusetts.   1948.   Robert Hillyer

2318   Pisk, Paul
         SCHATTENSEITE

2319   Polgar, Tibor
         A EUROPEAN LOVER

2320   ______.
         THE GLOVE

2321   ______.
         THE TROUBLEMAKER

2322   Poston, Elizabeth
         THE BRIERY BUSH.   R. M. Crawford

2323   Potter, Edward C.
         ISHTAR.   Margaret Horton Potter

Additional Operas

2324   Pound, Ezra
        CAVALCANTI. Composer; written in Italian

2325   ______.
        COLLIS O HELICONII

2326   Poutney, David
        THE DONKEY. 1974. Stephen Oliver

2327   Powell, John
        JUDITH AND HOLOFERNES

2328   Presser, William
        THE BELGIAN DOLL. Tallahassee, Florida. Uni-
        versity of Florida. 1962

2329   Procter, Leland
        EVE OF CROSSING. Composer

2330   Randegger, G. Aldo
        THE PROMISE OF MEDEA. Henriette Brinker-
        Randegger

2331   Raphling, Sam
        JOHNNY PYE AND THE FOOL-KILLER

2332   ______.
        LIAR, LIAR

2333   ______.
        PRESIDENT LINCOLN

2334   Rapoport, Eda
        THE FISHERMAN AND HIS WIFE. Composer

2335   ______.
        G. I. JOE. 1945

Additional Operas

2336   Rasbach, Oscar
        DAWN BOY

2337   ______.
        OPEN HOUSE

2338   Ratner, Leonard
        THE NECKLACE.   Composer

2339   Ravosa, Carmino
        JOHNNY APPLESEED

2340   ______.
        PINOCCHIO.   Hartford, Connecticut.   Hartt
        College

2341   Read, Gardiner
        VILLON

2342   Reif, Paul
        CAMPAIGN.   Composer

2343   Reiser, Alois
        DAPHNE.   1945

2344   Repper, Charles
        THE COBBLER AND THE ELVES.   Bertha Elsmith

2345   Réti, Rudolf
        DAVID AND GOLIATH.   1935

2346   ______.
        IVAN AND THE DRUM

2347   Reynolds, Alfred
        FOUNTAIN OF YOUTH

2348   ______.
        LIONEL AND CLARISSA

2349   _____.
        LOVE IN A VILLAGE

2350   Rich, Gladys
        THE TOY-SHOP.   Phyllis McGinley

2351   Richter, Ada
        THE HARE AND THE TORTOISE

2352   _____.
        JACK AND THE BEANSTALK

2353   _____.
        THE LION AND THE MOUSE

2354   _____.
        THREE LITTLE PIGS

2355   Richter, Francis William
        THE GRAND NAZAR

2356   Ridley, Ursula
        SIX AND FOUR ARE TEN

2357   Rieti, Vittorio
        THE CLOCK.   Composer

2358   _____.
        MARYAM.   Composer and Claire Nichols

2359   Roberts, Jeremy Dale
        RECONCILIATION.   London.   Morley College.   1972

2360   Robertson, Hugh S.
        THE ATHEIST

2361   Robinson, Earl
        GIANTS IN THE LAND.   Joseph Moncure March

Additional Operas

2362   Robinson, Earl
        SANDHOG

2363   Robinson, Stanford
        THE SAVOYARDS

2364   Ronald, Sir Langdon
        A CAPITAL JOKE

2365   Rorem, Ned
        THE ANNIVERSARY

2366   Rosen, Lewis
        HESTER

2367   Roy, Klaus George
        THE EASTER GUEST

2368   Rubbra, Edmund
        BEE-BEE-BEI. 1933

2369   Ruggles, Carl
        THE SUNKEN BELL. Charles Henry Meltzer

2370   Russell, Robert
        END OF DAY

2371   ______.
        SO HOW DOES YOUR GARDEN GROW?

2372   Russo, John
        JOHN HOOTEN. Chicago. Chicago Public Schools.
        1966-1967

2373   Saminsky, Lazare
        THE DAUGHTER OF JEPHTA. 1929

2374   ______.
        JULIAN, THE APOSTATE CAESAR

Additional Operas

2375   Scarmolin, A. Louis
       THE CALIPH

2376   ______.
       THE MAGIC DRUM

2377   ______.
       THE OATH

2378   Schad, W. C.
       PLANGO. Islip, Long Island. 1938

2379   Schaeffer, Murray
       GITA. Lenox, Massachusetts. 1967

2380   Schaeffer, William
       THE NIGHTINGALE AND THE ROSE. Composer

2381   Schickele, Peter
       THE STONED GUEST: A HALF-ACT OPERA

2382   Schlein, Irving
       STACKLEE

2384   Schoenefeld, Henry
       ATALA, OR, THE LOVE OF TWO SAVAGES. Bernard
       McConville

2385   Schryock, Buren
       FLAVIA. Composer

2386   ______.
       MALENA AND NORDICO. Composer

2387   ______.
       MARY AND JOHN. 1948. Composer

2388   ______.
       NANCY AND ARTHUR. 1951. Composer

Additional Operas

2389   Schryock, Buren
        TANSHE AND SANCHI. 1955. Composer

2390   Scott, Tom
        THE FISHERMAN. 1956

2391   Seymour, John Laurence
        THE AFFECTED MAIDS

2392   _____.
        ANTIGONE

2393   _____.
        THE BACHELOR BELLES

2394   _____.
        THE DEVIL AND TOM WALKER. H. C. Tracy

2395   _____.
        GOLDEN DAYS

2396   _____.
        HOLLYWOOD MADNESS

2397   _____.
        THE PROTÉGÉE OF THE MISTRESS

2398   _____.
        THE SNAKE WOMAN

2399   Shaw, Francis
        THE SELFISH GIANT. Caerphilly Castle, Wales.
        1972. Michael Finch

2400   Shelley, Harry Rowe
        LEILA

2401   _____.
        LOTUS SAN

2402   ______.
        ROMEO AND JULIET

2403   Shields, Alice
        ODYSSEY. Composer and John Dowland

2404   Siegmeister, Elie
        DARLING CORIE

2405   Silver, Alfred
        A SLAVE IN ARABY

2406   Silverman, Faye-Ellen
        THE MIRACLE OF NEMIROV. Composer

2407   Silverman, Stanley
        A MIDSUMMER NIGHT'S DREAM

2408   ______.
        UP FROM PARADISE. Ann Arbor, Michigan. Uni-
        versity of Michigan. 1974

2409   Simeone, Harry
        THE EMPEROR'S NEW CLOTHES. New York. 1956.
        Jay Johnson

2410   Simon, Netty
        THE BELL WITCH OF TENNESSEE. Joan Simon

2411   Singer, Andre
        ALCOTTIANG

2412   Skilton, Charles Sanford
        THE DAY OF GAYOMAIR

2413   ______.
        KALOPIN. 1927

Additional Operas

2414   Slade, Julian
         SALAD DAYS

2415   Slater, Walter L.
         JAEL

2416   Slaughter, Walter
         LADY TATTERS. London. 1907. Herbert Leonard
         and Roland Carse

2417   Sloane, Alfred Baldwin
         THE MOCKING BIRD. Sydney Rosenfeld

2418   _____.
         SARGEANT KITTY. R. H. Burnside

2419   Smit, Leo
         THE ALCHEMY OF LOVE. Fred Hoyle

2420   Smith, David Stanley
         MERRYMOUNT. Lee Wilson Dodd

2421   Smith, Hale
         BLOOD WEDDING. Cleveland. 1953

2422   Smith, Leland
         SANTA CLAUS, A MORALITY. 1955

2423   Smith, Zelma
         THE GALLANT TAILOR. Edith Rothrock

2424   Smith-Masters, Anthony
         THE PIED PIPER

2425   Smolanoff, Michael
         VERCINTEGORIX. Frank Quilkin

2426   Sokoloff, Noel
         THE PARDONER'S TALE. Ted Hart

Additional Operas

2427   Somers, Harry
THE FOOL. Toronto. 1956

2428   Sousa, John Phillip
THE AMERICAN MAID. 1913

2429   _____.
THE CHARLATON. New York

2430   _____.
CHRIS AND THE WONDERFUL LAMP. 1900

2431   _____.
THE GLASS BLOWERS. 1911

2432   _____.
VICTORY. 1913

2433   Spaulding, V. M.
YANKI SAN

2434   Spelman, Timothy Mather
THE COURTSHIP OF MILES STANDISH

2435   _____.
LA MAGNIFICA. 1920. Leolyn Louise Everett

2436   _____.
THE SEA ROVERS. 1928

2437   _____.
THE SUNKEN CITY. 1930. Composer

2438   Sprenger, Cyril H. and M. Attley
SNOW WHITE AND THE SEVEN DWARFS. Composer

2439   Stanford, Charles Villiers
THE MARRIAGE OF HERO. Julian R. Sturgis

Additional Operas

2440   Stanford, Charles Villiers
THE MINER OF FALUN. W. Barclay Squire and
H. F. Wilson

2441   Stein, Leon
DEIRDRE

2442   Stenberg, Jordan
THE CLOCK STRUCK ONE. 1970

2443   ______.
MIND OVER MATTER. 1969

2444   Stern, Arthur
A RARE BIRD, OR, LOVE WINS OUT. Composer

2445   Stewart, Humphrey J.
THE CONSPIRATORS. San Francisco. 1906. Clay M.
Green

2446   ______.
KING HAL. San Francisco. 1911. Daniel O'Connor

2447   Still, William Grant
BLUE STEEL. Carlton Moss and Bruce Forsythe

2448   ______.
COSTASO. Verna Avery

2449   ______.
MINETTE FONTAINE. Verna Avery

2450   ______.
MOTA. Verna Avery

2451   ______.
THE PILLAR. Verna Avery

Additional Operas

2452   ______.
        A SOUTHERN INTERLUDE. Verna Avery

2453   Stoughton, Roy Spaulding
        MOUNT VERNON. Frederick H. Martens

2454   ______.
        THE PRINCE OF MARTINIQUE. Frederick H. Martens

2455   Stringfield, Lamar
        CAROLINA CHARCOAL. 1952

2456   ______.
        THE MOUNTAIN SONG. 1931

2457   Strouse, Charles
        THE COSY. Williamsburg, Virginia. 1954. Lee
        Adams

2458   Stuart, Leslie
        THE SLIM PRINCESS. Henry Blossom

2459   Sweet, Reginald
        RIDERS TO THE SEA

2460   Sydeman, William
        FULL CIRCLE. New York. 1971. Composer

2461   ______.
        MALEDICTION. New York. 1970. Composer

2462   Symonds, Norman
        THE SPIRIT OF FUNDY. Ontario. 1972

2463   Tate, Phyllis
        A PRIDE OF LIONS. Ian Serraillien

2464   ______.
        TWICE IN A BLUE MOON

Additional Operas

2465 Tavener, John
   THE WHALE. Composer

2466 Thomas, Vincent
   A TALE OF ALSATIA

2467 Thompson, Randall
   THE NATIVITY ACCORDING TO ST. LUKE

2468 Tippett, Michael
   LOVE IN A VILLAGE

2469 ______.
   ROBERT OF SICILY. 1938. Christopher Fry

2470 ______.
   SEVEN AT ONE STROKE. 1939. Christopher Fry

2471 Toch, Ernst
   THE LAST TALE. Melchior Lengyel

2472 Townsend, Peter
   TOMMY

2473 Tracy, George Lowell
   THE MAID AND THE MIDDY. David Stevens

2474 Tregillus, H. G.
   GASPARILLA

2475 ______.
   GOOD QUEEN BESS

2476 Treharne, Bryceson
   THE MAGI'S GIFT

2477 Trimble, Lester
   THE NIGHTINGALE. George M. Ross

Additional Operas

2478   Trythall, Gilbert
        THE MUSIC LESSON

2479   Turner, Robert C.
        THE BRIDESHIP. Vancouver. 1967. George
        Woodstock

2480   Twombly, Mary Lynn
        THE LITTLE MATCH GIRL

2481   Vander, Judith
        THE SNOW QUEEN

2482   Vaughan Williams, Ralph
        ON CHRISTMAS NIGHT. A. Bolm

2483   Venth, Carl
        ALEXANDER'S HORSE. Composer

2484   ______.
        CATHAL

2485   ______.
        DOLLS. Composer

2486   ______.
        JACK

2487   ______.
        THE JUGGLER. Composer

2488   ______.
        LIMA BEANS. Composer

2489   ______.
        THE SUN GOD

2490   Victory, Gerald
        NITA. 1944

Additional Operas

2491   Victory, Gerard
        ONCE UPON A MOON. 1949

2492   Vincent, Henry Betheul
        ESPERANZA. Washington. 1906

2493   ______.
        INDIAN DAYS

2494   Waddington, Louis Van
        WHIMLAND

2495   Wagner, Thomas
        THE BEGGAR

2496   Wald, Max
        GAY LITTLE WORLD. 1942

2497   ______.
        MIRANDOLINA. 1936

2498   Wales, Evelyn
        LITTLE GYPSY BOY. Milwaukee. 1955

2499   Walker, Raymond
        THE GOLDEN FLUTE

2500   ______.
        TURKISH DELIGHT

2501   Wallace, Maude
        RODDY RIDDLE FROM MARS

2502   Walsh, Helen Mary
        DANIEL IN THE LION'S DEN

2503   Ward, Arthur Edward
        NORWEGIAN NIGHTS

Additional Operas

2504   Ward-Steinman, David
        THE TALE OF ISSOUMBOCHI

2505   ______.
        TAMAR. William Adams

2506   Ware, Harriet
        WALTZ FOR THREE

2507   Warren, Mel
        DANNY, THE DARK GREEN DINOSAUR

2508   ______.
        DAVID AND GOLIATH

2509   Webb, Roy D.
        THE FORBIDDEN CITY. 1913

2510   Webber, Andrew Lloyd
        JESUS CHRIST SUPERSTAR. Composer and Tim Rice

2511   Wehner, George
        THE HEAVENLY PARTY. Composer

2512   ______.
        PRAIRIE PEACE DAY

2513   Weigel, Eugene
        THE LION MAKERS. 1953

2514   Weil, Oscar
        THE SEVEN OLD LADIES OF LAVENDER TOWN

2515   Weinberg, Jacob
        THE PIONEERS. Composer

2516   Weisgall, Hugo
        HENRY IV

Additional Operas

2517   Weisgall, Hugo
        LILITH

2518   ______.
        NIGHT. 1934

2519   Weiss, Adolph
        THE LIBATION BEARERS

2520   Werder, Felix
        AGAMEMNON. Composer

2521   ______.
        THE GENERAL. Leonard Radic

2522   ______.
        KISSES FOR A QUID. Melbourne. 1956.
        A. Marshall

2523   ______.
        PRIVATE. P. Rorke

2524   Whitely, Bessie M.
        HIAWATHA'S CHILDHOOD. Composer

2525   Wicker, Irene
        ABRAHAM LINCOLN THE BOY

2526   ______.
        GEORGE WASHINGTON THE BOY. Composer and Beatrice
        Faber

2527   ______.
        HAIL NEW WORLD, OR, TOBACCO BRIDE

2528   ______.
        LOOK AND LONG

2529   Wiley, Bob
        A BONE OF CONTENTION

2530   Willan, Healey
        DEIRDRE. John Coulter

2531   Williams, John Gerrard
        KATE, THE CABIN BOY. London. 1924

2532   ______.
        SWEET WINTER

2533   Williams, Joseph
        THE FAIRY MAIDEN

2534   Williamson, Malcolm
        ANIMAL CAPERS

2535   ______.
        GENESIS

2536   ______.
        RED SEA. Composer

2537   ______.
        WINTER STAR

2538   Wilson, Don
        THE MODEL BRIDE

2539   Wilson, Stanley
        MIDAS. Gladys Mathew

2540   Windsor, Helen J.
        THE ADVENTURES OF THUMBELINA

2541   ______.
        THE EMPEROR'S NIGHTINGALE

Additional Operas

2542   Winslow, Richard
         ADELAIDE. Middleton, Connecticut. Wesleyan
         University. 1957

2543   Witni, M.
         THE DARK OF SUMMER

2544   Wolfe, Jacques
         JOHN HENRY

2545   Yeamans, Laurel Everett
         IN ROBOT LAND. Composer

2546   Zador, Eugene
         FOREVER REMBRANDT

2547   Zaninelli, Luigi
         SPEAK UP! Trenton, New Jersey. 1963. Composer

2548   Zech, Frederick
         LA PALOMA. Mrs. M. Fairweather

2549   ———.
         WA-KIN-YON, OR, THE PASSING OF THE RED MAN.
         Mrs. M. Fairweather

2550   Zeckwer, Richard
         JANE AND JANETTA

2551   ZEISL, Eric
         JOB

2552   Ziffrin, Marilyn
         CAPTAIN KIDD. Composer

2553   Zur, Menachem
         THE AFFAIRS. New York. Mannes College of Music.
         1970. Composer

III. APPENDIX

A. OPERAS BASED ON LITERARY WORKS

This is an alphabetical list by opera title
of those operas which are known to be based on
literary works. Only those operas which are
definitely known to originate from literary works
are included. Title congruence has not been
considered as sufficient criteria for listing
works in this Appendix. The format for entries
in this section is:

OPERA TITLE (Composer's last name)
Author of the literary work. Title of work

When the title of the opera and the literary
work are exactly the same, "Same" is written in
the space for the title of the literary work.
When the author of the literary work is unknown,
but the title of the work is not, the title
space is blank.

A1   THE ADVENTURES OF THUMBELINA (Windsor)
     Hans Christian Anderson

A2   THE AFFECTED MAIDS (Seymour)
     Molière. <u>Les Précieuses Ridicules</u>

A3   AGINCOURT (Boughton)
     William Shakespeare

A4   AIR RAID (Laderman)
     Archibald MacLeish. Same

Literary Works

A5   ALICE (Winslow)
Lewis Carroll. <u>Alice's Adventures in Wonderland</u>

A6   ALICE IN WONDERLAND (DuPage)
Lewis Carroll. <u>Alice's Adventures in Wonderland</u>

A7   ALKESTIS (Boughton)
Euripedes. Same; Gilbert Murray's translation

A8   ALL'S WELL THAT ENDS WELL (Castelnuovo-Tedesco)
William Shakespeare. Same

A9   AMERIKA (Kohs)
Franz Kafka. Same

A10   THE AMOROUS JUDGE (Gross)
Heinrich von Kleist. <u>Zerbrochene Krug</u>

A11   ANNE OF GREEN GABLES (Campbell)
L. M. Montgomery

A12   ANTONY AND CLEOPATRA (Barber)
William Shakespeare. Same

A13   ARIA DA CAPO (Baska)
Edna St. Vincent Millay. Same

A14   ARIA DA CAPO (Blank)
Edna St. Vincent Millay. Same

A15   AT THE BOAR'S HEAD (Holst)
William Shakespeare. <u>Henry IV</u>

A16   ATALA, OR THE LOVE OF TWO SAVAGES (Schoenfeld)
François-Rene de Chateaubriand. <u>Atala</u>

A17   ATHALIAH (Weisgall)
Jean Racine. <u>Athalie</u>

Literary Works

A18   THE BALD PRIMA DONNA (Kalmanoff)
       Eugène Ionesco. La cantatrice chauve

A19   BARNSTABLE (OR SOMEONE IN THE ATTIC) (Burt)
       James Saunders. Same

A20   BEACH OF FALSEA (Hoddinott)
       Robert Louis Stevenson

A21   THE BEAR (Walton)
       Anton Chekov

A22   THE BEAUTY AND THE BEAST (Murray)
       ? Beaumont

A23   THE BELL-TOWER (Krenek)
       Herman Melville. Same

A24   BERTHA (Rorem)
       Kenneth Koch. Same

A25   BETHLEHEM (Boughton)
       Anonymous. The Coventry Nativity Play

A26   BILLY BUDD (Britten)
       Herman Melville. Same

A27   THE BIRDS (Maconchy)
       Aristophanes. Same

A28   BLACK WIDOW (Pasatieri)
       Miguel de Unamuno. Dos Madres

A29   BLIND MAN'S BLUFF (P. M. Davies)
       Georg Büchner. Leonce und Lena

A30   BLOOD WEDDING (H. Smith)
       Federico Garcia Lorca. Bodas de sange

Literary Works

A31   BOATSWAIN'S MATE (Smyth)
        W. W. Jacobs

A32   THE BOOR (U. Kay)
        Anton Chekov

A33   THE BOOR (Bucci)
        Anton Chekov

A34   THE BROKEN PITCHER. (E. Gross)
        Heinrich von Kleist

A35   THE BRUTE (L. Moss)
        Anton Chekov

A36   CALANDRINO (Bimboni)
        Boccaccio

A37   CALVARY (Pasatieri)
        William Butler Yeats. Same

A38   CAMILLE (Forrest)
        Alexandre Dumas (fils). La dame aux camélias

A39   CANTERVILLE GHOST (Kalmanoff)
        Oscar Wilde. Same

A40   CAPONSACCHI (Hageman)
        Robert Browning. The Ring and the Book

A41   CAPTAIN LOVELOCK (J. Duke)
        Ludvig Holberg. Changed Bridegroom

A42   CARRION CROW (Fletcher)
        John Jacob Niles

A43   THE CASK OF AMONTILLADO (Hamm)
        Edgar Allan Poe. Same

Literary Works

A44   THE CAT AND THE MOON (Putsché)
       William Butler Yeats. Same

A45   THE CATILINE CONSPIRACY (I. Hamilton)
       Cicero

A46   CAUCASIAN CHALK CIRCLE (M. Fink)
       Bertolt Brecht. Der kaukasische Kreidekreis

A47   THE CENCI (Coke)
       Percy Bysshe Shelley. Same

A48   THE CHAPEL IN LYONESSE (Boughton)
       William Morris

A49   THE CHILD (Bernardo)
       José Marti

A50   A CHILDHOOD MIRACLE (Rorem)
       Nathaniel Hawthorne. The Snow Image

A51   A CHRISTMAS CAROL (Samuel)
       Charles Dickens. Same

A52   A CHRISTMAS TALE (Freer)
       Maurice Boucher. Same

A53   CHRISTOPHER SLY (Argento)
       William Shakespeare. The Taming of the Shrew

A54   CLEOPATRA (P. Allen)
       Victorien Sardou

A55   CLEOPATRA'S NIGHT (Hadley)
       Théophile Gautier

A56   THE COMMITTEE (Doran)
       Marcel Ayme

Literary Works

A57   CRESSIDA (MacDermott)
William Shakespeare. Troilous and Cressida

A58   THE CRITIC, OR AN OPERA REHEARSED (Stanford)
Richard Brinsley Sheridan. The Critic

A59   THE CROCODILE (T. Wagner)
Fyodor Dostoyevsky

A60   THE CRUCIBLE (R. Ward)
Arthur Miller. Same

A61   CYRANO (Damrosch)
Edmond Rostand. Cyrano de Bergerac

A62   CYRANO DE BERGERAC (Jarrett)
Edmond Rostand. Same

A63   CYRANO DE BERGERAC (Effinger)
Edmond Rostand. Same

A64   DAMASK DRUM (D. Gordon)
Fifteenth century Noh drama

A65   DARK SONNET (Chisholm)
Eugene O'Neill. Before Breakfast

A66   DAVID GARRICK (Somerville)
T. W. Robertson

A67   DEATH IN DECEMBER (Barab)
Stanley Ellin. "Death on Christmas Eve"

A68   DEATH IN VENICE (Britten)
Thomas Mann. Same

A69   THE DEATH OF TINTAGILES (Collingwood)
Maurice Maeterlinck. La mort de Tintagiles

A70   THE DEATH OF TINTAGILES (Isaacs)
      Maurice Maeterlinck. La mort de Tintagiles

A71   DEIRDE (L. Stein)
      William Butler Yeats. Same

A72   THE DEVIL AND DANIEL WEBSTER (D. Moore)
      Stephen Vincent Benét. Same

A73   THE DEVIL AND TOM WALKER (Seymour)
      Washington Irving. Same

A74   DISAPPEARING ACT (Cox)
      Alfred Bester

A75   DOCTOR JEKYLL AND MR. HYDE (Depue)
      Robert Louis Stevenson. Same

A76   DON JUAN DE MAÑARA (Goosens)
      Arnold Bennett. Same

A77   DON PERLIMPLIN (Rieti)
      Federico Garcia Lorca

A78   DONA ROSITA (Hackett)
      Federico Garcia Lorca. Los Titeres de
          Catchiporra

A79   THE DOOR (Mopper)
      Robert Louis Stevenson. "The Sire de Maletroit's
      Door"

A80   DORIAN GRAY (Flick-Stegner)
      Oscar Wilde. Same

A81   DOUBLE-TROUBLE (Mohaupt)
      Plautus

Literary Works

A82   DR. HEIDEGGER'S EXPERIMENT (Raphling)
       Nathaniel Hawthorne. Same

A83   DR. JEKYLL AND MR. HYDE (Fragale)
       Robert Louis Stevenson. Same

A84   THE DUMB WIFE (Gruenberg)
       Anatole France

A85   THE EMPEROR CLOTHED ANEW (Jenni)
       Hans Christian Anderson

A86   THE EMPEROR JONES (Gruenberg)
       Eugene O'Neill. Same

A87   THE EMPEROR'S NEW CLOTHES (Gingold)
       Hans Christian Anderson

A88   THE EMPEROR'S NEW CLOTHES (D. Moore)
       Hans Christian Anderson

A89   THE EMPEROR'S NEW CLOTHES (Simeone)
       Hans Christian Anderson

A90   THE EMPEROR'S NEW CLOTHES (R. Wood)
       Hans Christian Anderson

A91   THE EMPEROR'S NIGHTINGALE (Windsor)
       Hans Christian Anderson

A92   ENDGAME (Winslow)
       Samuel Beckett. Same

A93   ENGLISH ECCENTRICS (Williamson)
       Edith Sitwell. Same

A94   ESCORIAL (Levy)
       Michel de Ghelerode. Same; Lionel Abel
           translation

A95   EVENTIDE (Fennimore)
        James Purdy

A96   THE EXPERIMENT (P. Schwartz)
        Nathaniel Hawthorne. "Dr. Heidegger's Experiment"

A97   FABLES (Rorem)
        Jean de la Fontaine. Same; Marianne Moore
            translation

A98   THE FALL OF ROME (H. Moore)
        Wilkie Collins

A99   THE FALL OF THE CITY (Cohn)
        Archibald MacLeish. Same

A100   THE FALL OF THE HOUSE OF USHER (Claflin)
        Edgar Allan Poe. Same

A101   THE FALL OF THE HOUSE OF USHER (Klauss)
        Edgar Allan Poe. Same

A102   THE FALL OF THE HOUSE OF USHER (Loomis)
        Edgar Allan Poe. Same

A103   THE FALL OF THE HOUSE OF USHER (Sitsky)
        Edgar Allan Poe. Same

A104   THE FALL OF THE HOUSE OF USHER (Ruger)
        Edgar Allan Poe. Same

A105   THE FATAL OATH (Koutzen)
        Honoré de Balzac. "La Grande Bretèche"

A106   FENNIMORE UND GERDA (Delius)
        J. P. Jacobsen

A107   THE FISHERMAN (T. Scott)
        Oscar Wilde

Literary Works

A108   THE FISHERMAN AND HIS WIFE (Rapoport)
        Brothers Grimm

A109   THE FISHERMAN AND HIS WIFE (Schuller)
        Brothers Grimm

A110   THE FISHERMAN'S WIFE (L. Stein)
        Brothers Grimm

A111   FOUR READINGS FROM MARLOWE'S 'DR.'FAUSTUS'
        (Nelhybel)
            Christopher Marlowe. Same

A112   THE FRANKLIN'S TALE (Sokoloff)
        Geoffrey Chaucer. Same

A113   FULL CIRCLE (R. Orr)
        Sydney Goodsir-Smith. The Stick-Up

A114   GAGLIARDA OF A MERRY PLAGUE (Saminsky)
        Edgar Allen Poe. "The Masque of the Red Death"

A115   THE GALLANT TAILOR (Z. Smith)
        Brothers Grimm

A116   A GAME OF CHANCE (Barab)
        Ryerson and Clements. All on a Summer's Day

A117   THE GARDEN OF MYSTERY (Cadman)
        Nathaniel Hawthorne. "Rappacini's Daughter"

A118   THE GIANT'S GARDEN (Krane)
        Oscar Wilde

A119   GIANTS IN THE EARTH (D. Moore)
        O. E. Rølvaag. Same

A120   THE GIFT OF THE MAGI (Gillis)
        O. Henry. Same

A121   THE GLITTERING GATE (Glanville-Hicks)
         Lord Dunsany. Same

A122   GLORIANA (Britten)
         Lytton Strachey. Elizabeth and Essex

A123   GOODMAN BROWN (H. Fink)
         Nathaniel Hawthrone. "Young Goodman Brown"

A124   LA GRANDE BRETECHE (Claflin)
         Honoré de Balzac. Same

A125   LA GRANDE BRETECHE (Hollingsworth)
         Honoré de Balzac. Same

A126   THE GREAT STONE FACE (Kalmanoff)
         Nathaniel Hawthorne. Same

A127   GREEN MANSIONS (Gruenberg)
         W. H. Hudson. Same

A128   GREYSTEEL, OR THE BEARSARKS COME TO SURNADALE
         (N. Gatty)
             Saga of Gisli, the Soursop. G. W. Dasent
             translation

A129   THE GROWING CASTLE (Williamson)
         August Strindberg. Ett drömspel

A130   GUIDO FERRANTI (Etten)
         Oscar Wilde. The Duchess of Padua

A131   THE HAIRCUT (Morgenstern)
         Ring Lardner. Same

A132   HAMLET (Kagen)
         William Shakespeare. Same

Literary Works

A133   HAMLET (Searle)
        William Shakespeare.   Same

A134   THE HAPPY PRINCE (W. Fisher)
        Oscar Wilde.   Same

A135   THE HAPPY PRINCE (Raines)
        Oscar Wilde.   Same

A136   THE HAPPY PRINCE (Williamson)
        Oscar Wilde.   Same

A137   THE HAWKEYES SENTINEL (Drummond)
        Miguel de Cervantes Saavedra

A138   THE HEADLESS HORSEMAN (D. Moore)
        Washington Irving.   "The Legend of Sleepy Hollow"

A139   HELEN IN EGYPT (Elkus)
        H. D.   Same

A140   HELLO OUT THERE (Beeson)
        William Saroyan.   Same

A141   HELOISE AND ABELARD (C. Wilson)
        Eugene Benson.   Same

A142   HENRY IV (Weisgall)
        Luigi Pirandello.   Same

A143   HESTER (Rosen)
        Nathaniel Hawthorne.   The Scarlet Letter

A144   HESTER, OR THE SCARLET LETTER (Carlson)
        Nathaniel Hawthorne.   The Scarlet Letter

A145   HESTER PRYNNE (Claflin)
        Nathaniel Hawthorne.   The Scarlet Letter

A146   HOSKI-SAN (Leps)
        John Luther Long.   "Andon"

A147   HUCKLEBERRY FINN (Overton)
        Mark Twain.   Same

A148   THE HUNTING OF THE SNARK (Laderman)
        Lewis Carroll.   Same

A149   THE HUNTING OF THE SNARK (E. Roberts)
        Lewis Carroll.   Same

A150   IDIOTS FIRST (Blitzstein)
        Bernard Malamud

A151   IF THE CAP FITS (G. Bush)
        Molière. Les Précieuses Ridicules

A152   IL FILTRO (P. H. Allen)
        L. Capuana

A153   'ILE (Laufer)
        Eugene O'Neill.   Same

A154   THE IMMORTAL HOUR (Boughton)
        "Fiona Macleod" [William Sharp].   (Various works)

A155   THE IMPORTANCE OF BEING EARNEST (Castelnuovo-
        Tedesco)
            Oscar Wilde. Same

A156   IN A GARDEN (Kupferman)
        Gertrude Stein.   Same

A157   IN PASHA'S GARDEN (Seymour)
        Harrison Griswold Dwight

A158   IN WONDERLAND (Pascal)
        Lewis Carroll. Alice's Adventures in Wonderland

Literary Works

A159   INCIDENT AT OWL CREEK (Whelen)
        Ambrose Bierce.   "An Occurrence at Owl Creek
           Bridge"

A160   ISHTAR (Potter)
        Margaret Horton Potter.   Ishtar of Babylon

A161   IVAN AND THE DRUM (Réti)
        Leo Tolstoy

A162   JERICHO ROAD (Aria)
        Isabel Harris Barr.   Same

A163   JOAN OF ARC (Leginska)
        Mark Twain

A164   JOE HILL (A. D. Bush)
        Barrie Stavis.   The Man Who Never Died

A165   THE JUGGLER OF OUR LADY (U. Kay)
        Anatole France

A166   THE JUMPING FROG OF CALAVERAS COUNTY (Foss)
        Mark Twain.   "The Notorious Jumping Frog of
           Calaveras County"

A167   KARLA (Lehrman)
        Bernard Malamud.   Same

A168   THE KING'S BREAKFAST (Barthelson)
        Maurice Barring.   Catherine Parr

A169   KNICKERBOCKER HOLIDAY (Weill)
        Washington Irving.   A History of New York by
           Diedrich Knickerbocker

A170   THE LAND BETWEEN THE RIVERS (Van Buskirk)
        Robert Penn Warren.   "The Ballad of Billy Potts"

A171   THE LAST PUPPET (Strilko)
Grace Dorcas Ruthenburg. Same

A172   THE LEGEND OF SLEEPY HOLLOW (Lora)
Washington Irving. Same

A173   THE LEGEND OF SLEEPY HOLLOW (J. D. White)
Washington Irving. Same

A174   THE LEGEND OF THE PIPER (Freer)
Robert Browning. "The Pied Piper of Hamelin"

A175   A LETTER TO EMILY (Johnson, L.)
Robert Hupton. Consider the Lilies

A176   THE LIB: 393 B.C. (Kirk)
Aristophanes. Lysistrata

A177   A LIGHT FROM ST. AGNES (Harling)
Minnie Fisk. Same

A178   LILITH (Taff)
George McDonald. Same

A179   LITTLE MOON OF ALBAN (Ferris)
James Costigan. Same

A180   THE LODGER (Tate)
Mrs. Belloc-Lowndes. Jack, the Ripper

A181   THE LONG CHRISTMAS DINNER (Hindemith)
Thornton Wilder. Same

A182   LOOK AND LONG (M. Schwartz)
Gertrude Stein. Same

A183   LORD ARTHUR SAVILE'S CRIMES (G. Bush)
Oscar Wilde. Same

Literary Works

A184   LORD BYRON'S LOVE LETTER (DeBanfield)
Tennessee Williams.   Same

A185   LOVE'S LABOR LOST (Nabokov)
William Shakespeare.   Same

A186   THE LUCK OF GINGER COFFEY (Pannell)
Brian Moore.   Same

A187   LUCKY PETER'S JOURNEY (Williamson)
August Strindberg.   Ett drömspel

A188   MACBETH (Collingwood)
William Shakespeare.   Same

A189   MACBETH (Gatty)
William Shakespeare.   Same

A190   MACBETH (Halpern)
William Shakespeare.   Same

A191   A MADCAP PRINCESS (Engländer)
Charles Major.   When Knighthood Was in Flower

A192   THE MAGIC BARREL (Blitzstein)
Bernard Malamud.   Same

A193   THE MAGIC MIRROR (Oberndorfer)
Hans Christian Anderson

A194   MALEDICTION (Sydeman)
Laurence Sterne.   Tristram Shandy

A195   MANY MOONS (Dougherty)
James Thurber

A196   MARKHEIM (Floyd)
Robert Louis Stevenson.   Same

A197   MARKHEIM (Miles)
         Robert Louis Stevenson. Same

A198   MARRIAGE PROPOSAL (Murray)
         Anton Chekov

A199   THE MARTYRED (Wade)
         Richard E. Kim and Kim Ki-Pal

A200   THE MASQUE OF PANDORA (Freer)
         Henry Wadsworth Longfellow

A201   MAURYA (Kosteck)
         John Millington Synge. Riders to the Sea

A202   THE MAYOR OF CASTERBRIDGE (Tranchell)
         Thomas Hardy. Same

A203   MEDEA (Elkus)
         Euripedes. Same

A204   MEDEA (Henderson)
         Robinson Jeffers. Same

A205   A MEDICINE FOR MELANCHOLY (Underwood)
         Ray Bradbury

A206   THE MERCHANT OF VENICE (Carlson)
         William Shakespeare. Same

A207   THE MERCHANT OF VENICE (Castelnuovo-Tedesco)
         William Shakespeare. Same

A208   MERRY MOUNT (Hanson)
         Nathaniel Hawthorne. "The Maypole of Merrymount."
            Michael Wigglesworth. "The Day of Doom."
            Cotton Mather. Wonders of the Invisible
            World and Magnalis Christi Americana. King
            James Bible. Thomas Morton (?) Sports and
            Pastimes of the English People

Literary Works

A209   MERRYMOUNT (D. A. Smith)
Nathaniel Hawthorne. "The Maypole of Merrymount"

A210   METAMORPHOSIS (M. White)
Franz Kafka. Same

A211   A MIDSUMMER NIGHT'S DREAM (Britten and Pears)
William Shakespeare. Same

A212   A MIDSUMMER NIGHT'S DREAM (Silverman)
William Shakespeare. Same

A213   MISS JULIE (Rorem)
August Strindberg. Same

A214   MISTRESS INTO MAID (Duke)
Alexandr Pushkin

A215   MOBY DICK (Low)
Herman Melville. Same

A216   THE MONKEY'S PAW (Combs)
William Jacobs. Same

A217   MONTEZUMA (Sessions)
Bernal Diaz. <u>True History of the Conquest of Mexico</u>

A218   THE MOON AND SIXPENCE (Gardner)
Somerset Maugham. Same

A219   MORALS A LA MODE (R. Stewart)
Simon Raven

A220   THE MOTHER (Hollingsworth)
Hans Christian Anderson

A221   THE MOTHER (J. Wood)
Hans Christian Anderson

Literary Works

A222   MOURNING BECOMES ELECTRA (Levy)
        Eugene O'Neill.   Same

A223   MR. AND MRS. DISCOBBOLOS (Westergaard)
        Edward Eager.   Same

A224   MUCH ADO ABOUT NOTHING (Stanford)
        William Shakespeare.   Same

A225   MY HEART'S IN THE HIGHLANDS (Beeson)
        William Saroyan.   Same

A226   MYSHKIN (Eaton)
        Fyodor Dostoyevsky.   The Idiot

A227   NATALIA PETROVNA (Hoiby)
        Ivan Turgenev.   A Month in the Country

A228   NAUSICAA (Glanville-Hicks)
        Robert Graves.   Homer's Daughter

A229   THE NECKLACE (Ratner)
        Guy de Maupassant

A230   NELSON (Berkeley)
        C. Oman.   Life of Nelson

A231   NEW ENGLAND SAMPLER (J. Wagner)
        Anton Chekov.   "The Proposal"

A232   A NEW WORLD FOR NELLIE (DuPage)
        R. Emmett

A233   THE NIGHTINGALE (Clokey)
        Hans Christian Anderson

A234   THE NIGHTINGALE (Rogers)
        Hans Christian Anderson

Literary Works

A235   THE NIGHTINGALE AND THE ROSE (Lessner)
        Oscar Wilde.   Same

A236   THE NIGHTINGALE AND THE ROSE (Schaeffer, W.)
        Oscar Wilde.   Same

A237   NINE RIVERS FROM JORDAN (Weisgall)
        Dennis Johnston.   Same

A238   NO TIME FOR FUNERALS (Tom Hammond)
        Guy de Maupassant.   "The Old Man"

A239   THE NOSE (Papale)
        Nikolay Gogol.   Same

A240   NOTES FROM A LADY AT A DINNER PARTY (Lehrman)
        Bernard Malamud

A241   NOTRE DAME (Phillipus)
        Victor Hugo.   Notre-Dame de Paris

A242   OF MICE AND MEN (Floyd)
        John Steinbeck.   Same; play version

A243   OLAF (Kirkpatrick)
        Louise Cox.   Same

A244   ON CHRISTMAS NIGHT (Vaughan Williams)
        Charles Dickens.   A Christmas Carol

A245   ONCE UPON A CHRISTMAS (Hatch)
        Leo Tolstoy.   "Where Love Is, God Is Also"

A246   ONE CHRISTMAS LONG AGO (W. Mayer)
        MacDonald Alden.   "Why the Chimes Ring"

A247   THE OPEN WINDOW (Arnold)
        Saki

A248   THE OTHER WISE MAN (Van Grove)
        Henry Van Dyke

A249   OUR AMERICAN COUSIN (Clokey)
        Tom Taylor.   Same

A250   THE OUTCASTS OF POKER FLAT (Adler)
        Bret Harte.   Same

A251   THE OUTCASTS OF POKER FLAT (Beckler)
        Bret Harte.   Same

A252   THE OUTCASTS OF POKER FLAT (Elkus)
        Bret Harte.   Same

A253   OWEN WINGRAVE (Britten)
        Henry James.   Same

A254   PANTAGLEIZE (Starer)
        Michel de Ghelerode.   Same

A255   PANTALOON (R. Ward)
        Leonid Adnreyev

A256   THE PARDONER'S TALE (John Davis)
        Geoffrey Chaucer.   Same

A257   THE PARDONER'S TALE (Lubin)
        Geoffrey Chaucer.   Same

A258   THE PARDONER'S TALE (Ridout)
        Geoffrey Chaucer.   Same

A259   THE PARDONER'S TALE (Sokoloff)
        Geoffrey Chaucer.   Same

A260   THE PARLOUR (Grace Williams)
        Guy de Maupassant.   "En famille"

Literary Works

A261   THE PEARL (D. Crawford)
          John Steinbeck. Same

A262   A PENNY FOR A SONG (Richard Rodney Bennett)
          John Whiting

A263   PERELANDRA (Swann)
          C. S. Lewis. Same

A264   PETER GRIMES (Britten)
          George Crabbe. "The Borough"

A265   PETER IBBETSON (D. Taylor)
          George DuMaurier. Same

A266   PHELIAS (Carlson)
          Stephen Phillips. "Iola"

A267   PHOTOGRAPH--1920 (Kalmanoff)
          Gertrude Stein. Same

A268   PICKWICK (Burnand)
          Charles Dickens. Pickwick Papers

A269   PICKWICK (Coates)
          Charles Dickens Pickwick Papers

A270   THE PIED PIPER (Berger)
          Robert Browning. "The Pied Piper of Hamelin"

A271   THE PIED PIPER (Brumleu)
          Robert Browning. "The Pied Piper of Hamelin"

A272   THE PIED PIPER (Dubbiosi)
          Robert Browning. "The Pied Piper of Hamelin"

A273   THE PIED PIPER (Farmer)
          Robert Browning. "The Pied Piper of Hamelin"

Literary Works

A274   PIED PIPER (Mennin)
        Robert Browning. "The Pied Piper of Hamelin"

A275   THE PIED PIPER (Smith-Masters)
        Robert Browning. "The Pied Piper of Hamelin"

A276   THE PIED PIPER OF HAMELIN (Bergh)
        Robert Browning. Same

A277   THE PIED PIPER OF HAMELIN (Clokey)
        Robert Browning. Same

A278   THE PIED PIPER OF HAMELIN (Flagello)
        Robert Browning. Same

A279   PILGRIM'S PROGRESS (Vaughan Williams)
        John Bunyan. Same

A280   PIPPA'S HOLIDAY (Beach)
        Robert Browning. Pippa Passes

A281   THE PLOUGH AND THE STARS (Siegmeister)
        Sean O'Casey. Same

A282   THE POISONED KISS, OR THE EMPRESS AND THE
        NECROMANCER (Vaughan Williams)
            Richard Garnett. "The Poison Maid"

A283   PORGY AND BESS (Gershwin)
        DuBose Heyward. Porgy

A284   PORTRAIT IN BROWNSTONE (Reif)
        Louis Auchincloss. Same

A285   THE POT OF FAT (Chanler)
        Brothers Grimm

A286   THE PRINCESS AND THE FROG PRINCE (H. Phillips)
        Hans Christian Anderson

Literary Works

A287   PRISCILLA, THE MAID OF PLYMOUTH (Famciulli)
        Henry Wadsworth Longfellow. The Courtship of
            Miles Standish

A288   THE PUMPKIN (Kondorossy)
        Beta Pasztor. Same

A289   PURGATORY (Crosse)
        William Butler Yeats. Same

A290   PURGATORY (Weisgall)
        William Butler Yeats. Same

A291   THE QUEEN AND THE REBEL (L. Moss)
        Ugo Betti

A292   THE QUEEN OF CORNWALL (Boughton)
        Thomas Hardy. Same and six Hardy poems

A293   QUENTIN DURWARD (Maclean)
        Sir Walter Scott. Same

A294   RAMUNTCHO (D. Taylor)
        Pierre Loti. Same

A295   RAPPACINI'S DAUGHTER (Kirchner)
        Nathaniel Hawthorne. Same

A296   THE RAPE OF LUCRETIA (Britten)
        André Obey. Le Viol de Lucrèce

A297   REBA (Barab)
        William March. "The Funeral"

A298   RED CARNATIONS (Baska)
        Gleen Hughes

A299   REGINA (Blitzstein)
        Lillian Hellman. Little Foxes

Literary Works

A300   REHEARSAL CALL (Giannini)
        Francis Swann. <u>Out of the Frying Pan</u>

A301   REIGN OF TERROR (Pimsleur)
        Clifford Odets. <u>Till the Day I Die</u>

A302   RHINOCEROS (Kohs)
        Eugene Ionesco. Same

A303   RIDERS TO THE SEA (Betts)
        John Millington Synge. Same

A304   RIDERS TO THE SEA (Sweet)
        John Millington Synge. Same

A305   RIDERS TO THE SEA (Vaughan Williams)
        John Millington Synge. Same

A306   THE ROAD TO SALEM (Blumenfeld)
        Nathaniel Hawthorne. "The Gentle Boy"

A307   ROBERT OF SICILY (Tippett)
        Robert Browning

A308   ROMEO AND JULIET (Barkworth)
        William Shakespeare. Same

A309   ROMEO AND JULIET (Chignell)
        William Shakespeare. Same

A310   ROMEO AND JULIET (Liota)
        William Shakespeare. Same

A311   ROMEO AND JULIET (Mullins)
        William Shakespeare. Same

A312   ROMEO AND JULIET (Shelley)
        William Shakespeare. Same

Literary Works

A313   THE ROPE (Mennini)
         Eugene O'Neill.   Same

A314   THE ROSE AFFAIR (N. Kay)
         Alun Owen.   Same

A315   THE ROYAL HUNT OF THE SUN (Hamilton, Iain)
         Peter Schaeffer.   Same

A316   THE RUBY (Dello Joio)
         Lord Dunsany.   Night at the Inn

A317   SANTA CLAUS, A MORALITY (L. Smith)
         e.e. cummings.   Same

A318   SAPPHO (Glanville-Hicks)
         Lawrence Durrell.   Same

A319   THE SCARLET LETTER (Giannini)
         Nathaniel Hawthorne.   Same

A320   THE SCARLET LETTER (Kaufmann)
         Nathaniel Hawthorne.   Same

A321   THE SCARLET LETTER (Lybbert)
         Nathaniel Hawthorne.   Same

A322   THE SCARLET LETTER (Mann)
         Nathaniel Hawthorne.   Same

A323   THE SCARLET LETTER (Mullins)
         Nathaniel Hawthorne.   Same

A324   THE SCARLET MILL (Zador)
         Ference Molnar.   Same

A325   THE SEAGULL (Pasatieri)
         Anton Chekov.   Same

A326   THE SECRET LIFE OF WALTER MITTY (Hamm)
        James Thurber.   Same

A327   THE SELFISH GIANT (Burtch)
        Oscar Wilde.   Same

A328   THE SELFISH GIANT (Cabena)
        Oscar Wilde.   Same

A329   THE SELFISH GIANT (Perry)
        Oscar Wilde.   Same

A330   THE SELFISH GIANT (F. Shaw)
        Oscar Wilde.   Same

A331   THE SERVANT OF TWO MASTERS (Giannini)
        Carlo Goldoni

A332   SGANARELLE (Kaufmann)
        Molière.   Le Medecin malgré lui

A333   SGANARELLE (Zito)
        Molière.   Le Medecin malgré lui

A334   THE SHINING CHALICE (Van Grove)
        Janice Lovood.   Same

A335   SHOEMAKER'S HOLIDAY (Argento)
        Thomas Dekker.   Same

A336   SIGNOR DELUSO (Pasatieri)
        Molière

A337   SILAS MARNER (Joubert)
        George Eliot.   Same

A338   SIR GAWAIN AND THE GREEN KNIGHT (Feliciano)
        "The Pearl Poet".   Same

Literary Works

A339   SIR JOHN IN LOVE (Vaughan Williams)
        William Shakespeare. The Merry Wives of Windsor

A340   SIX CHARACTERS IN SEARCH OF AN AUTHOR (Weisgall)
        Luigi Pirandello. Same

A341   SLEEPING BEAUTY (Faith)
        Brothers Grimm

A342   THE SLIM PRINCESS (Stuart)
        George Ade. Same

A343   THE SNOW QUEEN (Gerrish-Jones)
        Hans Christian Anderson

A344   THE SNOW QUEEN (Vander)
        Hans Christian Anderson

A345   SOLOMON AND BALKIS (Thompson)
        Rudyard Kipling. "The Butterfly That Stamped"

A346   THE SONG OF HIAWATHA (E. Roberts)
        Henry Wadsworth Longfellow. Same

A347   THE STONE PRINCESS (Love)
        Karl Bratton. Same

A348   THE STORY OF VASCO (Crosse)
        Georges Schehadé. L'Histoire de Vasco; Ted
            Hughes translation

A349   STREET SCENE (Weill)
        Elmer Rice. Same

A350   THE STRONGER (Kosteck)
        August Strindberg. Same

A351   THE STRONGER (Weisgall)
        August Strindberg. Same

Literary Works

A352   THE STUDENT PRINCE (Romberg)
        Mansfield. Old Heidelberg

A353   SUD (Coe)
        Julien Green. Same

A354   SUMMER AND SMOKE (Hoiby)
        Tennessee Williams. Same

A355   THE SUN GOD (Hugo)
        Bartlett B. James. Same

A356   THE SUNKEN BELL (Ruggles)
        Gerhart Hauptmann. Same

A357   THE SYSTEM (Bach)
        Edgar Allan Poe.   "The System of Doctor Tarr"

A358   A TALE OF TWO CITIES (Benjamin)
        Charles Dickens. Same

A359   TAMAR (Ward-Steinman)
        Robinson Jeffers. Same

A360   TAMAR AND JUDAH (Lavry)
        Rabbi Newman. The Woman at the Wall

A361   THE TAMING OF THE SHREW (Giannini)
        William Shakespeare. Same

A362   TARTUFFE (Benjamin)
        Molière. Same

A363   THE TELL-TALE HEART (Horacek)
        Edgar Allan Poe. Same

A364   THE TEMPEST (N. C. Gatty)
        William Shakespeare. Same

Literary Works

A365   THE TEMPTATION OF ST. ANTHONY (C. Gray)
        Gustave Flaubert. Same

A366   THE TENOR (Weisgall)
        Frank Wedekind. Der Kammersänger

A367   TESS (D'Erlanger)
        Thomas Hardy. Tess of the D'Urbervilles

A368   LE TESTAMENT (Pound)
        François Villon. Various

A369   THAÏS AND TALMAAE (C. M. Campbell)
        Anatole France. Thaïs

A370   THREE SISTERS WHO ARE NOT SISTERS (Rorem)
        Gertrude Stein. Same

A371   THE THREE STRANGERS (Maconchy)
        Thomas Hardy. Same

A372   TRANSFORMATIONS (Susa)
        Anne Sexton. Same

A373   THE TRIAL OF LUCULLUS (Sessions)
        Bertolt Brecht. Same

A374   TROILUS AND CRESSIDA (Walton)
        Geoffrey Chaucer. Troylus and Criseide

A375   THE TURN OF THE SCREW (Britten)
        Henry James. Same

A376   TWELFTH NIGHT (Amram)
        William Shakespeare. Same

A377   TWELFTH NIGHT (James Wilson)
        William Shakespeare. Same

A378   L'ULTIMO DEI MOICANI (P. H. Allen)
        James Fennimore Cooper. Same

A379   UNCLE TOM'S CABIN (Claflin)
        Harriet Beecher Stowe. Same

A380   UNDER WESTERN EYES (Joubert)
        Joseph Conrad. Same

A381   VICTORY (Richard Rodney Bennett)
        Joseph Conrad. Same

A382   A VILLAGE ROMEO AND JULIET (Delius)
        Gottfried Keller. Same

A383   VILLON (Read)
        James Forsyth. The Other Heart

A384   THE VISITORS (J. Gardner)
        Oliver Goldsmith. Same

A385   THE VOICE OF ARIADNE (Musgrave)
        Henry James. "The Last of the Valerii"

A386   VOLPONE (Burt)
        Ben Jonson. Same

A387   THE WALL (Hahn)
        Verne Bowers

A388   THE WANDERING SCHOLAR (Holst)
        Helen Waddell. The Tale of the Wandering Scholar

A389   THE WEDDING KNELL (Verrall)
        Nathaniel Hawthorne. Same

Literary Works

A390   WHIRLIGIG (Brisman)
        O. Henry

A391   A WHITE BUTTERFLY (Leichtling)
        Gabriella Roepke.   Same

A392   THE WHITE SISTER (Giglio)
        Marion Crawford.   Same

A393   WINDOW GAMES (Bentz)
        Guy de Maupassant

A394   WUTHERING HEIGHTS (Barri)
        Emily Brontë.   Same

A395   WUTHERING HEIGHTS (Floyd)
        Emily Brontë.   Same

A396   WUTHERING HEIGHTS (Herrmann)
        Emily Brontë.   Same

A397   YERMA (Apivor)
        Federico Garcia Lorca

A398   YOUNG GOODMAN BROWN (Lenel)
        Nathaniel Hawthorne.   Same

A399   YOUNG GOODMAN BROWN (Mollicone)
        Nathaniel Hawthorne.   Same

A400   YZDRA (Forrest)
        Louis V. Leddux.   <u>Alexander the Great</u>

B. PUBLISHED OPERAS

This appendix lists alphabetically by composer published scores, vocal scores, and libretti, except in a few instances when the libretto of an opera has been published separately by the librettist and does not carry the composer's name. The format for entries in this section is:

Composer's name
Opera Title. Place of publication: Publisher,
    date.

After each entry is a parenthetical notation of what form the opera is available in: (s) score; (vs) vocal score; (1) libretto. Only those forms for which evidence of existence has been located are listed.

B1   Adams, Carrie Bell
      The National Flower. Cincinnati: J. Church,
          1921. (vs)

B2   Adaskin, Murray
      Grant, Warden of the Plains. Toronto: Canadian
          Music Center, 1969. (microfilm) (vs)

B3   Addinsell, Richard
      Adam's Opera. Garden City: Doubleday, Doran,
          1929. (1)

B4   Alford, Harry L.
      Sunny of Sunnyside. Chicago: T. S. Denison,
          1929. (vs)

Published Operas

B5   Allen, Paul Hastings
<u>Il Filtro</u>. Milano: Casa Musicale L. Sonzogno,
     1912. (vs)

B6   ______.
<u>Manzelle Figaro</u>. New York: Whitney Blake, 1944.
     (vs)

B7   ______.
<u>Milda</u>. Milano: L. Sonzogno, 1913. (vs)

B8   ______.
<u>The Monastery</u>. New York: Whitney Blake, 1944.
     (vs)

B9   ______.
<u>L'Ultimo dei Moicani</u>. Milano: G. Ricordi, 1916.
     (vs)

B10   Apivor, Dennis
<u>Yerma</u>. Mainz: Schoot, 1960. (vs)

B11   Argento, Dominick
<u>The Boor</u>. New York: Boosey and Hawkes, 1960.
     (vs)

B12   ______.
<u>Christopher Sly</u>. New York: Boosey and Hawkes,
     1968. (vs)

B13   ______.
<u>The Masque of Angels</u>. New York: Boosey and
     Hawkes, 1964. (vs)

B14   ______.
<u>Postcard From Morocco</u>. New York: Boosey and
     Hawkes, 1972. (1, vs)

Published Operas

B15
    _____.
The Shoemaker's Holiday. New York: Boosey and
    Hawkes, 1971. (vs)

B16 Aschaffenburg, Walter
Bartleby. Bryn Mawr: Theodore Presser, 1967.
    (vs)

B17 Ashley, Robert
In Memoriam Kit Carson. Davis, California:
    Composer/Performer Edition, 1967. (vs)

B18 Aston, Peter
Sacrapant the Socerer. London: Novello, 1968.
    (1, vs)

B19 Auden, W. H.
"The Ballad of Barnaby." New York Review of
    Books, XIII (18 Dec. 1969), 1. (1)

B20 _____ and Chester Kallman.
Delia or a Masque of Night. Botteghe Oscura,
    XII (1953), 164-210.

B21 Bantock, Granville
Caedmar. London: London Music, n.d. (vs)

B22
    _____.
The Seal Woman. London: Boosey, 1924. (vs)

B23 Barab, Seymour
Chanticleer. New York: Boosey and Hawkes, 1964.
    (vs)

B24
    _____.
A Game of Chance. New York: Boosey and Hawkes,
    1960. (vs)

Published Operas

B25   Barber, Samuel
        Antony and Cleopatra. New York: G. Schirmer,
            1966. (1, vs)

B26   ______.
        A Hand of Bridge. New York: G. Schirmer, 1960.
            (vs)

B27   ______.
        Vanessa. New York: G. Schirmer, 1958, 1964.
            (1, vs)

B28   Barkworth, John Edmund
        Romeo and Juliet. London: MacDongh, Capdeville,
            1926. (vs)

B29   Barlow, Samuel L.
        Mon Ami Pierrot. Paris: Choudens, 1934. (vs)

B30   Barton, Andrew
        The Disappointment, or the Force of Credulity.
            New York: n.p., 1938. (vs)

B31   Beckler, Stanwork
        The Outcasts of Poker Flat. New York: Belwin,
            1961. (s)

B32   Beckwith, John
        Night Blooming Cereus. Toronto: Canadian Music
            Center, 1969. (microfilm) (vs)

B33   Beeson, Jack
        Hello Out There. New York: Mills Music, 1960.
            (vs)

B34   ______.
        Lizzie Borden. New York: Boosey and Hawkes,
            1967. (vs)

Published Operas

B35   _____.
         My Heart's In the Highlands. New York: Boosey
             and Hawkes, 1973. (vs)

B36   _____.
         The Sweet Bye and Bye. New York: Boosey and
             Hawkes, 1966. (1, vs)

B37   Benedict, Allan
         Robin Hood, Inc. Chicago: M. T. Fitzsimmons,
             1928. (vs)

B38   Benjamin, Arthur
         The Devil Take Her. London: Boosey and Hawkes,
             1932. (vs)

B39   _____.
         Prima Donna. London: Boosey and Hawkes, n.d.
             (vs)

B40   _____.
         A Tale of Two Cities. London: Hawkes, 1954.
             (vs)

B41   Bennett, Richard Rodney
         All the King's Men. London: Universal Edition,
             1969. (1, vs)

B42   _____.
         The Ledge. London: Mills Music, 1963. (vs)

B43   _____.
         The Midnight Thief. London: Mills Music, 1963.
             (vs)

B44   _____.
         The Mines of Sulphur. London: Universal Edition,
             1966. (vs)

Published Operas

B45   Bennett, Richard Rodney
       A Penny for a Song. London: Universal Edition,
           1967.   (1, vs)

B46   ______.
       Victory. London: Universal Edition, 1970.
           (1, vs)

B47   Berezowsky, Nicolai
       Babar the Elephant. New York: Carl Fischer,
           1953.   (vs)

B48   Berger, Jean
       The Pied Piper. New York: G. Schirmer, 1971.
           (1, vs)

B49   ______.
       Yiptah and His Daughter. New York: Carl Fischer,
           1972.   (s)

B50   Bergh, Arthur
       In Arcady. Boston: C. C. Birchard, 1924.   (vs)

B51   Berio, Luciano
       Circles. London: Universal Edition, 1960.   (vs)

B52   ______.
       Traces. London: Universal Edition, 1965.
           (1, vs)

B53   Berkeley, Lennox
       Castaway. London: J. & W. Chester, 1967.
           (1, vs)

B54   ______.
       A Dinner Engagement. London: J. & W. Chester,
           1955.   (vs)

Published Operas

B55   ______.
            Ruth. London: J. & W. Chester, 1960. (vs)

B56   Berners, Lord
            Le Carrosse due Saint-Sacrement. London:
                J. & W. Chester, 1923. (vs)

B57   Bernstein, Leonard
            Candide. New York: G. Schirmer, 1958. (vs)

B58   ______.
            Mass. New York: Amberson Enterprises, 1971.
                (1, vs)

B59   ______.
            Trouble in Tahiti. New York: Amberson
                Enterprises, 1953. (vs)

B60   Bezanson, Philip
            Golden Child. Kansas City: Hallmark Cards,
                1960. (vs)

B61   Birtwistle, Harrison
            Down by the Greenwood Side. London: Universal
                Edition, 1971. (vs, s)

B62   ______.
            The Mark of the Goat. London: Universal
                Edition, 1966. (vs)

B63   ______.
            Punch and Judy. London: Universal Edition,
                1968. (1, vs)

B64   Bissell, Keith
            His Majesty's Pie. Waterloo, Ontario: Waterloo
                Music, 1966.

Published Operas

B65   Blatch, Herbert
       Rip Van Winkle, Jr. London: Bach, 1910. (vs)

B66   Bliss, Sir Arthur
       The Olympians. London: Novello, 1950. (1, vs)

B67   ______.
       Tobias and the Angel. London: Novello, 1962.
          (1, vs)

B68   Blitzstein, Marc
       The Cradle Will Rock. New York: Chappell, 1938.
          (vs)

B69   ______.
       I've Got the Tune. New York: Chappell, 1938.
          (vs)

B70   ______.
       Regina. New York: Chappell, 1954. (vs)

B71   ______.
       Triple Sec. Mainz: B. Schott's Söhne, 1930.
          (vs)

B72   Boughton, Rutland
       Alkestis. London: Goodwin and Tabb, 1923. (vs)

B73   ______.
       Bethlehem. London: Curwen, 1920. (vs)

B74   ______.
       The Immortal Hour. London: Stainer and Bell,
          1920. (vs)

B75   ______.
       The Queen of Cornwall. London: Joseph Williams,
          1926. (vs)

Published Operas

B76   Breil, Joseph
The Legend. London: Chappell, 1919. (vs)

B77   Brent-Smith, Alexander
The Captain's Parrot. London: Novello, 1950.
(vs)

B78   Bridge, Frank
The Christmas Rose. London: Augener, 1931.
(vs)

B79   Briggs, Mary Elizabeth
Our Night Out. New York: S. French, 1952.
(vs)

B80   Brindle, Reginald Smith
The Death of Antigone. London: Edition Peters,
1972. (s)

B81   Britten, Benjamin
Albert Herring. London: Boosey and Hawkes,
1948. (1, vs, s)

B82   ______.
Billy Budd. London: Boosey and Hawkes, 1952,
1961. (1, vs)

B83   ______.
The Burning Fiery Furnace. London: Faber Music,
1966. (1, s)

B84   ______.
Curlew River. London: Faber and Faber, 1964.
(1, s)

B85   ______.
Death in Venice. London: Faber Music, 1973.
(1, vs)

Published Operas

B86   Britten, Benjamin
       Gloriana. London: Boosey and Hawkes, 1953.
          (1, vs)

B87   ______.
       The Golden Vanity. London: Faber Music, 1967.
          (1)

B88   ______.
       Let's Make an Opera! London: Boosey and Hawkes,
          1949.   (1)

B89   ______.
       The Little Sweep. London: Boosey and Hawkes,
          1966.   (s)

B90   ______.
       Noye's Fludde. London: Boosey and Hawkes, 1958.
          (1, vs)

B91   ______.
       Owen Wingrave. London: Faber Music, 1970.
          (1, vs)

B92   ______.
       Peter Grimes. London: Boosey and Hawkes, 1945,
          1961.   (1, vs)

B93   ______.
       The Prodigal Son. London: Faber Music, 1968.
          (1, s)

B94   ______.
       The Rape of Lucretia. London: Boosey and
          Hawkes, 1946.   (1, vs)

B95   ______.
       The Turn of the Screw. London: Boosey and
          Hawkes, 1955.   (1, vs)

Published Operas

B96   Britten, Benjamin and Peter Pears
        Midsummer Night's Dream. London: Hawkes, 1960.
            (1, vs)

B97   Brumby, Colin
        The Seven Deadly Sins. Ipswick: T. W. Shapcott
            in conjunction with the Queensland Opera
            Company, 1970. (1)

B98   Bucci, Mark
        The Dress. New York: Chappell, 1956. (vs)

B99   _____.
        A Tale for a Deaf Ear. New York: Frank Music,
            1958. (vs)

B100   Bullock, W. H.
        The Count of Como, or, A Bandit's Bride. London:
            J. Curwen, 1928. (vs)

B101   Burroughs, Bob
        David. Nasheville: Broadman Press, 1968. (1)

B102   _____.
        Now Hear It Again! Nasheville: Broadman Press,
            1970. (1)

B103   Burt, Francis
        Volpone. Wien: Universal Edition, 1962. (vs)

B104   Bush, Alan Dudley
        The Ferryman's Daughter. London: Novello, 1963.
            (vs)

B105   _____.
        Men of Blackmoor. London: Williams, 1959. (vs)

B106   _____.
        The Spell Unbound. London: Novello, 1945. (vs)

Published Operas

B107   Bush, Alan Dudley
        Wat Tyler. London: Novello, 1957. (1, vs)

B108   Bush, Geoffrey
        The Blind Beggar's Daughter. London: Elkin,
            1953. (vs)

B109   ______.
        The Equation X = 0. London: Elkin, 1967. (vs)

B110   ______.
        If the Cap Fits. London: Galliard, 1964. (vs)

B111   Butler, Eugene S.
        Samuel. Nasheville: Broadman Press, 1970. (s)

B112   Butterworth, Neil
        Rumplestilzkin. London: Mills Music, 1961. (1)

B113   Cadman, Charles Wakefield
        The Belle of Havana. Boston: White-Smith Music,
            1928. (vs)

B114   ______.
        The Garden of Mystery. New York: J. Fischer,
            1925. (vs)

B115   ______.
        The Ghost of Lollypop. Boston: Oliver Ditson,
            1926. (vs)

B116   ______.
        Hollywood Extra. Boston: C. C. Birchard, 1938.
            (vs)

B117   ______.
        Meet Arizona. Boston: C. C. Birchard, 1947.
            (vs)

B118   ______.
          Shanewis. Boston: White-Smith, 1918. (vs)

B119   ______.
          The Sunset Trail. Boston: White-Smith, 1918.
             (vs)

B120   ______.
          Two Selections from the Opera "Ramala". New
             York: n.p., 1946. (vs)

B121   ______.
          A Witch of Salem. Boston: Oliver Ditson, 1925.
             (1, vs)

B122   Cage, John
          Theatre Piece. New York: C. F. Peters, 1960.
             (vs)

B123   Caldwell, Mary Elizabeth
          A Gift of Song. New York: Boosey and Hawkes,
             1963. (vs)

B124   ______.
          Pepito's Golden Flower. Delaware Water Gap:
             Shawnee Press, 1959. (vs)

B125   Campbell, Norman
          Anne of Green Gables. London: Chappell, 1973.
             (vs)

B126   Carter, Ernest Trow
          The Blonde Donna, or, The Fiesta of Santa
             Barbara. New York: Composer's Press, 1936.
             (vs)

B127   Caryll, Ivan
          The Cherry Girl. London: Chappell, 1903. (vs)

Published Operas

B128   Castelnuovo-Tedesco, Mario
        The Merchant of Venice. Milano: G. Ricordi,
           1961. (1, vs)

B129   Chadwick, George Whitefield
        Judith. New York: G. Schirmer, 1901. (vs)

B130   ______.
        Love's Sacrifice. Boston: C. C. Birchard, 1917.
           (vs)

B131   Chapin, Frederic
        The Forbidden Land. New York: M. Witmark, 1904.
           (vs)

B132   Chappell, Herbert
        Mak, the Sheep Stealer. London: Universal
           Edition, 1967. (1, vs)

B133   Clark, Palmer John
        Carrie Comes to College, or Campus Daze.
           Chicago: Gamble Hinged Music, 1926. (vs)

B134   Clarke, Henry Leland
        The Loafer and the Loaf. New York: American
           Composer's Alliance, 1957. (vs)

B135   Clokey, Joseph W.
        In Grandmother's Garden. Chicago: C. F. Summy,
           1922. (vs)

B136   ______.
        The Pied Piper of Hamlin. Boston:
           C. C. Birchard, 1923. (vs)

B137   Coates, Albert
        Pickwick. London: Universal Edition, 1936.
           (vs)

Published Operas

B138   Cockshott, Gerald
        A Faun in the Forest. New York: S. Fox, 1971.
            (vs)

B139   Coerne, Louis Adolphe
        The Bells of Beaujolais. Boston: C. C. Birchard,
            1921. (vs)

B140   ____.
        Zenobia. Leipzig: H. Seeman, 1903. (vs)

B141   Cole, Hugo
        Jonah. Sevenoaks, Kent: Novello, 1967. (vs)

B142   ____.
        Persephone. London: Novello, 1958. (vs)

B143   Collison, William Alexander
        The Irish Girl. London: Boosey, 1918. (vs)

B144   Converse, F. S.
        The Pipe of Desire. New York: H. W. Gray,
            1907. (vs)

B145   ____.
        The Sacrifice. New York: H. W. Gray, 1910.
            (vs)

B146   Copland, Aaron
        The Second Hurricane. New York: Boosey and
            Hawkes, 1957. (vs, 1)

B147   ____.
        The Tender Land. New York: Boosey and Hawkes,
            1954. (1, vs)

B148   Crosse, Gordon
        Ahmet the Woodseller. London: Oxford Univer-
            sity Press, 1965. (vs)

Published Operas

B149   Crosse, Gordon
         The Grace of Todd. London: Oxford University
              Press, 1969. (1, vs)

B150   ______.
         Purgatory. London: Oxford University Press,
              1968. (vs)

B151   ______.
         The Story of Vasco. London: Oxford University
              Press, 1974. (1, vs)

B152   Curtis, Louis Woodsen
         Briar Rose. n.p.: J. Church, 1929. (vs)

B153   Damrosch, Walter.
         Cyrano. New York: G. Schirmer, 1913. (vs)

B154   ______.
         The Dove of Peace. New York: G. Schirmer, 1912.
              (vs)

B155   ______.
         The Man Without a Country. New York:
              G. Schirmer, 1937. (vs)

B156   ______.
         The Opera Cloak. n.p.; n.p., 1942. (vs)

B157   Davies, Sir Henry Walford
         What Luck! London: H. F. W. Deane, 1931. (vs)

B158   Davies, Peter Maxwell
         Taverner. London: Boosey and Hawkes, 1972.
              (1, vs)

B159   DeBanfield, Raffaello
         Lord Byron's Love Letter. New York: G. Ricordi,
              1955. (1, vs)

B160   DeKoven, Reginald
        The Canterbury Pilgrims. Cincinnati: J. Church,
           1916. (vs)

B161   ______.
        Happyland, or, The King of Elysia. New York:
           J. W. Stern, 1905. (vs)

B162   ______.
        Maid Marian. New York: E. Schuberth, 1901.
           (vs)

B163   ______.
        Red Feather. New York: J. W. Stern, 1903. (vs)

B164   ______.
        Rip Van Winkle. New York: G. Schirmer, 1919.
           (vs)

B165   ______.
        The Student King. New York: J. W. Stern, 1906.
           (vs)

B166   ______.
        The Wedding Trip. New York: J. H. Remick, 1911.
           (vs)

B167   DeLara, Isidore
        Les Trois Masques. Paris: Choudens, 1911. (vs)

B168   ______.
        Solea. Paris: Choudens, 1911. (vs)

B169   DeLeone, Francesco B.
        Algala. New York: G. Schirmer, 1924. (vs)

B170   Delius, Frederick
        Fennimore und Gerda. London: Universal Edition,
           1919. (vs)

Published Operas

B171   Delius, Frederick
        Irmelin. London: Boosey and Hawkes, 1953.
            (1, vs)

B172   ______.
        Koanga. London: Boosey and Hawkes, 1935. (vs)

B173   ______.
        A Village Romeo and Juliet. London: Universal
            Edition, 1910. (vs, s)

B174   Dello Joio, Norman
        The Ruby. New York: G. Ricordi, 1955. (vs)

B175   ______.
        The Triumph of St. Joan. New York: G. Ricordi,
            1959. (1)

B176   DeWitt, S. A.
        The Agony of St. Joan. New York: Greenberg,
            n.d. (1)

B177   Dickinson, Peter
        The Judas Tree. London: Novello, 1965. (1)

B178   Dougherty, Cecius
        Many Moons. New York: G. Schirmer, 1964. (vs)

B179   Dunhill, Thomas Frederick
        Tantivy Towers. London: J. B. Cramer, 1930.
            (vs)

B180   Edwards, Julian
        Dolly Varden. New York: M. Witmark, 1901. (vs)

B181   ______.
        The Gay Musician. New York: M. Witmark, 1908.
            (vs)

Published Operas

B182 _____.
     Love's Lottery. New York: M. Witmark, 1904.
        (vs)

B183 _____.
     The Patriot. New York: M. Witmark, 1907. (vs)

B184 _____.
     The Princess Chic. New York: M. Witmark, 1900.
        (vs)

B185 _____.
     When Johnny Comes Marching Home Again. New York:
        M. Witmark, 1902

B186 Effinger, Cecil
     Pandora's Box. New York: G. Schirmer, 1962.
        (vs)

B187 Elkus, Jonathan
     The Mandarian. New York: Carl Fischer, 1969.
        (1, vs)

B188 _____.
     Tom Sawyer. London: Novello, 1956. (vs)

B189 Elton, Antony
     The Minister of Justice. Durham: Antony Elton,
        1973.

B190 Engel, Carl
     Way Down South in Dixie. Boston: C. C. Birchard,
        1924. (vs)

B191 Engel, Lehman
     Malady of Love. New York: H. Flammer, 1954.
        (vs)

Published Operas

B192   Engländer, Ludwig
          A Madcap Princess. New York: J. W. Stern, 1904.
              (vs)

B193   ______.
          The Office Boy. New York: J. W. Stern, 1903.
              (vs)

B194   ______.
          The Two Roses. New York: J. W. Stern, 1904.
              (vs)

B195   Erskine, John
          Helen Retires. Indianapolis: Bobbs-Merrill,
              1934.   (1)

B196   ______.
          Jack and the Beanstalk. Indianapolis: Bobbs-
              Merrill, 1931.   (1)

B197   Fink, Harold
          Goodman Brown. Paineville, Ohio: Lake Erie
              College Press, 1968.   (vs)

B198   Flanagan, William
          Bartleby. New York: Composers Facimile
              Edition, 1968.   (vs)

B199   Floyd, Carlisle
          Markheim. New York: Boosey and Hawkes, 1968.
              (vs)

B200   ______.
          Of Mice and Men. New York: Belwin-Mills, 1971.
              (1, vs)

B201   ______.
          Slow Dusk. New York: Boosey and Hawkes, 1957.
              (vs)

Published Operas

B202   _____,
          The Sojourner and Mollie Sinclair. New York:
              Boosey and Hawkes, 1968. (vs)

B203   _____.
          Susannah. New York: Boosey and Hawkes, 1956.
              (1, vs)

B204   _____.
          Wuthering Heights. New York: Boosey and Hawkes,
              1958. (1, vs)

B205   Forrest, Hamilton
          Camille. New York: F. Rullman, 1930. (1)

B206   Foss, Lukas
          Introductions and Goodbyes. New York: Carl
              Fischer, 1961. (vs)

B207   _____.
          The Jumping Frog of Calaveras County. New York:
              Carl Fischer, 1951. (vs)

B208   Foster, Arnold
          Lord Bateman. London: Novello, 1961. (vs)

B209   Fraser-Simpson, Harold
          Bonita. London: Keith, Prowse, 1911. (vs)

B210   Freeman, Harry Lawrence
          Voodoo. New York: Negro Opera Company, 1926.
              (vs)

B211   Freer, Eleanor Everest
          The Brownings Go to Italy. Chicago: Music
              Library of Chicago, 1936. (vs)

B212   _____.
          The Chilkoot Maiden. Milwaukee: William A.
              Kaun, 1926. (vs)

Published Operas

B213   Freer, Eleanor Everest
        A Christmas Tale. Milwaukee: William A. Kaun,
            1928. (vs)

B214   _____.
        Fritihof. Milwaukee: William A. Kaun, 1929.
            (vs)

B215   _____.
        Joan of Arc. Milwaukee: William A. Kaun, 1926.
            (vs)

B216   _____.
        The Legend of the Piper. Boston: C. C. Birchard,
            1922. (vs)

B217   _____.
        A Legend of Spain. Milwaukee: William A. Kaun,
            1931. (vs)

B218   _____.
        Little Women. Chicago: Music Library of
            Chicago, 1934. (vs)

B219   _____.
        The Masque of Pandora. Milwaukee: William A.
            Kaun, 1930. (vs)

B220   _____.
        Massimilliano. Chicago: Rayner, Daheim Music,
            1925. (vs)

B221   _____.
        Preciosa. Milwaukee: William A. Kaun, 1928.
            (vs)

B222   Friml, Rudolf
        The Firefly. New York: G. Schirmer, 1912. (vs)

Published Operas

B223   Gatty, Nicholas Comyn
        Prince Ferelon, or, The Princess's Suitors.
           London: Stainer and Bell, 19   (vs)

B224   German, Sir Edward
        Fallen Fairies, or, The Wicked World. London:
           Chappell, 1909. (vs)

B225   ______.
        Merrie England. London: Chappell, 1902. (vs)

B226   ______.
        A Princess of Kensington. London: Chappell,
           1903. (vs)

B227   ______.
        Tom Jones. London: Chappell, 1907. (vs)

B228   Gershwin, George
        Porgy and Bess. New York: Gershwin Publishing,
           1935. New York: Random House, 1935. (vs)

B229   Giannini, Vittorio
        Beauty and the Beast. New York: F. Colombo,
           1951. (1, vs)

B230   ______.
        The Taming of the Shrew. New York: G. Ricordi,
           1945, 1953, 1954. (1, vs)

B231   Glanville-Hicks, Peggy
        Nausicaa. New York: F. Colombo, 1963. (vs)

B232   ______.
        Transposed Heads. New York: Associated Music,
           1940. (vs)

B233   Goehr, Alexander
        Arden Must Die. London: Schott, 1967. (vs)

Published Operas

B234   Goehr, Alexander
        Triptych. London: Schott, 1973. (vs)

B235   Goosens, Eugene
        Don Juan de Mañara. London: J. & W. Chester,
            1935. (vs)

B236   ______.
        Judith. London: J. & W. Chester, 1929. (vs)

B237   Gould, Doris
        Love's a Gamble. London: Oxford University
            Press, 1961. (vs)

B238   Gray, Cecil
        The Temptation of Saint Anthony. London:
            Chappell, 1954. (vs)

B239   ______.
        The Women of Troy. London: Chappell, 1955.
            (vs)

B240   Gray, David
        A Christmas Carol. London: Novello, 1966. (vs)

B241   Greenberg, Noah
        The Play of Daniel. New York: Oxford Univer-
            sity Press, 1959. (vs)

B242   ______.
        The Play of Herod. London: Oxford University
            Press, 1965. (vs)

B243   Grey, Julian
        Beautiful Dreamer. Minneapolis: T. S. Denison,
            1956. (vs)

B244   Griffiths, Philip
        My Daughter Coppelia. London: Oxford Univer-
        sity Press, 1971. (vs)

Published Operas

B245   Gruenberg, Louis
        The Emperor Jones. New York: Cos-Cob-Press,
            1932. (vs)

B246   ______.
        The Witch of Brocken. Boston: C. C. Birchard,
            1931. (vs)

B247   Gulesian, Grace
        Dick Whittington. New York: Boosey, Hawkes,
            and Belwin, 1941. (1)

B248   Hadley, Henry Kimball
        Azora, The Daughter of Montezuma. New York:
            G. Schirmer, 1917. (vs)

B249   ______.
        Bianca. New York: H. Flammer, 1918. (vs)

B250   ______.
        Cleopatra's Night. Boston: Oliver Ditson, 1920.
            (vs)

B251   ______.
        Happy Jack. Boston: C. C. Birchard, 1927. (vs)

B252   Hageman, Richard
        Caponsacchi. Berlin: Edition Adler, 1931. (vs)

B253   Hagemann, Virginia
        The Bird's Christmas Carol. Bryn Mawr: Theodore
            Presser, 1957. (vs)

B254   Hamill, Roseann
        The Blessed Event. Interlochen: Interlochen
            Press, 1958. (vs)

B255   Hand, Colin
        The King of the Golden River. Borough Green:
            Novello, 1969. (vs)

Published Operas

B256   Hanson, Howard
        Merry Mount. New York: Harms Music, 1933. (vs)

B257   Hart, Peter
        A Christmas Carol. London: Dash Music, 1960.
            (vs)

B258   Haverson, Leslie
        Suzannah With the Bell. London: Schott, n.d.
            (vs)

B259   Hector, Chastey
        The Golden Argosy. London: J. Curwen, 1934.
            (vs)

B260   Henekker, David
        Jorrocks. London: Chappell, 1968

B261   Henze, Hans Werner
        The Bassarids. Mainz: B. Schott's Söhne, 1966.
            (1, vs)

B262   ______.
        Elegy for Young Lovers. Mainz: B. Schott's
            Söhne, 1961. (1, vs)

B263   Herbert, Victor
        Babette. New York: M. Witmark, 1903. (vs)

B264   ______.
        The Duchess. New York: M. Witmark, 1911. (vs)

B265   ______.
        Eileen. New York: M. Witmark, 1917. (vs)

B266   ______.
        The Enchantress. New York: M. Witmark, 1911.
            (vs)

Published Operas

B267 ______.
    Her Regiment. New York: T. B. Harms and Francis,
      Day and Hunter, 1917. (vs)

B268 ______.
    The Madcap Duchess. New York: G. Schirmer,
      1913. (vs)

B269 ______.
    Madeleine. New York: G. Schirmer, 1914. (vs)

B270 ______.
    Mlle. Modiste. New York: M. Witmark, 1905.
      (vs)

B271 ______.
    Mlle. Rosita. New York: M. Witmark, 1911. (vs)

B272 ______.
    Natoma. New York: G. Schirmer, 1911. (1, vs)

B273 ______.
    Naughty Marietta. New York: M. Witmark, 1910.
      (vs)

B274 ______.
    The Prima Donna. New York: M. Witmark, 1908.
      (vs)

B275 ______.
    Princess Pat. New York: M. Witmark, 1915.
      (vs)

B276 ______.
    Sweethearts. New York: G. Schirmer, 1913. (vs)

B277 ______.
    The Tattooed Man. New York: M. Witmark, 1907.
      (vs)

Published Operas

B278   Herbert, Victor
          The Viceroy. New York: M. Witmark, 1900. (vs)

B279   Herrmann, Bernard
          Wuthering Heights. London: Novello, 1965.
              (1, vs)

B280   Heywood, Percival Meredith
          The Batsman's Bride. London: Oxford University
              Press, 1957. (vs)

B281   Hindemith, Paul
          The Long Christmas Dinner. Mainz: B. Schott,
              1961. (1, vs)

B282   Hoiby, Lee
          Natalia Petrovna. New York: Boosey and Hawkes,
              1965. (1, vs)

B283   ______.
          The Scarf. New York: G. Schirmer, 1959. (vs)

B284   ______.
          Summer and Smoke. New York: Belwin-Mills, 1972.
              (1, vs)

B285   Holbrooke, Josef
          Bronwen. London: J. & W. Chester, n.d. (vs)

B286   ______.
          The Children of the Don. London: London Opera
              House, 1912. (vs)

B287   ______.
          Dylan, Son of the Wave. London: Novello, 1910.
              (vs)

B288   ______.
          Pierrot et Pierrette. London: Goodwin and Tabb,
              1923. (vs)

Published Operas

B289   _____.
             The Wizard. London: Goodwin and Tabb, 1924.
                (vs)

B290   Hollingsworth, Stanley
             The Mother. New York: G. Ricordi, 1961.

B291   Holst, Gustav
             At the Boar's Head. London: Novello, 1925.
                (vs)

B292   _____.
             The Perfect Fool. London: Novello, 1923. (vs)

B293   _____.
             Savitri. London: J. Curwen, 1923. (vs)

B294   _____.
             The Wandering Scholar. Ed. Benjamin Britten and
                Imogen Holst. London: Faber Music, 1971.
                (vs, s)

B295   Hopkins, Anthony
             Crown of Gold. London: Pentagon Press, 1945.
                (vs)

B296   _____.
             Doctor Musicus. London: J. & W. Chester, 1971.
                (vs)

B297   _____.
             Three's Company. London: J. & W. Chester, 1955.
                (vs)

B298   Hopkins, Edwin
             Crosstown Stroll. New York: n.p., 1947. (vs)

B299   Horovitz, Joseph
             Gentleman's Island. London: J. & W. Chester,
                1960.   (vs)

Published Operas

B300   Hosmer, Lucius
        The Rose of Alhambra. New York: T. B. Harms,
            1905. (vs)

B301   Hovhaness, Alan
        Afton Water. New York: C. F. Peters, 1951.
            (vs)

B302   ________.
        The Burning House. New York: C. F. Peters,
            1962. (vs)

B303   ________.
        Pilate. New York: C. F. Peters, 1964. (vs)

B304   ________.
        Spirit of the Avalanche. New York: C. F. Peters,
            1962.

B305   ________.
        The Travellers. New York: C. F. Peters, 1965.
            (vs)

B306   Howell, Alice
        Christmas in Coventry. Boston: C. C. Birchard,
            1953. (vs)

B307   Hugo, John Adam
        The Temple Dancer. Bridgeport, Connecticut:
            J. A. Hugo, 1918. (vs)

B308   Hunkins, Eusebia
        Smoky Mountain. New York: Carl Fischer, 1954.
            (vs)

B309   ________
        Young Lincoln. New York: Private Printing,
            1958. (vs)

Published Operas

B310   Hurd, Michael
        Little Billy. London: Novello, 1966. (vs)

B311   ______.
        Mr. Punch. Sevenoaks, Kent: Novello, 1971.
           (vs)

B312   Jerome, Benjamin
        The Royal Chief, or, The Mythical Isle of Oolong.
           New York: F. B. Haviland, 1904. (vs)

B313   Johnson, Tom
        The Fournote Opera. New York: Associated Music,
           1973. (vs)

B314   Johnston, Edward F.
        The Drum-Major. New York: J. Fischer, 1912.
           (vs)

B315   Johnstone, Alexander
        Fiddlers Three. New York: M. Witmark, 1918.
           (vs)

B316   Joplin, Scott
        Treemonisha. Ed. Vera Brodsky. Chicago:
           Dramatic Publishing, 1972. (vs)

B317   Joubert, John
        The Quarry. London: Novello, 1966. (1, vs)

B318   ______.
        Under Western Eyes. London: Novello, 1960.
           (vs)

B319   Kanitz, Ernest
        Perpetual. Bryn Mawr: Theodore Presser, 1971.
           (vs)

Published Operas

B320   Kellam, Ian
        The Journey. London: Oxford University Press,
            1965. (vs)

B321   Kelly, Brian
        Herod, Do Your Worst. London: Novello, 1968.
            (1, vs)

B322   Klein, Manuel
        Bow Sing. New York: M. Witmark, 1911. (vs)

B323   ______.
        The Pied Piper. New York: M. Witmark, 1909.
            (vs)

B324   Kleinsinger, George
        Archy and Mehitabel. New York: Chappell, 1957.
            (vs)

B325   ______.
        Tommy Pitcher. New York: Chappell, 1954. (vs)

B326   ______.
        A Tree That Found Christmas. New York: Chappell,
            1956. (vs)

B327   Knight, Morris
        A Legend. Athens, Georgia: n.p., 1963. (vs)

B328   Kondorossy, Leslie
        The Pumpkin. Cleveland: n.p., 1954. (vs)

B329   Kreutz, Arthur
        Sourwood Mountain. New York: F. Colombo, 1963.
            (vs)

B330   Kurka, Robert
        The Good Soldier Schweik. New York: Program
            Publishing, 1958. (1, vs)

Published Operas

B331   LaMontaine, John
        Erode the Great. Hollywood: Paul J. Sifler,
            1969. (vs)

B332   ______.
        Novellis, Novellis. New York: G. Schirmer,
            1962. (vs)

B333   ______.
        The Shepherdes Play. Hollywood: Paul J. Sifler,
            1967. (vs)

B334   Landgrave, J. Philip
        Living in the Spirit. Nashville: Broadman
            Press, 1970. (vs)

B335   LeFleming, Christopher Kaye
        Squirrel Nutkin. London: F. Warne, 1967. (1)

B336   Lehman, Liza
        Everyman. London: Dinham and Blyth, 1916. (vs)

B337   ______.
        The Vicar of Wakefield. London: Boosey, 1907.
            (vs)

B338   Lester, William
        Manabozo. London: J. & W. Chester, 1929. (vs)

B339   ______.
        Se-a-wan-a. Boston: Oliver Ditson, 1919. (vs)

B340   Levy, Marvin David
        Escorial. New York: Boosey and Hawkes, 1966.
            (vs)

B341   ______.
        Mourning Becomes Electra. New York: Boosey and
            Hawkes, 1967. (vs)

Published Operas

B342   Lewis, Carrie
          The Rose and the Ring. Boston: White-Smith
              Music, 1934.   (s)

B343   ______.
          The Queen of the Garden. Boston: C. C.
              Birchard, 1914.   (vs)

B344   Luders, Gustav
          The Sho-Gun. New York: M. Witmark, 1904.   (vs)

B345   ______.
          Woodland. New York: M. Witmark, 1904.   (vs)

B346   Lyford, Ralph
          Castle Agrazant. Cincinnati: R. Lyford, 1922.
              (vs)

B347   Mackaye, Percy
          The Canterbury Pilgrims. New York: Macmillan,
              1916.   (1)

B348   Maconchy, Elizabeth
          The Birds. London: Boosey and Hawkes, 1974.
              (vs, s)

B349   Marshall, Nicholas
          Arion and the Dolphins. London: J. & W. Chester,
              1972.   (1)

B350   Marshall-Hall, George W.
          Romeo and Juliet. London: Enoch, 1914.   (vs)

B351   Marzo, Eduardo
          Santa Claus, Junior. New York: G. Schirmer,
              1907.   (vs)

B352   Mathias, William
          Culwch ac Olwen, difyrrwch. Cardiff: University
              of Wales Press, 1971.   (vs)

Published Operas

B353   Matteson, Maurice
        <u>Southrons All</u>. Beaufort, South Carolina: n.p.
            1961. (vs)

B354   Maw, Nicholas
        <u>One-Man Show</u>. London: Boosey and Hawkes, 1968.
            (1, vs)

B355   ______.
        <u>The Rising of the Moon</u>. London: Boosey and
            Hawkes, 1971. (1, vs)

B356   Mayer, William
        <u>Brief Candle</u>. Bryn Mawr: Theodore Presser,
            1971

B357   McCabe, John
        <u>The Lion, the Witch, and the Wardrobe</u>. Borough
            Green, Kent: Novello, 1971. (1, vs)

B358   Menotti, Gian-Carlo
        <u>Amahl and the Night Visitors</u>. New York: G.
            Schirmer, 1952. (1, vs)

B359   ______.
        <u>Amelia Goes to the Ball (Amelia al Ballo)</u>.
            Trans. George Mead. New York: G. Ricordi,
            1938. (1, vs)

B360   ______.
        <u>The Consul</u>. New York: G. Schirmer, 1950.
            (1, vs)

B361   ______.
        <u>Help, Help, the Globolinks</u>. New York: G.
            Schirmer, 1969. (vs)

B362   ______.
        <u>The Last Savage</u>. Trans. George Mead. New York:
            Franco Colombo, 1964. (1, vs)

Published Operas

B363   Menotti, Gian-Carlo
         Maria Golovin. New York: G. Ricordi, 1959.
             (1, vs)

B364   ______.
         The Medium. New York: G. Schirmer, 1947.
             (1, vs)

B365   ______.
         The Old Maid and the Thief. New York: G.
             Ricordi, 1942. (1, vs)

B366   ______.
         The Saint of Bleeker Street. New York: G.
             Schirmer, 1954. (1, vs)

B367   ______.
         The Telephone. New York: G. Schirmer, 1947.
             (1, vs)

B368   ______.
         The Unicorn, the Gorgon, and the Manticore, or,
             the Three Sundays of a Poet. New York: G.
         Ricordi, 1956. (1, vs)

B369   Meyerowitz, Jan
         Esther. New York: Independent Music Publishers,
             1956. (vs)

B370   Millay, Edna St. Vincent
         The King's Henchman. New York: Harper, 1927.
             (1)

B371   Montgomery, Bruce Eglinton
         John Barleycorn. London: Novello, 1962. (vs)

B372   Moore, Douglas
         The Ballad of Baby Doe. New York: Chappell,
             1958. (1, vs)

Published Operas

B373   _____.
          Carrie Nation. New York: Galaxy Music, 1968.
             (1, vs)

B374   _____.
          The Devil and Daniel Webster. New York: Boosey
             and Hawkes, 1939. (vs)

B375   _____.
          The Emperor's New Clothes. New York: Carl
             Fischer, 1948. (vs)

B376   _____.
          Gallantry. New York: G. Schirmer, 1958. (vs)

B377   _____.
          The Greenfield Christmas Tree. New York: G.
             Schirmer, 1963. (vs)

B378   _____.
          The Headless Horseman. Boston: E. C. Schirmer,
             1937. (vs)

B379   _____.
          The Wings of the Dove. New York: G. Schiermer,
             1961. (1, vs)

B380   Moore, Homer
          Selections from the Puritans. St. Louis: Free-
             yard Press, 1902. (vs)

B381   Moore, Mary Carr
          The Cost of Empire. Seattle: Stuff Printing
             Concern, 1912. (vs)

B382   _____.
          David Rizzio. San Bruno, California: W.
             Webster, 1937. (vs)

Published Operas

B383   Moore, Mary Carr
            Narcissa. New York: M. Witmark, 1912. (vs)

B384   Musgrave, Thea
            The Decision. London: J. Curwen, 1967. (1,
               vs)

B385   Nabokov, Nicholas
            Rasputin's End. Paris: S. A. Editions Ricordi,
               1959. (vs)

B386   Naylor, Edward Woodall
            The Angelus. London: G. Ricordi, 1908. (vs)

B387   Nicholson, Sydney Hugo
            The Mermaid. London: J. Curwen, 1928. (vs)

B388   Nixon, Roger A.
            The Bride Comes to Yellow Sky. New York: Inde-
               pendent Music Publishers, 1968. (vs)

B389   Norman, Ruth and Hardy Wieder
            The Gypsies' Reward. New York: Mills Music,
               1958. (vs)

B390   Odam, George
            St. George and the Dragon. London: J. & W.
               Chester, 1969. (1)

B391   O'Dwyer, Robert
            Eithne. Dublin: Kramer, Wood, 1910. (vs)

B392   O'Gorman, Denis
            The Shepherd's Story. Pinner, Middlesex: The
               Grail, 1973. (vs)

B393   O'Hara, Geoffrey
            Harmony Hall. New York: S. French, 1934. (vs)

Published Operas

B394   ______.
         Little Women. New York: S. French, 1940. (vs)

B395   ______.
         Peggy and the Pirate. Boston: C. C. Birchard,
              1927. (vs)

B396   ______.
         The Princess Runs Away. New York: S. French,
              1935. (vs)

B397   Orr, Robin
         Full Circle. London: International Music, 1968.
              (vs)

B398   Paine, John Knowles
         Azara. Leipzig: Breitkopfand Härtel, 1901.
              (vs)

B399   Parker, Horatio
         Fairyland. New York: G. Schirmer, 1912. (vs)

B400   ______.
         Mona. New York: G. Schirmer, 1911. (vs)

B401   Parrott, Ian
         The Black Ram. London: J. Curwen, 1957. (vs)

B402   Pasatieri, Thomas
         Black Widow. New York: Belwin-Mills, 1972.
              (1, vs)

B403   ______.
         Calvary. Bryn Mawr: Theodore Presser, 1972.
              (vs)

B404   ______.
         La Divina. Bryn Mawr: Theodore Presser, 1968.
              (vs)

Published Operas

B405   Pasatieri, Thomas
        Padrevia. Bryn Mawr: Theodore Presser, 1971
           (vs)

B406   ______.
        The Seagull. New York: Belwin-Mills, 1974.
           (1, vs)

B407   ______.
        The Women. Bryn Mawr: Theodore Presser, 1970.
           (vs)

B408   Patterson, Pat
        The Dandy Lion. Toronto: New Press, 1972. (vs)

B409   ______.
        The Popcorn Man. Toronto: New Press, 1972.
           (vs)

B410   ______.
        Red Riding Hood. Toronto: New Press, 1972.
           (vs)

B411   Patterson, Frank
        Beggars Love. Boston: C. C. Birchard, 1930.
           (vs)

B412   ______.
        The Echo. New York: G. Schirmer, 1922. (vs)

B413   Paynter, John
        The Space Dragon of Galatar. London: Universal
           Edition, 1972. (vs)

B414   Penn, Arthur A.
        Captain Crossbones, or, The Pirate's Bride. New
           York: M. Witmark, 1918. (vs)

B415   _____.
The Lass of Limerick Town. New York: M.
  Witmark, 1917. (vs)

B416   _____.
Mam'zelle Taps, or the Silver Bugler. New York:
  M. Witmark: 1919. (vs)

B417   _____.
Yokohama Maid. New York: M. Witmark, 1916.
  (vs)

B418 Poston, Elizabeth
The Briery Bush. London: Novello, 1961. (vs)

B419 Putsché, Thomas
The Cat and the Moon. New York: Seesaw Music,
  1972. (vs)

B420 Ramsier, Paul
The Man on the Bearskin Rug. New York: Boosey
  and Hawkes, 1963. (vs)

B421 Raphling, Sam
Liar! Liar! Hastings-on-Hudson, New York:
  General Music, 1972. (vs)

B422 Ravosa, Carmino Carl
Johnny Appleseed. New York: G. Schirmer, 1958.
  (vs)

B423 Redding, Joseph Deighm
Fay-Yen-Fah. Paris: Durand, 1925. (vs)

B424 Richards, Samuel
Daniel Boone. Boston: C. C. Birchard, 1931.
  (vs)

Published Operas

B425   Robinson, Earl
        Sandhog. New York: Chappell, 1956. (vs)

B426   Robinson, Stanford
        The Savoyards. London: Boosey and Hawkes,
            1973. (vs)

B427   Robyn, Alfred George
        The Bandit. New York: Shapiro, Bernstein, 1915.
            (vs)

B428   Romberg, Sigmund
        Student Prince. New York: Harms Music, 1932,
            (vs)

B429   Rorem, Ned
        Bertha. New York: Boosey and Hawkes, 1973.
            (vs)

B430   _____.
        A Childhood Miracle. New York: Southern Music,
            1972. (vs)

B431   _____.
        Fables. New York: Boosey and Hawkes, 1974.
            (vs)

B432   _____.
        Miss Julie. New York: Boosey and Hawkes, 1965.
            (1, vs)

B433   _____.
        Three Sisters Who Are Not Sisters. New York:
            Boosey and Hawkes, 1974. (vs)

B434   Saminsky, Lazare
        Julian, the Apostate Caesar. London: J. & W.
            Chester, 19   (vs)

Published Operas

B435
    ________.
The Vision of Ariel. New York: Bloch, 1950.
    (vs)

B436
Schickele, Peter
The Stoned Guest: A Half-Act Opera. Bryn Mawr:
    Theodore Presser, 1968. (vs)

B437
Schumann, William
The Mighty Casey. New York: G. Schirmer, 1954.
    (vs)

B438
Scott, Cyril
The Alchemist. Mainz: B. Schott's Söhne, 1924.
    (vs)

B439
Searle, Humphrey
The Diary of a Madman. Mainz: B. Schott's
    Söhne, 1959. (vs)

B440
    ________.
Hamlet. London: Faber Music, 1971. (vs)

B441
    ________.
The Photo of the Colonel. London: Schott, 1968.
    (vs)

B442
Sessions, Roger
Montezuma. New York: Marks Music, 1962. (vs)

B443
Seymour, John Laurence
The Bachelor Belles. New York: S. French, 1935.
    (vs)

B444
    ________.
Golden Days. New York: S. French, 1936. (vs)

B445
    ________.
In Pasha's Garden. New York: Harms Music, 1934.
    (vs)

Published Operas

B446   Shelley, Harry Rowe
        Romeo and Juliet. New York: New York: E.
          Schuberth, 1901. (vs)

B447   Siegmeister, Elie
        Darling Corie. New York: Chappell, 1954. (vs)

B448   ______.
        The Mermaid in Lock Number Seven. New York:
          Henmar Press, 1958. (vs)

B449   ______.
        Miranda and the Dark Young Man. New Rochelle:
          Alec Templeton, 1957. (vs)

B450   Silver, Alfred
        A Slave in Araby. London: J. Curwen, 1931.
          (vs)

B451   Slade, Julian
        Salad Days. London: Francis, Day and Hunter,
          1957. (vs)

B452   Slaughter, Walter
        Lady Tatters. Francis, Day and Hunter, 1907.
          (vs)

B453   Sloane, Alfred Baldwin
        The Mocking Bird. New York: J. W. Stern, 1902.
          (vs)

B454   ______.
        Sargeant Kitty. New York: C. K. Harris, 1903.
          (vs)

B455   Smith, Russell
        The Unicorn in the Garden. New York: G.
          Schirmer, 1958. (vs)

Published Operas

B456   Smith-Masters, Anthony
        The Pied Piper. London: Novello, 1964. (vs)

B457   Smyth, Ethel
        The Boatswain's Mate. London: Forsyth, 1915.
            (vs)

B458   _____.
        Entente Cordiale. London: J. Curwen, n. d.
            (vs)

B459   _____.
        Der Wald. Mainz: B. Schott's Söhne, 1902. (vs)

B460   _____.
        Fête Galante. Vienna: Universal Edition, 1923.
            (vs)

B461   _____.
        The Wreckers. London: Forsyth, 1916. (vs)

B462   Somerville, Reginald
        David Garrick. London: Ascherberg, Hopwood and
            Crew, 1920. (vs)

B463   Spaulding, V. M.
        Yanki San. Cincinnati: Willis Music, 1919. (vs)

B464   Stanford, Charles Villiers
        The Critic. London: Boosey, 1915. (vs)

B465   _____.
        Much Ado About Nothing. London: Boosey, 1901

B466   _____.
        The Travelling Companion. London: Stainer and
            Bell, 1919, 1923. (vs)

Published Operas

B467   Stein, Gertrude
        Four Saints in Three Acts. New York: Random
            House, 1934.   (1)

B468   _____.
        Last Operas and Plays. Ed. Carl Vechten. New
            York: Rinehart, 1949.   (1)

B469   _____.
        Operas and Plays. Paris: Plain Edition, 1932.
            (1)

B470   Stewart, H. J.
        King Hal. New York: J. Fischer, 1911.   (vs)

B471   Stoessel, Albert Frederic
        Garrick. New York: J. Fischer, 1937.   (vs)

B472   Stoker, Richard
        Johnson Preserv'd. London: Edition Peters,
            1971.   (vs)

B473   Stoughton, Roy Spaulding
        Mount Vernon. Boston: Oliver Ditson, 1932.   (vs)

B474   _____.
        The Prince of Martinique. Boston: Oliver
            Ditson, 1926.   (vs)

B475   Stravinsky, Igor
        The Flood. London: Boosey and Hawkes, 1963.

B476   _____.
        The Rake's Progress. New York: Boosey and
            Hawkes, 1951.   (1, s)

B477   Stuart, Leslie
        The Slim Princess. New York: Chappell, 1910.
            (vs)

Published Operas

B478   Tate, Phyllis
        A Pride of Lions. London: Oxford University
            Press, 1971. (vs)

B479   ______.
        Twice in a Blue Moon. London: Oxford University
            Press, 1971. (vs)

B480   ______.
        The What D'ye Call It. London: Oxford Univer-
            sity Press, 1966. (vs)

B481   Tavener, John
        The Whale. London: J. & W. Chester, 1969. (s)

B482   Taylor, Deems
        The King's Henchman. New York: J. Fischer,
            1926. (vs)

B483   ______.
        Peter Ibbetson. New York: J. Fischer, 1930.
            (1, vs)

B484   ______.
        Ramuntcho. New York: J. Fischer, 1941. (vs)

B485   Thompson, Randall
        Solomon and Balkis. Boston: E. C. Birchard,
            1942. (vs)

B486   Thomson, Virgil
        Four Saints in Three Acts. New York: G.
            Schirmer, 1948. (vs)

B487   ______.
        The Mother of Us All. New York: Music Press,
            1947. (vs)

Published Operas

B488   Tippett, Michael
        King Priam. London: Schott, 1962. (1, vs)

B489   ______.
        The Knot Garden. London: Schott, 1969. (1, vs)

B490   ______.
        The Midsummer Marriage. London: Schott, 1954.
            (1, vs)

B491   Townsend, Peter D.
        Tommy. Miami Beach: C. Hansen, 1969. (vs)

B492   Tracy, George Lowell
        The Maid and the Middy. Boston: C. C. Birchard,
            1918. (vs)

B493   Treharne, Bryceson
        The Magi's Gift. Cincinnati: Willis Music,
            1927. (vs)

B494   Turner, Charles
        The Ballad of Barnaby. New York: G. Schirmer,
            1969.

B495   Van Grove, Isaac
        The Music Robber. n.p.: n.p., n.d. (1)

B496   Vaughan Williams, Ralph
        The First Nowell. London: Oxford University
            Press, 1959

B497   ______.
        Hugh the Drover, or 'Love in the Stocks'.
            London: J. Curwen, 1924. (vs)

B498   ______.
        Pilgrim's Progress. London: Oxford University
            Press, 1952. (vs)

Published Operas

B499   ______.
          The Poisoned Kiss, or The Empress and the
               Necromancer. London: Oxford University
               Press, 1936. (vs)

B500   ______.
          Riders to the Sea. London: Oxford University
               Press, 1936. (vs)

B501   ______.
          Sir John in Love. London: Oxford University
               Press, 1930. (vs)

B502   Walker, Raymond
          Turkish Delight. Sevenoaks, Kent: Novello,
               1968. (1)

B503   ______.
          The Golden Flute. Sevenoaks, Kent: Novello,
               1972. (1, vs)

B504   Walton, William
          The Bear. London: Oxford University Press,
               1967. (1, vs)

B505   ______.
          Troilus and Cressida. London: Oxford University
               Press, 1954. (1, vs)

B506   Ward, Arthur Edward
          Norwegian Nights. New York: American Book
               Company, 1936. (vs)

B507   Ward, Robert
          The Crucible. n.p.; Highgate Press, 1963. (vs)

B508   Webber, Andrew Lloyd
          Jesus Christ Superstar. London: Leeds Music,
               1970. (1)

Published Operas

B509   Weil, Oscar
         The Seven Old Ladies of Lavender Town. New
             York: Harper, 1910. (vs)

B510   Weill, Kurt
         Down in the Valley. New York: G. Schirmer,
             1948. (vs)

B511   _____.
         Lost in the Stars. New York: Chappell, 1950.
             (vs)

B512   _____.
         Street Scene. New York: Chappell, 1948. (vs)

B513   Weinberg, Jacob
         The Pioneers. New York: J. Fischer, 1932. (vs)

B514   Weisgall, Hugo
         Nine Rivers from Jordan. Bryn Mawr: Merion
             Music, 1965. (1, vs)

B515   _____.
         Purgatory. Bryn Mawr: Merion Music, 1959. (vs)

B516   _____.
         Six Characters in Search of an Author. Bryn
             Mawr: Merion Music, 1957. (1, vs)

B517   _____.
         The Stronger. Bryn Mawr: Merion Music, 1956.
             (vs)

B518   _____.
         The Tenor. Bryn Mawr: Merion Music, 1957.
             (1, vs)

B519   Westergaard, Peter
         Mr. and Mrs. Discobbolos. New York: Alexander
             Broude, 1968. (vs)

Published Operas

B520   White, Clarence Cameron
        Ouanga. New York: S. Fox, 1930, 1955. (vs)

B521   Wicker, Irene
        George Washington the Boy. New York: ABC
            Music, 1941. (1)

B522   _____.
        Abraham Lincoln the Boy. New York: ABC Music,
            1941. (1)

B523   Wilder, Alec
        Kittiwake Island. New York: G. Schirmer, 1955.
            (vs)

B524   _____.
        The Lowland Sea. New York: G. Schirmer, 1952.
            (vs)

B525   _____.
        Sunday Excursion. New York: G. Schirmer, 1953.
            (vs)

B526   Willan, Healey
        Deidre. Scarborough, Ontario: Berandol Music,
            1972. (vs)

B527   Williams, John Gerrard
        Sweet Winter. London: J. Curwen, 1926. (vs)

B528   Williams, Joseph
        The Fairy Maiden. London: J. Williams, 1907.
            (vs)

B529   Williams, William Carlos
        The First President in Many Loves and Other
            Plays. New York: New Directions, 1961,
            pp. 301-358. (1)

Published Operas

B530   Williamson, Malcolm
          Dunstan and the Devil. London: Josef Weinberger,
              Weinberger, 1969. (s)

B531   ______.
          Genesis. London: Josef Weinberger, 1971. (1)

B532   ______.
          The Happy Prince. London: Josef Weinberger,
              1965. (vs)

B533   ______.
          Julius Caesar Jones. London: Josef Weinberger,
              1966. (vs)

B534   ______.
          Lucky-Peter's Journey. London: Josef
              Weinberger, 1969. (1, vs)

B535   ______.
          The Moonrakers. London: Josef Weinberger, 1967.
              (vs)

B536   ______.
          Red Sea. London: Josef Weinberger, 1973. (vs)

B537   ______.
          The Stone Wall. London: Josef Weinberger,
              1971. (1)

B538   ______.
          The Violins of Saint-Jacques. London: Josef
              Weinberger, 1966. (1, vs)

B539   Windsor, Helen
          The Emperor's Nightingale. New York: G.
              Schirmer, 1966. (vs)

B540   Yeamans, Laurel Everett
          In Robot Land. Philadelphia: Theodore Presser,
              1942. (vs)

Index

Index